Luminos is the Open Access monograph publishing program from UC Press. Luminos provides a framework for preserving and reinvigorating monograph publishing for the future and increases the reach and visibility of important scholarly work. Titles published in the UC Press Luminos model are published with the same high standards for selection, peer review, production, and marketing as those in our traditional program. www.luminosoa.org

The publisher and the University of California Press Foundation gratefully acknowledge the generous support of the Joan Palevsky Imprint in Classical Literature.

1. *Language, Nation, Race: Linguistic Reform in Meiji Japan (1868–1912)*, by Atsuko Ueda

2. *A Proximate Remove: Queering Intimacy and Loss in the* Tale of Genji, by Reginald Jackson

A Proximate Remove

A Proximate Remove

Queering Intimacy and Loss in The Tale of Genji

Reginald Jackson

UNIVERSITY OF CALIFORNIA PRESS

University of California Press
Oakland, California

© 2021 by Reginald Jackson

Suggested citation: Jackson, R. *A Proximate Remove: Queering Intimacy and Loss in* The Tale of Genji. Oakland: University of California Press, 2021.
DOI: https://doi.org/10.1525/luminos.106

Names: Jackson, R., author.
Title: A proximate remove : queering intimacy and loss in The tale of Genji / Reginald Jackson.
Description: Oakland, California : University of California Press, [2021] | Includes bibliographical references and index.
Identifiers: LCCN 2020053167 (print) | LCCN 2020053168 (ebook) | ISBN 9780520382541 (paperback) | ISBN 9780520382558 (ebook)
Subjects: LCSH: Murasaki Shikibu, 978?– Genji monogatari—Criticism and interpretation.
Classification: LCC PL788.4.G43 J33 2021 (print) | LCC PL788.4.G43 (ebook) | DDC 895.63/14—dc23
LC record available at https://lccn.loc.gov/2020053167
LC ebook record available at https://lccn.loc.gov/2020053168

28 27 26 25 24 23 22 21
10 9 8 7 6 5 4 3 2 1

To Hideki Okada and his partner, Azusa Nishimoto.

Theirs is a lasting, barely fathomed love.

CONTENTS

ACKNOWLEDGMENTS

Like intimacy and loss, gratitude can feel like a queer thing: visceral, yet difficult to ever grasp or calculate fully. In writing this book, I benefited from many people's contributions. I'll always be eternally grateful to Jonathan Beçanson, my first Japanese teacher, whose remarkable sensitivity, kindness, and exacting musicianship continue to inspire me. Patrick Caddeau got me reading Tanizaki in college, and Tony Chambers stoked that curiosity, so blame them for the weirdest bits of the book. Hideki Okada fostered the habit of imagining otherwise, absent knee-jerk judgments or pretense. Tom Hare continues to engage my ideas with warmth and an open mind. Jason Weidemann's proposal made me retool the book I thought I was writing. Lauren Berlant's advice helped me realize the book's limitations and potentials. Michael Bourdaghs retains his impeccable taste in music, and he remains the wisest, most constructive and generous colleague I've known. I can't thank him enough.

Sabine Frühstück has been a welcoming steward in leading the New Interventions in Japanese Studies imprint. At University of California Press, I've had the pleasure to work with Reed Malcolm, Archna Patel, Enrique Ochoa-Kaup, Genevieve Thurston, and Cindy Fulton, who have supervised a smooth publishing process. Two anonymous readers for the press and *Japanese Language and Literature* offered vital commentary. Judi Gibbs indexed the book. Any remaining errors are mine. I am also grateful to Anne Walthall, whose generosity subsidized the book's open-access version, and to the Tokugawa Museum, for lending images.

I thank participants of 2015's Rethinking Premodern Japan: Territory, Embodiment, Exposure workshop at the University of Chicago—Charlotte Eubanks and Paul Atkins, especially—for weighing in. Karen Thornber kindly invited me to share work at Harvard's Reischauer Institute, where she and other smart folks like David Howell, Terry Kawashima, Melissa McCormick, and Tomiko Yoda offered valuable commentary at a formative stage. Abé Markus Nornes's close reading is always appreciated, and Christi Merrill's keen comments energized the introduction. Annalisa Zox-Weaver did an excellent job editing an earlier version of this manuscript, and I owe her a belated expression of gratitude. Helen Findley provided outstanding research support. Enormous thanks go to Edith Sarra and Charo D'Etcheverry, whose extraordinarily learned and conscientious comments made for a better book. Ellen Tilton-Cantrell's thoughtful editorial work was transformative. Rachel Willis's attentive annotations helped me finish strong.

Grace Ting's sparkling critiques refined and emboldened the prose. She's a fabulous coconspirator. Similar sentiments hold for Frieda Ekotto, Raya Naamneh, Hakem Al-Rustom, and Rana Barakat. Arvind-Pal Mandair is a brilliant thinker whose camaraderie has meant tons. Tiffany Ng is a stellar friend whose hustle and humanity continually floor me. Not for nothing, Denise Galarza-Sepúlveda's literary sensibility and *cariño* set a high bar two decades running. The incredible Victor Mendoza and Pardip Bolina let Ana and Simone sing "Happy Birthday" for my first book, *Textures of Mourning*; the postpandemic cake train will not skip their stop. Marvelous interlocutor Ava Purkiss shall conduct said train. Carla "Sunshine" Nappi continues to rock the house, along with Emily Greene, Dan Shulman, and Emilie Chesnutt Boone. The Berger-Richman family needs more aliens in their Korean cinema. Abrazos always to the Aimee and Juan Rodriguez household. Ron Brunette, Allen Finkel, and Alana; Patricio Herbst, Vilma Mesa, Bruno, and Ana Sofia; and Sarah Arehart, Ivy, and Steve Cavaness are neighbors akin to relatives (the good kind). And Hideki Okada's partner, Azusa Nishimoto, is family forever.

I gratefully acknowledge financial support from the Fulbright Foundation, Japan Foundation, and Michigan's Center for Japanese Studies. My gratitude also goes to Kevin Carr, Rosie Ceballo, Haely Chang, Tamara Chin, Steven Chung, Abi Cochran, Deirdre de la Cruz, Christopher Dryer, Yukiko Endō, Norma Field, Jim Fujii, Yuri Fukazawa, Diana Fuss, Anita Gonzalez, Miyabi Goto, Bradly Hammond, Yucong Hao, Kaoru Hayashi, Christopher Hill, Sue Juster, Swarnim Khare, Steven Kile, Ungsan Kim, Astrid Lac, Kim Larrow, Ashton Lazarus, Minna Lee, Hoyt Long, Mimi Long, Stephanie Lovelace, Christine Marran, Alex Murphy, Agnes Lugo-Ortiz, Do-Hee Morsman, Elizabeth Oyler, Sonya Ozbey, Esperanza Ramirez-Christensen, David Rolston, Patrick Schwemmer, Jayanthi Selinger, Rob Sellers, Matthew Stavros, Jocelyn Stitt, Kiyoteru Tsutsui, Patrice Whitney, Nicole Wright, and Keiko Yokota-Carter.

A massive shout out to the University of Michigan's Accelerated Master's Program in Transcultural Studies' "Quaranteam": Bailey Compton, Allie Hodge, Kaley Makino, Alex Prosi, Jeremy Ray, and Rachel Willis. Their sincerity and intellectual agility in engaging with this material puts many an expert to shame. Our ongoing educational exchange buoys my hopes for styles of study the university can't ruin. Brian Jackson, Sallie, Tiffany, and Thandi Townsend keep me rooted. Along with the Roland-Forney reunion crew, Eulinda and Moriya Smith's faith lifts my spirits. My heartfelt thanks and love go to the phenomenal Allison Alexy—the most competent person I know—for her support and killer editorial chops. Alice Gorham's caring, righteous anger provides clarity. Eunice Jackson's singular warrior spirit continues to pay dividends that nary a soul can steal. Arthur L. Jackson Jr.'s abundant love, humor, and insight remain indelible.

Benefits of the Doubt: Questioning Discipline
and the Risks of Queer Reading

What does giving the benefit of the doubt cost? And how should we assign value to questions that raise doubts about disciplinary values we've learned to take for granted? Before I delve into queer readings of *The Tale of Genji* or even frame this book's goals, interventions, and debts to previous scholarship, it felt important to address some concerns, in hopes of smoothing entry into the book proper. This preface reflects on the value of queer approaches to specialists in premodern Japanese literature. In the subsequent introduction, I outline how each chapter's arguments challenge or improve on existing models of understanding in premodern Japanese literary studies and queer studies. I explain, for instance, why I draw on certain strains of queer theory more than others, and I unpack the value of a phenomenological approach across the chapters. Here, however, I contextualize how certain disciplinary locations might condition one's expectations toward *A Proximate Remove*.

First, an observation: this project has met with more resistance than any other I've undertaken. *A Proximate Remove* connects Heian literary studies and queer studies in a manner not done before. This is no easy task. And some of the difficulty stems from larger social, historical, and disciplinary structures that configure these fields and influence reactions within them.

I've noticed that the topic of performing queer readings of *Genji* tends to make many scholars of premodern Japanese literature uneasy. This unease manifests in various ways. Sometimes it crops up in a crossing of arms at the project's mention, while other times reservations are expressed about the validity of the project—without the commenter having read a page. Some scholars admit the premise sounds interesting, small talking toward inquiring if I myself identify as queer. Informal reservations are mentioned, like, "Try not to overdo it" (Is this an encouragement or a warning?); and, "But Genji only has sex with the boy [Kogimi] once." A host of soft or hard protestations have arisen about the historical validity of the inquiry, such as, "But that's more Edo"; and, "But that's more modern"; or, "But these aren't real people" (as though I don't realize this is a fictional narrative); and, "But these aren't modern people" (as though I don't realize these are characters in an eleventh-century fictional narrative). Written reactions go further, including, "He has no evidence any of these [readings] are what Murasaki Shikibu intended" (as though that was actually the author's real name, or as though the very notion of authorial intention for an eleventh-century tale should be seriously entertained by literary scholars as a guarantor of meaning); and, "The author repeatedly injects sexual innuendo into scenes" (as though *Genji* needed a shred of help on that score). I mention these examples to do four things: (1) share and think through the nature of the unease they register, with the ideological and disciplinary resistance underpinning it; (2) outline some perceived risks attending my inquiry; (3) anticipate some of the project's potential benefits; and (4) perform solidarity with those who might have encountered similar responses or who seek to bring new energy to their fields.

Rather than discount this pushback as peripheral, theorizing it upfront seems valuable as a critical gesture in itself. This entails not taking negativity for granted but rather, in a queer theoretical spirit, weighing it as a way to consider some of the thematic textual concerns examined in subsequent chapters—such as disorientation, temporal dilation, and disenchantment with normative structures. This might seem like hand-wringing to some, particularly audiences more conversant with queer theory; if you're in that category, please proceed to the introduction proper. However, for readers less versed in that style of inquiry, and perhaps more skeptical toward it, this section attempts to lay out the analytical terrain at a meta level.

A Proximate Remove will in some ways be a challenging book. This is because of the book's arguments and engagement with a varied conceptual archive unfamiliar to many scholars in the field of premodern Japanese studies, on the one hand, and a historiography alien to queer studies scholars, on the other. My goal is not to incite a love-hate relationship but rather to expand the horizon of interpretive possibilities currently available in premodern Japanese literary studies. Without belaboring the point, I should merely say up front that a lack of a sustained engagement with queer theory within the field is precisely what my manuscript seeks to address.

Part of what makes the book challenging is that it questions fundamental and often unmarked beliefs about the nature of desire and disciplinary orientations toward reading and writing themselves. Consequently, it seemed prudent in this preface to identify certain disciplinary habits and expectations and indicate potential instances of friction. So from the outset we should ask, How does posing queer questions accentuate, reinforce, or erode disciplinary norms—within premodern Japanese literary studies primarily? And how should we understand the risks and benefits of that doubt?

Although queer studies grew out of antidiscriminatory activism centered on sexual identity, and some critiques still hew close to that legacy, the field has expanded beyond those concerns since its early 1990s inception in the United States. Some recent approaches in queer studies recognize facets of everyday experience that speak to possibilities overshadowed by normalizing regimes, with compulsory heterosexuality being just one draconian example; others reconsider antinormativity's dominant role in queer theorization or pursue posthuman critiques inclined to minimize human sexuality's privileged position through a broader focus on animacy.[1] On this point, I am careful to never capitalize *queer theory* so as to not reify it as some monolithic entity or flatten its conceptual diversity.

Often, the analytical object of queer theory is not queerness, which is associated vernacularly with nonnormative or LGBTQ+ identities, but rather complex processes that structure exclusion or reproduce repressive styles of sociality. Thus, one way to understand queer studies is as a practice of asking questions more openly—be it in love, law, or literature—without taking prohibitive assertions at face value. Insofar as queer theory ideally pursues better, less constrained circumstances for living, it works to diagnose or critically intuit stimuli, gestures, turns of phrases, and irruptions large and small that disclose chinks in the armor of dominant logics or signal ways to imagine otherwise.

By positing such an array of phenomena as deserving analysis, some scholars protest that queer theory becomes a "theory of everything." This complaint can precede a dismissal indicative of deeper-seated issues. My hunch is that this qualm stems more from unspoken homophobia, which lets a closeted prejudice masquerade as dispassionate appraisal. I wouldn't claim this sort of homophobia constitutes full-blown bigotry; rather, it persists as a constitutive element of heteronormative society. Against such judgments, I would counter that queer theory is no more a theory of everything than theories examining class, gender, or race. On the one hand, Black feminists like Kimberlé Crenshaw have made clear that these powerfully structuring social categories must be considered in their intersectional relation to one another.[2] On the other hand, intersectionality in a Black feminist context or queer-of-color critique has yet to secure cachet within Japanese studies. Although younger than Marxist or psychoanalytic criticism, queer theory both overlaps and exceeds some of those more established lenses' concern about economies, inequalities, and subjectivities.

This book practices a form of queer reading composed of several interpretive approaches. Importantly, as used here, the term *queer* does not index erotic exchange or identity politics. Generally speaking, queer approaches question the dominant, normative logics governing the embodied experience of space, time, and feeling. Within literary analysis, queer approaches pause over irruptions or aporias in a text—fissures of space, time, or feeling—as intervals in which to suspend belief in predominant logics, reorient critical attention, reassess normalized styles of sociality, and rethink habituated patterns of inhabiting the world.

In *The Tale of Genji*'s case, these normative logics include the workings of aristocratic patriarchy and imperial succession, and the multifaceted desires undergirding them. To be sure, the eleventh-century narrative depicts the entwinement of heterosexual reproduction with political fortune that conditioned aristocratic consciousness of the time. Yet the text continually dramatizes desire's propensity to veer off track and features a range of "nonproductive" relations that literary scholars like Kimura Saeko stress as central to Heian narratives.[3] Accordingly, queer textual approaches involve apprehending conspicuous and subtle encounters with uncertainty and disorientation, without necessarily centering on sexuality and antinormative subversion. My goal is to locate moments askew of the text's prevailing vectors of authority, temporality, and social intercourse. I therefore emphasize the visual, aural, tactile, and spatial attributes of scenes to provide a sensorial account that accentuates embodied experiences of contingency: encounters where institutional, physical, or psychic stability falters. My own use of *queer* as a figure of indeterminacy is strategic, and my readings of *Genji* demonstrate the irreducibility of queerness to matters linked exclusively or even primarily to sexuality, as *queer* entails a far broader array of affections, orientations, and social relations.

That said, raising the issue of sexuality can prove valuable—pedagogically and conceptually. For instance, as I delineate in chapter 1, where I explain the notion of false flags and problematize the matter of misreading suggestions of sexual contact, my decision to sometimes concentrate on scenes surrounding erotic desire is not simply a matter of injecting innuendo for kicks. Rather, this tendency reflects a deliberate choice to raise such possibilities precisely to demonstrate their limitations. A more limited reading strategy would trawl the text for "gay" desire—ideally hidden—to expose and diagnose. In short, I perform readings that play up this capacity for misreading to undercut them and accentuate potentials irreducible to sexuality—despite its potent resonance throughout the narrative. To queer *The Tale of Genji* is not simply to magnify its scenes of homosocial camaraderie or amplify homoerotic murmurs but rather to take cues from the text's own intense circumspection toward all normative social formations: a productive unease from which past and present readers might draw lessons.

Hence both the Heian text and the discipline currently enclosing it seem enriched by a turn to queer reading. *A Proximate Remove*'s larger critical project—echoing *Genji*'s own—is to practice a mode of reading wary of absolutist pronouncements regarding desire, politics, textuality, or method. Indeed, one benefit of that queer theoretical emphasis is its instructive skepticism toward aspirations for empiricist certitude or epistemological closure. But how might we pursue such a project, especially given the fascinating skepticism queer reading itself arouses among premodernists in Japanese studies in particular?

In raising the question of queer approaches to Heian literature, I'm reminded of something Norma Field wrote about *The Tale of Genji* more than thirty years ago. Extrapolating from her feminist approach, we get a better idea of what reading *Genji* might teach us about how to read queer theory—as a mode of attention deserving the benefit of the doubt. Field argues for "novelistic" reading in an enlightening manner:

> A novel is lost if its reader refuses to think novelistically. This means in part that at a certain point every reader—and this point will be different for each reader and each reading—must gain some distance from inherited points of view (principles of theory, tools of the trade such as information on historical allusion, rules of etiquette, fashions in incense concoction) simply to make room for other perceptions. . . . In fact, a great deal of my book is an appeal to other readers of the *Genji* to *notice*, for example, a form of address, or the presence of a certain musical instrument.[4]

Like Field, I am also "continually struck by minute points of resonance, by extraordinarily complicated and unfamiliar configurations," that *Genji* presents, and my response to these textual irruptions is to read them through a queer frame. Field's suggestion that open, attentive readers "gain some distance from inherited points of view . . . to make room for other perceptions" anticipates a basic premise of *A Proximate Remove*. This recommendation to "gain some distance" applies to the "principles of theory" and "tools of the trade" germane to both more and less theoretical approaches. Made in 1987, before theorizing the everyday became customary in queer studies, Field's parenthetical admonition to "never underestimate the potency of the banal" recuperates the banal as a resource for theorizing—even when the textual object or cultural practices are far removed from that familiar everyday:

> Take, for example, the pervasive aestheticism of the Heian period [794–1185]. Much has been made of the refinement of Heian sensibilities—the excruciating devotion to details of color, scent, hand, or season. . . . For now I would like to caution the reader to be attentive to these aesthetic matters as languages that are deployed throughout the tale. Certainly, from our own point of view, some of these interests seem precious at best and perniciously frivolous at worst.[5]

These details stir attention for both the intricacy of their respective grammars and for the way they might estrange or obstruct present-day perspectives. Importantly, Field here supplements the question of aesthetic interpretation by anticipating the negative feelings that accompany it. Shades of disgust seep from the chasm between "our point of view," or recourse to accustomed disciplinary regimens, and Heian courtiers' "excruciating devotion" to sensibilities that can frustrate our interpretive encounter. I stress this last sentence about how our disciplinary norms discredit certain alienating forms of critical interest because it recalls the dubious, defensive, or dismissive tinges that have colored several responses I've gotten in proposing queer readings of *Genji*. Such responses—be they principled, cynical, well-informed, or otherwise—signify symptoms of a devotion to insular disciplinary norms according to which *queer* does not translate smoothly. As a remedy to this misapprehension, Field recommends that "we learn to follow the other languages—of dress, of calligraphy, of floral and musical preference, of incense concoction. This implies, of course, expenditure of effort to learn about these matters. We must be cautious, however, so as not to force the novel to conform to such expertise as we have gained but rather to use it to help us apprehend that incense concoction, for instance, is one language among others within the novel."[6]

Fluency in all these languages is impossible in a non-Heian world, thus Field concedes that effort spent learning to follow the other languages is enough. What matters here is the recognition of potential value added: the lending of a benefit of the doubt to subsidize the effort needed to fathom less familiar idioms. Alongside calligraphy or incense concoction, why not position queer theory as another language worth learning to follow, an idiom whose capacity to enhance our sense of these other Heian idioms has yet to be explored sufficiently?

Viewed another way, queer theory signifies a style of paying attention to these multiple languages already present in *Genji*. In this sense, far from being an imposition of the foreign, a recourse to queer theory represents a means of engaging those native idioms anew in hopes of discerning different, formerly subdued scents and frequencies. In other words, queer theory should not be seen as a wholesale displacement of more familiar styles of analysis but instead be embraced for its refinement and extension of them. Field's point extends beyond *Genji*. It applies to thinking about the type of work that literary scholars in general can pursue in terms of being open to aesthetic grammars circulating alongside written languages.[7]

Some will counter that the crucial difference between these idioms is that where calligraphy or incense belong to *Genji*'s world, queer theory does not. Fair enough. Yet none of these aesthetic/political languages is sovereign, regardless of its provenance. Even *Genji*'s "native" languages (e.g., incense blending, calligraphy, painting, kickball) are partial; each of them at some level supplements another, calling to be read beside its counterparts. Moreover, a millennium's gap estranges these idioms from any post-Heian critic. Fantasies of absolute accuracy or access aside, interpreting them might thus require all the help we can get. Therefore, let's pose the question this way: What might queer theory teach us about Heian calligraphy and incense that prevailing historiographies or patterns of expertise cannot?

Such questions can feel promising or menacing, depending partly on the disciplines to which one feels most beholden. Alongside personal preference, different disciplinary homes trigger a range of inclinations toward or against a mode of questioning I describe as *queer*. Sketching some of these inclinations helps us recognize how *queer*'s potential as an interpretive tool is managed among different audiences that are more (or less) inclined to give it the benefit of the doubt. Indeed, queer theory prompts doubt about the authority of critics who might avoid or embrace it and raises productive, if possibly unsettling, questions about the ideological and pedagogical stakes of reading within and beyond our disciplinary comfort zones.

Queer resonates as a magnetic term; it attracts and repels across a range of intellectual orientations. *Queer* shines as more attractive (or sexier) for certain editors who have a sense of the term's contemporary market value within the beleaguered realm of academic publishing. Meanwhile, some scholars resent the term on the basis of this very same perceived appeal, therefore dismissing this project out of hand as merely trendy or expedient. This has happened more among premodern Asianists than in other company, and generally with more established scholars; it has been less of an issue with female, queer, or junior scholars.

Some suspicion stems from a concern about the applicability of queer theory to medieval Asian texts. Sometimes, this is a concern about subsuming a particular old Asian example beneath the hegemonic banner of a Western paradigm sprouting from the United States in the 1990s. This concern can stem from legitimate apprehensions about legacies that subordinate Asia as a passive object ripe for analysis through non-Asian methods. Folks bearing this mindset don't want the Asian object to be overtaken by the (implicitly American) *queer*. Granted, a conscientious desire for reciprocity or parity seems reasonable enough—admirable, even. However, sometimes it's a ruse—a way to register discomfort about other, less formalized or more embarrassing worries through righteous posturing.

The amount of concern—or defensiveness—hinges on how much of a burden or incursion queer represents. A recent roundtable among Japanese scholars on queer reading mentions various factors hampering queer studies' impact on modern Japanese literary studies in Japan. These range from celebrated feminist scholar Ueno Chizuko's indictment of "a theory phobia among Japanese literature scholars" (nihon bungaku kenkyūsha ni okeru riron fobia) to the link between sexual identity and queer studies.[8] This perception, that doing queer work requires a particular identity, breeds a reluctance in literary studies that doesn't exist in fields like sociology, where queer studies in Japan is most advanced.[9]

Meanwhile, for some scholars in Japan and elsewhere, queer theory epitomizes an outer limit. Where thematic, new historicist, or feminist criticism seems permissible enough, queer critique makes some folks more uneasy with the aura of excess it emits. It can code as too vanguard, too antiestablishment, too flimsy, too neoliberal, too consumerist, too foreign, too irreverent, too sexual, too smug, too permissive or promiscuous in its methods and choice of analytical objects, too slippery or soft to reckon suitably with hard textual or historical evidence. These perceptions coat disciplinary boundaries and assumptions that tend to go unmentioned. But then this privileged silence is what makes them such sturdy norms.

I've had scholars proceed to explain why this queer stuff was ill-suited or just wouldn't work with *Genji* without engaging queer studies texts I referenced or acknowledging their ignorance of the issues. Mansplaining of this sort revolved around notions of scholarly rigor without the acknowledgment of even rudimentary literacy in queer studies as a component of due diligence. Such an implicit or explicit devaluation of a queer theoretical approach speaks to disciplinary norms—regarding legibility, empiricism, and proper object choices, for instance— that surface in comportments where shades of unease, bemusement, condescension, and low-key paranoia try to coalesce into the guise of sound advice.

Not that this style of negativity stays anchored to a single disciplinary home or demographic. For, as Lauren Berlant and Michael Warner explain, "even inside the academy, questions about queer theory's political utility are occasionally not in the best faith. Sometimes they serve to ward off theory from a model of gay studies that has a more affirmative relation to its imagined constituency. In this context, queer commentary provides exactly what some fear it will: perspectives and archives to challenge the comforts of privilege and unself-consciousness."[10] This challenge goes both ways. It applies as much to queer theorists as to premodern East Asianists, each with their respective comforts, expertises, biases, pretensions, and claims to authority. To be sure, queer studies has been quite limited in scope, with ancient Greece and early modern Europe getting the most attention after modern Western societies. This habit no doubt contributes to the worry that queer theory might not work with premodern Asian material.

Some folks are more sympathetic, though, and a robust benefit of the doubt offsets their skepticism. For these scholars of premodern Asia, queer theory might still feel suspect, but is not dismissed outright as unviable, partially because it seems consonant with feminist critiques that have burgeoned since the mid-1980s. For instance, among scholars in the Japanese academy aligned with or influenced by the Narrative Research Association (*monogatari kenkyūkai*), a turn toward queer theory reads as a natural outgrowth of explorations of textuality, sexuality, and phenomenology already undertaken for decades by figures like Mitani Kuniaki, Kawazoe Fusae, Mitamura Masako, and Matsui Kenji, whose contributions I outline in the introduction. Conversations with scholars of this sort have a different quality than ones with the mansplainers. There's genuine curiosity, less posturing, less visible tension. Talk turns to which textual depictions might deserve most scrutiny and why. *Queer* signifies less as threat than as opportunity in this case, and any pushback feels more measured and constructive, not reactionary.

My experience suggests that queer theory perturbs to a degree that tropes like status, gender, performance, space, and agency don't currently. A main difference is that unlike *queer*, those terms function more as interchangeable, relatively benign thematic lenses than as comprehensive challenges per se. These other lenses can feel more comfortable or applicable, partly because they don't carry the same ambient stigma born of homophobic culture and partly because they don't spotlight the critic's sexual identity to a comparable extent. This makes me think that this book's topic taps a reservoir of feelings that well up in unexpected ways. Reactions I've received have made it feel like invoking the term *queer* highlights larger presumptions and expectations—within and beyond disciplinary boundaries.

Berlant and Warner's "What Does Queer Theory Teach Us about X?" (1995) helps explain the sensitivities that surface when queer scrapes such normative structures. They write, "The critical mass of queer theory is more a matter of perception than of volume. Queer is hot. . . . The association with the star system and with graduate students makes this work the object of envy, resentment, and suspicion. As often happens, what makes some people queasy others call sexy."[11]

Queer theory, in other words, attracts bad affective energy because of its perceived popularity—or some sort of imperative to be more contemporary, politically correct, and caring toward minorities?—regardless of its potential interpretive efficacy. But if this negativity arrives from outside queer studies, a friction also exists within queer studies, one stemming from the same ubiquitous reach its detractors condemn with the "theory of everything" rhetoric. Thus, as Berlant and Warner observe, the value of queer commentary also wavers among commentators committed to it: "The panicky defensiveness that many queer and non-queer-identified humanists express has to do with the multiple localities of queer theory and practice. Separately, these localities often seem parochial, or simply local—like little ornaments appliquéd over real politics or real intellectual work. They carry the odor of the luxuriant."[12]

In either context, *queer* transmits an excess that solicits resistance at varying degrees, from multiple sectors of the academy. We could downplay this claim by highlighting the time that's passed since Berlant and Warner's essay was published, assuming that bad feelings have mellowed with age. But that would overlook structural realities of the contemporary academy. Feelings have no doubt changed, but where and how much? The academy's topography is far from uniform. Specifically, asymmetrical disciplinary and institutional histories (relations to Cold War paradigms, activist movements, and marginalized communities) and prevailing attitudes (regarding the value of linguistic training, translation, theory, and popular/elite or modern/premodern objects) influence the differential rate at which queer theory earns currency within disciplines. Generally speaking, this cachet is higher in English, comparative literature, anthropology, gender studies, ethnic studies, performance studies, American studies, and Asian American studies than in history and East Asian studies, for example. And these disciplinary fissures get more jagged once we introduce historical period as a variable to differentiate further within fields of inquiry in Japanese studies: modern overshadows premodern and contemporary, and a project attempting to bring a premodern text and contemporary theory into conversation arguably suffers double.

Recognizing the structural unevenness of this valuation and the fluctuating structures of feeling that attend it, it becomes important to question the possibility—and desirability—of queer reading within environments prone to judge it as alien. Although "humanists" has a wide berth, Berlant and Warner (who were both tenured Americanists in English departments when they wrote the essay) might take for granted *queer*'s appraisal in less tolerant atmospheres. After all, a "luxuriant" odor cushions *queer* with the benefit of the doubt, but in other institutional "localities," it might just reek. Some of the judgments I've heard regarding queer theory disparage it as arbitrary. But the same applies for any number of routines in our fields—like European language requirements, say—that somehow feel more fragrant, cosmopolitan, serious, or valuable.

Which languages or idioms become naturalized as valuable or useful frames these recent scenes when I have shared my work on *Genji*. Returning to Field's insights about reading *Genji*, queer theory currently represents a language whose use value within the realm of Japanese literary studies remains relatively unacknowledged and untested. This predicament is not unlike that once faced by poststructuralism, postcolonial theory, or gender theory, critical idioms that now seem far less foreign and superfluous than they did in the not-so-distant past. I hope that the ensuing readings encourage others to engage this idiom to read beyond current conventions and rethink how we engage literature in our research, teaching, and broader lives.

There's a lesson here, one worth bearing in mind as this book gets underway. A caution toward our own expertise—be it empirical or conceptual, concrete or abstract—helps temper the mandate to domesticate or disregard those queer questions and impulses, the "minute points of resonance" and "unfamiliar configurations" that unsettle our prevailing professional sensibilities. The early '90s advent of queer commentary may have grated because of the "wrenching sense of recontextualization it gave."[13] But thirty years on, it needn't any longer. If it vexes us, we should at least be able to mark that feeling, take it seriously, historicize it, and attempt to theorize openly the overlapping norms and contexts that sparked it. We should, in other words, learn how to give that doubt the benefit of an attentive queer reading.

Introduction

Quiet as it's kept, *The Tale of Genji* is a queer text. But what might this mean, and how could engaging this medieval Japanese text's queerness alter and enrich how we read? *A Proximate Remove* contends that *Genji* queers, where to queer is to press into question predominant logics of thought, feeling, and movement. These logics both subsidize and compromise conditions of possibility for how characters in *Genji* live and how they relate to each other and to the wider world. Thus, in saying that *Genji* queers, I mean to emphasize how the text imagines alternatives through both portraying and encouraging a generative estrangement from inherited structures—within and beyond the text.

I argue that *The Tale of Genji* performs a queer critique in its insistence on the fictive, deficient, often unlivable nature of what prevails as the good life. Indeed, alongside its portrayals of intimacy and loss, especially, the narrative presents profound meditations on how—and even *if*—life should be lived. From the narrative's opening scene onward, stunning intimacies and losses trigger varied protagonists' fitful quests for viable ways to thrive. The narrative depicts destabilizing encounters that inspire the characters to question the environment they must inhabit. I read their questioning propensity as queer in its reluctance to take the configuring rhythms of the given world for granted or to accept them as sovereign. This book tells the story of how intimacy and loss spark that reluctance, kindling capacities to revise or reimagine the world.

A Proximate Remove explores the relationship between the aesthetic, affective, and phenomenological dimensions through which characters experience intimacy and loss. Part of this book's critical project is to explore desire's shifting topography through close thematic readings of *The Tale of Genji*. What I term "a proximate remove" assumes different forms over the book's chapters, figuring protagonists' embodied experiences of anticipation, disorientation, asynchrony, dispossession, and bereavement. Apprehending these experiences as queer, I theorize how intimacy and loss impact *Genji*'s characters' psychic and physical

1

sensitivities to the times and spaces they inhabit. A phenomenological method proves valuable insofar as I want to avoid positing relations as static or predetermined. Rather, my style of queer reading emphasizes the possibilities that emerge in the processual interface of bodies with the world through which they maneuver. I chart how a reshaping of sensitivities transpires as characters navigate loss and live on alongside it. And yet proximate removes are not chained to loss; they can also host the fragile promise of having.

My exploration proceeds by performing literary analysis of scenes in *The Tale of Genji*. Written during the Heian period (794–1185), commonly considered Japan's aristocratic golden age, Murasaki Shikibu's *Genji monogatari* (*The Tale of Genji*, 1008) has been called the world's first novel—albeit inaptly—and represents a canonical emblem of cultural identity.[1] Despite *Genji*'s roots in Heian Japan, the work's radiance scatters like a supernova's light, sparking countless remediations across centuries, among them stories, plays, paintings, clothing, comics, live-action and animated films, and even a special commemorative Japanese banknote in 2000 to toast the millennium and the twenty-sixth G8 summit.[2] Many of *The Tale of Genji*'s multigenerational plotlines detail the lusts and losses of the courtier "Shining" Genji, whose artistic brilliance and political wile allow him to seize power covertly and even illicitly father an emperor despite being unable to ever claim that title himself. For leading *Genji* scholar Mitamura Masako, this foundational paradox at imperial patriarchy's core drives masculine desire in the tale and shapes *Genji*'s circuitous narrative structure.[3] With its multiple registers, shifting perspective, and often elliptical style, the tale renders an elaborate portrait of the machinations undergirding Heian aristocratic society's decorous veneer. Across fifty-four chapters, the narrative chronicles dozens of protagonists through episodes of sexual intrigue, spirit possession, exile, death, and subtler relinquishments. Given its blend of gravity, intricacy, and comedic traces, *The Tale of Genji* names less a text than it does a galaxy.

Add to this mix an opacity that can both seduce and estrange readers of various eras, and our sense of *Genji*'s queerness deepens. *Genji* poses, by virtue of its very formation, certain fundamental yet unanswerable questions. We don't know the real name of the woman who wrote *Genji*, and no original manuscript in her hand exists. Like her text, the author leaves us no choice but to approach from an insurmountable remove. While *Genji*'s author is functionally nameless, we call her Murasaki Shikibu (973–1014?). Shikibu is derived from her father's post as senior secretary in the Bureau of Ceremonial (Shikibu no daijō). Meanwhile, Murasaki is a moniker ascribed by fans of *Genji* enamored of its most beloved female protagonist, the Lady Murasaki (Murasaki no Ue). Thus the makeshift "Murasaki Shikibu" fashions a phantom intimacy with readers that effaces the fact of perennial distance.

The Tale of Genji revels in that distance, estranging readers from inherited structures along the way. Steeped in the conventions of Heian court culture, the narrative highlights elites' reliance on marriage and heterosexual reproduction as strategic means of forging alliances, reinforcing lineages, and ensuring an ascendant path. Manifold desires and investments circulate under the banner of "Heian marriage politics."[4] Yet the text also dramatizes the mercurial capacity of aspiration to elude staid routes. Part of what makes *Genji* queer, then, is not the prevalence of homoerotic innuendo but rather the text's relentless illustration of how strictures designed to govern desire routinely stoke impulses that outstrip those constraints. Indeed, in showing the fatal torment Genji's mother suffers on becoming the emperor's favorite consort in the absence of a politically powerful father's backing, the narrator condemns the aspirational tropes of Heian marriage politics—and the enforced vulnerabilities it demands—in *Genji's* opening pages. As H. Richard Okada explains, "Rather than originating in 'love' or amorous passion as some would have it, the narrator seems to be showing us the tragic underside of a male desire that depends for the prosperity of a family on a feminine presence at the same time that it ignores the consequences of the practice for the women themselves."[5] This inaugural critique of male desire embodies a queer provocation, as readers are urged to rethink the value or viability of patriarchal aspiration. Doing so constitutes a disorientation that can amplify a protagonist's or reader's awareness of contingency—their own or that of the ideological structures to which they consciously or unconsciously adhere.

Accordingly, I would agree with Lili Iriye Selden's characterization that *Genji* reveals the presence "of a critical subtext that is juxtaposed against two hegemonic discourses of desire. The first of these hegemonic discourses is an aesthetic discourse of idealized love that reflects the ideology of [the imperial poetry anthology *Kokinwakashū*, 905], and the second is a discourse of amatory conquest (*irogonomi*) that arose from the practice of marriage politics in premodern Japan."[6] Conjectures about authorial intention aside, this critical subtext proves difficult to ignore. Importantly however, Rajyashree Pandey urges caution toward retrospective invocations of agency—or woman, or desire—that might skew our interpretation.[7] With this caveat in mind, an implicit critical subtext establishes the terrain through which queer readings can weave without snagging on hegemonic ideals of romantic sport.

A queer reading would consist partly of examining how ambiguities in textual mediation and intersubjective encounters pervade this narrative terrain, consequently keeping these reductive discourses in abeyance. Even in acknowledging the *Kokinwakashū's* role in promoting a hegemonic discourse of idealized love, we should also recognize, as Gustav Heldt argues concerning male homosocial desire, that "the court-sanctioned form of love poetry found in imperial anthologies encompassed a much more polymorphous spectrum of erotic desires than is commonly acknowledged in modern readings."[8] Awareness of such a spectrum—of desires and of the rhetorical techniques through which they are expressed—should encourage an awareness of correspondingly diverse ways to theorize them.

GENJI'S QUEERNESS / *GENJI* QUESTIONS

To suggest that *Genji* queers notions of romance, proximity, intimacy, or loss unspools an array of questions that exceed facile or familiar stances. Heterosexual romantic coupling; domestic security; material possession; procreation; the reproduction and maintenance of privilege; healthful longevity; an auspicious future—I argue that *The Tale of Genji* frequently presents this trajectory as a favored paradigm while undermining it as ultimately untenable, beset by instability, violence, and indelible ambivalence. To give just one example, we might consider Genji's prudence in fathering only three children—compared to characters like Tō no Chūjō and others, who father heaps of them; we can read this restraint as queer insofar as it suggests a wary disinclination toward favored modes of social reproduction.[9]

Genji in fact belongs to a longer lineage of such Heian literary critiques. Jonathan Stockdale notes that the *Genji* forbear *Taketori monogatari* (*The Tale of the Bamboo Cutter*, late ninth century) is striking for its "somewhat radical discontent" and "a deep antagonism toward Heian sexual politics and toward the constellation of power in court society that arose from Heian marriage practices."[10] Similarly, by emphasizing this system's injustice and fallibility, the *Genji* narrative exposes certain templates for ambitious living as brittle—if not lethal. Repeatedly, we witness compulsions to align with a vector of striving that may temporarily supply pleasure but eventually depletes lives. Consequently, when it comes to the intersubjective negotiations coordinating social intercourse, the text interrogates notions of normalcy and prosperity, laying bare an abiding queerness that suffused Heian courtly life.

But how specifically does this queerness surface in *Genji*, and what would queering the text—foregrounding less discernable encounters with uncertainty and disorientation—entail? In some ways, my project negotiates between two impulses in queer theory, distinguished historically as early versus later scholarship. As J. Keith Vincent explains, "Anglophone queer studies since the 1990s has been characterized by its rejection of fixed identity categories, its anti-normative stance, and its critique of linear and developmental temporality. One might call this 'classic' or 'first generation' queer studies."[11] As queer studies has shifted away from sexuality, identity, and embodiment and toward questioning broader normative paradigms such as, in the case of posthumanist queer theory, the category of the human itself, I have sought to incorporate these more recent ideas into my readings. Hence, *A Proximate Remove* takes cues from different moments in the history of queer reading as practiced in an Anglophone and Japanese context. Put schematically, the critical work queering does in this study involves (1) identifying homoerotic impulses as they get redirected to homosocial bonding; (2) showing how desires for authority, stability, and prestige underpinning Heian life are questioned; and (3) apprehending the affective and sensorial emergence of these impulses and desires through scenes of intimacy and loss to imagine alternative modes of living and becoming.

Moving beyond associations with sexuality or gender, I propose queering as an interpretive strategy that resists closure and observes aporias where desire, doubt, discomfort, disorientation, deferral, detachment, and disenchantment undo certainties of knowledge. All of these experiences accentuate a multimodal susceptibility to forces irreducible to pat notions of gender, agency, or embodiment. Moreover, they entail a heightened degree of distance from the familiar: a remove from routines that establish normative axes the text continually calls into question. Although gender and sexuality often provide a provisional departure point, my readings accent other aspects adjacent but not anchored to those categories. Rajyashree Pandey's realization resonates here: "What struck me as noteworthy in my readings of texts such as the *Genji* was not so much the presence of individuals as active agents, imbued with initiative and will and driven by desire, but rather the existence of a force field of erotic and affective sensations . . . which created a pleasurable ambience and generated in those who came under its spell a propensity, if you will, to react and respond."[12]

As I discuss below, this textual disposition challenges traditional tenets of feminist and queer theory. Methodologically, exploring the propensity Pandey describes involves lingering over hesitations or irruptions in the text, locating moments askew of the narrative's most prominent vectors of authority, sexuality, or temporality. More specifically, *A Proximate Remove* attends to spatial, visual, aural, and tactile attributes of scenes, "providing a sensorial account that aims to untether *Genji* scholarship from the questions of imperial power and gender that have dominated, and proposing sonic reverberations, architectural porosity, and bodily (dis-)orientation as literary devices that unspool what the text's logic may otherwise contain."[13]

When I say that *Genji* queers, I mean that it imagines alternatives through its questioning of inherited structures of thought, action, and feeling. Queering does not need to center on sexuality and antinormative subversion; it can instead bring attention to the embodied experience of contingency, instances where physical or psychic stability is threatened. Consider this inventory: "As Koremitsu hunted to and fro for Genji, the ages it took for dawn to break made that single night feel like it eclipsed a thousand years;"[14] "Because of Genji's aspect as he rode wobbly in an unsteadied saddle, Koremitsu was once again right by his side to help, but Genji still slid from his mount to the ground of the Kamo riverbank;"[15] "Thinking how awful it was that she'd let her guard down, Taifu felt so rueful for Her Highness that her face feigned ignorance and she withdrew to her quarters;"[16] "Taifu's face flushed red as she looked on;"[17] "Genji had very few people with him; as they slept he alone lay awake, his pillow propped to listen to the winds whirling from all directions as the waves felt as though they were washing right up to where he lay;"[18] "[Genji] pressed a sleeve to his face while [Yūgiri], his vision blurred by tears, squinted firmly to keep looking [at Murasaki's corpse], without getting his fill."[19]

Queer energies animate each of these scenes of intimacy and loss, emerging in the agonizing dilation of time Genji spends waiting to be rescued; the tottering saddle his servant steadies; Taifu's sympathetic downcast eyes and retreat; her flushed cheeks; Genji, lonesome, listening to ravishing waves; and Yūgiri's drawn-out melancholic stare, flickering to keep focused. The pauses, touches, approaches, and compressions we discern allude to disorientations and reorientations brought by brushes with compromised conditions of possibility. Far more than any inklings of seduction or insurgence, a disorganizing and vitalizing encounter with contingency is what marks these instances as queer. A queer theorization of these scenes helps us fathom their affective shape, their micropolitical intricacy, and their implications for our own present-day capacity to rethink—or transform—worldly relations beyond the text.

Queer approaches help me assess the disorganizing, vitalizing impulses saturating *Genji*'s world. They encourage a slowed consideration of such forces and their implications at individual and social levels. And yet I want to avoid affixing a thematic core that forecloses too much, since to posit that *The Tale of Genji* is "about" affect or love—not to mention loss or intimacy—can unduly occlude other perspectives. Therefore, throughout the book, I track a host of interrogative gestures presented in the narrative. In simple terms, "a proximate remove," refers to an embodied adjacency to familiar forms or relations that unsettles in critically generative ways. Proximate removes are spatiotemporal fissures, intervals in which to suspend belief in normalizing structures and to rethink habituated patterns of occupying the world. Proximate removes become openings that arouse questioning. Genji himself arouses, too, appealing to people across a range of ages, social stations, factional lines, and locales. But whatever sensuous appeal "Shining" Genji radiates, he simultaneously poses problems for established sensibilities; predominant logics of sociality and feeling thaw in his vicinity. Genji's encounters with the phenomenal world suggest shades of affection or apprehension unfastened from rote love or longing. Hence, Genji figures a provisional focal point in the narrative's insistent questioning of established patterns. Such questioning opens an interval to pause, and to reorient attention.

Queering a text therefore involves apprehending the extent to which these textual moments, in their uneasy adjacency to enduring social mores and hegemonic discourses, challenge the primacy or stability of such norms to suggest other modes of thinking, desiring, moving, living, and having. Proximate removes— whether wrought by exile's enforced privations or by mourning's ambivalent withdrawal—serve as nodes that can be used to track how desire travels and transforms. Through these sites, I theorize the repercussions of experiencing intimacy and loss. I contend that such encounters in *The Tale of Genji* foreground the precarious consistency of dominant discourses. Collectively, these portrayals question habits of feeling, affiliation, separation, and aspiration, urging readers to reckon with these divergences as queer and volatile.

Queer moments coax us to discern desires for proximity to entities or archetypes with renewed wariness—as presences ostensibly within reach yet receding out of hand. Indeed, *Genji* dilates on the question of aspiration itself, elaborating the casualties suffered for striving's sake. A queer reading of *Genji* recognizes its protagonists' experiences with intimacy and loss as being suffused by a contingency that makes them inescapably circuitous, and often only barely navigable. Although compromised capacities to thrive are unmistakably heightened in intervals of intimacy and loss, the narrative articulates these as ubiquitous features of its landscape. Therefore, I demonstrate that queer gestures are not peripheral to the text but pivotal. In *Genji*, misgivings permeate scenes of ostensible success to spotlight considerable potential for failure. This propensity for failure figures an excess that upends our sensibilities. Hence, I argue that the movements of *Genji*'s protagonists materialize as generative estrangements, queer questions that trouble any faith in business as usual—as shown by an ancient Japanese text, or as sanctioned by contemporary academic disciplines.

MINDING THE GAP

How might queer theory transform our interpretations of medieval Japanese literature, and how might medieval Japanese literature reorient the assumptions, priorities, and practices of queer theory? *A Proximate Remove* explores these questions by turning to *Genji* as a text through which to read these two fields in productive proximity to each other. One of my goals is to draw from scholars both within and outside of premodern Japanese literary studies to improve approaches in this discipline. The aim is not to use queer theory as a route away from Heian literature. To the contrary, my hope is that a dialogue between *Genji* and queer theory might bring us back to Heian literature with new questions and better ways to read.

Moving between the disciplines of premodern Japanese literary studies and queer studies, and building on previous scholarship in both areas, the book performs a critical engagement with medieval Japanese texts that integrates close thematic readings with queer conceptual tools. *A Proximate Remove* stages a dialogue between these contexts to pursue conceptual possibilities informed by both but confined by neither. Granted, perfect reciprocity proves elusive. While some of the conversation's asymmetry stems from the very nature of working between disparate fields, more of it owes to my formal disciplinary location in premodern Japanese literary studies. That said, I do hope the book generates interpretive tools that readers from diverse disciplinary locations removed from Japanese, literary, or premodern studies might draw from.

After all, my decision to pursue this project was partly influenced by a disappointment with the lack of queer theoretical scholarship dealing with archives that were both non-Western and nonmodern.[20] I have followed work in queer studies for more than a decade, and it has been exciting to observe the field expanding its scope, methods, and ambition to include queer of color, postcolonial, emergent media, and posthumanist critiques. And as a medievalist, I find that rigorous analyses of premodern discourse by scholars like Carolyn Dinshaw, Jonathan Goldberg, and Carla Freccero have been welcome counterweights to queer studies' overwhelmingly modern slant.[21] I'm intrigued by what kinds of insights surface once capitalist modernity and its attendant ideologies can't be presumed as a frame of reference. Such a backdrop provides a convenient basis for tracing confluences across boundaries of nations, media, or experience. But this backdrop's sweep can also overdetermine too much too soon.

Of course, certain touchstones of social organization also existed for premodern societies. But much of the appeal of medieval texts is their failure to align with capitalist modernity's categories of normativity, embodied subjectivity, and politics. My goal isn't to fetishize a continuous narrative across epochs or to posit some historical schism that would let me tout premodern Japan as a bastion of radical otherness. Rather, I want to underscore a gap in scholarship formed by several intersecting disciplinary proclivities: toward modern and early modern U.S. and European cultural production in queer studies; toward modern and early modern cultural production in Asian studies; and toward sexual discourse in modern and premodern queer studies. These interwoven dispositions have fostered blind spots that A Proximate Remove tries to address.

The book's overarching goal is to energize critical discourse on premodern Japanese literature and queer theory among established and emerging scholars alike. I offer these readings not as some final take on queerness or The Tale of Genji but as a cluster of pedagogically useful provocations for readers to find examples, ask questions, and develop approaches that this study can't predict. Moreover, I've written A Proximate Remove with students in mind, especially those who run into trouble when they encounter depictions of same-sex relations like this: "'Well, then, so be it. You, at least: don't ditch me,' Genji said, having the page boy lie down alongside him. Since the boy was so cheerily appreciative of Genji's youthful tenderness, it's said that Genji found him considerably sweeter than his cold-hearted sister."[22]

Such episodes can spark classroom discomfort, excitement, curiosity, and critical thinking. This can lead to the insight that "Genji's gay" (or, as one recent undergraduate emphasized, "hella gay"). As a class, we enjoy unpacking this earnest, if misleading claim, mostly because of how it highlights certain ill-suited cultural and historical assumptions about sexual identities and practices. I get to ask what gay denotes, exactly, and if our current lingo's connotations match what Genji was up to with the appreciative boy in a story written a millennium ago. I can propose that Genji is not necessarily gay, and my students listen to me skeptically: "He's lonely, ruined by his mother's death and his uncertain status in being denied the throne; he's also a connoisseur of pleasurable, advantageous intimate relations to people and things (partially and unconsciously because of these losses); plus, he's feeling a little more unloved than usual this particular night. He is wounded, tender, cunning, unapologetically radiant, and relentlessly affectionate, but gay?" Gay proves too glib and myopic to encompass the celestially smoking hot mess that is Genji. *Queer*, though, might characterize better his complicated breadth.

As the following chapter unpacks, textual episodes like this in *Genji* raise the issue of learning to differentiate between apt confluences and false flags. Such suggestive scenes yield opportunities to reconsider hasty misrecognitions of sexual identity. Yet the book's larger critical project is to practice an apprehensive mode of reading, warily distant from absolutist pronouncements regarding desire, politics, textuality, or method. Indeed, one benefit of a queer theoretical emphasis can be its skepticism toward aspirations for epistemological closure or empirical potency. "A proximate remove" can thus also refer to the tentativeness marking this style of inquiry. As a metaphor, the phrase names an interval where characters within the fictional realm—and, ideally, the attentive reader as well—come to regard these experiences of wanting. Hence, "a proximate remove" connotes a venue for mapping and questioning both desire and the often disorganizing sensory experiences that infuse it.

POSITIONING THE INTERVENTION

At its heart, *A Proximate Remove* is an act of literary criticism with commitments to queer conceptual approaches. Simply put, this monograph is the book about sexuality, spatial representation, and sensation I wish had existed when I first encountered premodern Japanese literature in college. It has been invigorating to see multiple pieces of scholarship arrive since that time to fill important gaps. Most exciting among these has been Rajyashree Pandey's *Perfumed Sleeves and Tangled Hair: Body, Woman, and Desire in Medieval Japanese Narratives* (2016), which delves deftly into questions of embodiment and sensation in *Genji* and other texts to a degree previously unseen in English-language scholarship. In its sensitive interrogation of fundamental categories of literary analysis, I consider Pandey's study an important touchstone for queer approaches to premodern Japanese literature, even if it doesn't couch itself in these terms.

Although scholarship on *The Tale of Genji* is vast, no full-length study in English or Japanese has yet examined the text explicitly through the lens of queer theory in a sustained manner. Despite this, delineating several strands of the broader mesh of Japanese and Anglophone scholarship surrounding these issues helps demonstrate how earlier contributions ground the readings performed here. *A Proximate Remove*'s intervention is to read Heian literature and queer theory in productive relation to each other. I see my work on Heian literature as a continuation of queer theory, which is not a fixed idiom but one I am trying to enrich and develop in new directions as a scholar of premodern Japan. After all, my readings are merely meant to contribute to a broader conversation that Japanese scholars, particularly those affiliated with the Narrative Research Association (*monogatari kenkyūkai*), have already been having for decades.

A poststructuralist recourse to phenomenology resulted both in a new focus on media and mediation and in heightened attention to the relationship between language and space, as pioneered by renowned *Genji* scholars such as Mitani Kuniaki beginning in the mid-1970s.[23] Broadly, this attention could analyze asymmetries between margin and center, especially as they framed factional gender politics. At a smaller scale, the phenomenological emphasis underscored the significance of natural barriers like mountains and rivers and man-made structures like gates, fences, and folding screens as mediating objects to be theorized in relation to their effects on discursive maneuvers and interpersonal intimacies within the narrative. This was a brand of textual criticism newly alert to well-worn objects and armed with fresh lenses through which to examine the political implications of these inanimate objects' animating narrative function.

With regard to scholarship in English related to the topics of love and loss in premodern Japanese literature, gender studies criticism in a feminist vein has proved most popular since the mid-1980s. Andrew Pekarik's influential edited volume *Ukifune: Love in the Tale of Genji* (1982) heralded later gender studies approaches to *Genji* in English. Crucially, Norma Field's *The Splendor of Longing in the Tale of Genji* (1987), the first full-length study of Heian literature in English to focus primarily on the literary representation of the narrative's "heroines," arguably inaugurated this trend of Anglophone feminist readings of *Genji*. Doris Bargen's *A Woman's Weapon: Spirit Possession in the Tale of Genji* (1997) joined a series of feminist readings of premodern literature appearing from the late 1990s, participating in a broader trend toward exploring the theme of gender within English-language scholarship. Besides Bargen's study, the following works form a thematic cohort: *The Woman's Hand: Gender and Theory in Japanese Women's Writing* (1996), edited by Janet Walker and Paul Gordon Schalow; *The Father-Daughter Plot: Japanese Literary Women and the Law of the Father* (2001), edited by Rebecca L. Copeland and Esperanza Ramirez-Christensen; Edith Sarra's powerful *Fictions of Femininity: Literary Inventions of Gender in Japanese Court Women's Memoirs* (1999); and Charo D'Etcheverry's *Love after the Tale of Genji: Rewriting the World of the Shining Prince* (2007). Within this broader mix, three of the most famous English-language monographs on *Genji* approach it explicitly from a feminist vantage: Field's *Splendor of Longing*, Bargen's *A Woman's Weapon*, and Tomiko Yoda's *Gender and National Literature: Heian Texts and the Constructions of Japanese Modernity* (2004). However, Kimura Saeko notes a tendency, visible in Japanese and Anglophone feminist scholarship, to unduly subsume Heian texts beneath modern discourses that might misread their treatments of sexuality or violence.[24]

Whereas Yoda, Kimura, and H. Richard Okada have drawn attention to the politics of discursive space, there have been comparatively few theoretically inclined treatments focused on more concrete Heian literary depictions of architectural or geographic space.[25] However, Terry Kawashima's *Writing Margins* (2001) and *Itineraries of Power* (2017) address the spatial tenor of gendered constructions and textual movement, respectively; and Jonathan Stockdale's *Imagining Exile in Heian Japan* (2015) interprets literary depictions of banishment from the court's political center. Similarly, Doris Bargen's *Mapping Courtship and Kinship in Classical Japan* (2015) considers the link between genealogical networks and their manifestation in social, spatial, and architectural terms within *Genji*.

One gap we find, however, is the absence of queer treatments of Heian literature, which stands out against the notable number of monographs offering feminist readings. This relative paucity can seem strange given the wealth of Japanese and English-language scholarship on other periods and in other disciplines that emphasize nonheterosexual relations. Stephen Miller's edited volume *Partings at Dawn: An Anthology of Japanese Gay Literature* (1996), which included texts from a range of eras, broke ground as the first such anthology of its kind and signifies an important contribution to queer studies research in Japanese literature. Research on medieval literature includes articles on *chigo* (adolescent males attached to Buddhist temples) by Margaret Childs (1980) and Paul Atkins (2008), which treat the post-Heian genres of "acolyte tales" (*chigo monogatari*) that portrayed relationships between monks and temple-boys.[26]

Most research on male-male or nonbinary sexuality has focused on the Edo period (1603–1868). This includes Gary Leupp's *Male Colors: The Construction of Homosexuality in Tokugawa Japan* (1997), which examined homosexuality primarily as a historical phenomenon; and Gregory Pflugfelder's influential *Cartographies of Desire: Male-Male Sexuality in Japanese Discourse, 1600–1950* (1999), which brought further attention to the topic of homosexuality within historical studies of Japanese modernity. Meanwhile, monographs by scholars such as James Reichert (2006), Michiko Suzuki (2009), and J. Keith Vincent (2012) pursue the topic of homosociality in modern fiction.

Articles related to these issues in a Heian context are a slightly different matter. They include Pflugfelder's "Strange Fates: Sex, Gender, and Sexuality in *Torikaebaya Monogatari*" (1992), pivotal for its sophisticated incorporation of contemporary gender theory into an analysis of *The Changelings* (*Torikaebaya monogatari*, twelfth century) that highlighted gender's provisional embodiment, the performance of androgyny, and Buddhist notions' role in shaping conceptions of intersexuality. Complementing work by scholars such as Susan Mann on the multiple styles of male bonding practiced in Chinese culture, Gustav Heldt's "Between Followers and Friends: Male Homosocial Desire in Heian Court Poetry" (2007) represents a valuable, more recent foray into queer literary studies.[27] Stressing the vital ambiguity infusing the "codes of poetic intercourse" men practiced, Heldt argues that "the slippery surface of the language through which Japanese court poetry expressed male-male desire enabled it to refer to these multiple [hierarchies of rank and kinship] while also maintaining the potential to call these hierarchies into question."[28] This type of linguistic ambiguity sets the stage for queer reading by maintaining both a proximity to male-male desire and a critical remove from it.

Paul Schalow's *The Poetics of Male Friendship in Heian Japan* (2007), which examines some of *The Tale of Genji*'s male-male relationships, would seem to occupy this space and gesture toward queer critique. Schalow's study explores what he terms "poetics of courtly male friendship" in Heian texts and "inherits these concerns about the transcendence of love and the suffering of women from feminist scholarship and carries it into a new realm of inquiry—of the suffering of noblemen and the literary record of their hopes for transcendence through friendship."[29] Although the book is helpful for its attention to this theme of male friendship in several works of Heian literature, it simultaneously seems to keep the potential for queer readings at arm's length, with friendship serving as a buffer by which this possibility is deflected. "Homosexuality" is mentioned only once in the book, during a reading of *Kagerō nikki* (ca. 974), with a fifteenth-century reading of male-love (*nanshoku*) in *Ise monogatari* (ca. 980) receiving a double mention.[30] Though he doesn't use the phrase in his work, Schalow details literary aspects of male friendship that Eve Sedgwick would place along a continuum of "male homosocial desire," one whose contiguity with homoeroticism warrants further investigation given her positing of "male friendship" and "mentorship" among possible manifestations of this desire.[31]

Unlike Schalow's account, my approach considers friendship as a form of intimacy whose affective and spatiotemporal features should be rethought in queer terms explicitly. As Heldt explains, multivalent terms like *tomo* (friend/follower) and *kimi* (my love/milord) highlight a degree of fluidity in male-male friendship that Schalow's account attenuates: "this homosocial category had the potential [*sic*] to confuse the boundary between private and public relationships, creating a type of bond that was defined by neither kinship nor kingship."[32] Hence, I would argue that this blurred boundary presents an opportunity for queer reading—namely, to examine how affinities formed outside these hierarchies potentially question them and can even generate other unanticipated modes of relation in the process. Heldt's analysis advocates for highlighting such linguistic ambiguity without rushing to resolve it, with the benefit of "breaking the habit of reading poems in a manner that forces us to choose between the sexual . . . and nonsexual."[33] This recommendation continues a trend pioneered by Japanese scholars of Heian literature more than a decade earlier.

LAYING THE GROUNDWORK: JAPANESE QUEER READINGS OF HEIAN TEXTS

In the context of Japanese-language Heian literary criticism, a queer studies approach develops largely out of the fertile research of Narrative Research Association scholars. In particular, Kawazoe Fusae and Kimura Saeko offer ways to think beyond simpler notions of social reproduction and to take seriously forms of sociality not defined primarily by an obsession with patrilineal succession. In

Japanese, an emblematic article considering *Genji* from what could be called a queer studies perspective is Kawazoe Fusae's "Genji monogatari no sei to bunka: andorogyunusu to shite no Hikaru Genji" (*The Tale of Genji*'s sex and culture: Hikaru Genji as androgynous, 1995), in which she examines Genji's ambiguous erotic depictions in relation to male homosociality. Kawazoe's article stands as a significant early experiment in the queer reading of Heian literature. Occasionally in the essay, Kawazoe registers some dissatisfaction about various terms' applicability to Genji's particular shifting disposition. She demonstrates how the terms *heterosexual, homosexual, bisexual,* and *androgynous* all fail to fit Genji, due largely to how his interactions play up the gap between shifting erotic practices and any static sexual identity. Kawazoe stresses that *The Tale of Genji*, like many premodern Japanese narratives, disallows any notion of sexual identity akin to that asserted later, in the early modern period or within modern societies.

Even as *androgyny* frames Genji's orientation less clunkily than *bisexual*, Kawazoe implies that the term *androgynous* itself might presume too harsh a gender binary. Usefully, she situates *The Tale of Genji*'s androgynous depictions of its main protagonist historically. She notes that although a 970 edict prohibited sex between men, by the time Fujiwara Sukefusa's journal *Shunki* was composed in 1039, attitudes toward such behavior had changed completely to become much more permissive heading into the *insei* period of cloistered rule by retired emperors.[34] Remarkably, this locates *Genji*'s composition, circa 1010, roughly midway between these two benchmarks, suggesting that Murasaki Shikibu's narrative registered and participated in the gradual normalization of male-male sexual relations and the gender expectations that slid along with them. Moreover, in a vein extended by scholars like Pandey, Kawazoe lays the groundwork for a radical rethinking of what even defines a body. In this way, Kawazoe parallels a conceptual turn taken within queer studies from initial critiques of gender systems and the politics of embodiment to more recent posthumanist approaches.

Two of Kawazoe's insights seem especially valuable. Firstly, the scenarios *Genji* depicts ultimately don't parse easily into modern categories of sexual identity or preference, where heterosexual and homosexual are counterposed: "Sexual love in *The Tale of Genji* is not something that tells of protagonists' sexual habits; it is narrating human reciprocal relationality itself [ningen sōgo no kankeisei sono mono]."[35] Secondly, Genji's interactions with various characters can actually suggest modes of relation (*yukari*) that are less rigid and overdetermined than what sexuality denotes. Kawazoe's argument challenges the significance of sexual object-choice in favor of affinity. Untethered from sexual object-choice, affinities of this sort imply more provisional, improvisational eroticism or affection that blooms momentarily and then evaporates or shifts course. Instructive is the way Kawazoe reads *Genji* closely to consider the utility of homosociality as an interpretive frame while remaining attuned to Heian concepts that helpfully refract such foreign terms.

One detail that highlights the complex scholarly environment in which these terms circulate is that Kawazoe's article, which invokes homosociality, doesn't cite Eve Sedgwick's foundational 1985 book, *Between Men: English Literature and Male Homosocial Desire*. Instead, it cites modern Japanese literature scholar Komori Yōichi's 1994 article, "*Kokoro* ni okeru dōseiai to iseiai" (Homosexuality and heterosexuality in *Kokoro*).³⁶ This citation speaks to the prevailing networks of translation (or lack thereof) for queer studies scholarship. As J. Keith Vincent notes, "Sedgwick's *Epistemology of the Closet* and Judith Butler's *Gender Trouble*, both published in English in 1990, made it into Japanese together in 1999, whereas Sedgwick's book had to wait until 2008 to be translated into French, and Butler's *Gender Trouble* until 2006. The same cannot be said, incidentally, of more recent works in queer theory."³⁷ Worth noting here are the relative speed with which certain works of queer theory were translated into Japanese and the relative slowness with which queer theory made it into premodern Japanese literary studies— as mediated through research on modern Japanese literature. Symptomatic of a politics of translation that differentially structures the rate and depth at which concepts from Anglophone academia enter subfields of Japanese literary studies, this secondhand citation itself symbolizes a proximate remove of sorts: a deferred access to queer theory despite an attraction to its interpretive promise.

Building on the work of scholars like Kawazoe, Kimura Saeko's *Koisuru monogatari no homosekushuariti: kyūtei shakai to kenryoku* (Love tales' homosexuality: Court society and authority, 2008) and "Kyūtei monogatari no kuia na yokubō" (The queer desire of court tales, 2014) exemplify a more recent move, especially by Japanese feminist scholars of Heian literature, to incorporate a queer studies emphasis into analyses of gender politics.³⁸ Kimura's investment in queer theory seems based on a desire to identify textual moments where prevailing gender politics yield a potential to imagine otherwise. I draw inspiration from Kimura's provocative ability to highlight how literary depictions can prompt us to reconsider aspects of gender and authority we might take for granted as being prescribed or totalized by Heian systems, such as wet-nursing and the serviceability of "nonproductive" female bodies to reproducing an aristocratic order.³⁹ Such an emphasis on nonproductive female bodies allows us to read them, and their relationships with Genji's own unusual body, as queer.

In her earlier research, Kimura unpacks the limiting assumptions of the term *homosexuality* while foregrounding the social utility of male-male sexuality despite its lack of reproductive value biologically. However, her later work names its concerns queer explicitly, loosening a customary analytical tie to bodies, sexuality, and gender politics per se. Instructively, Kimura shows how queer desire in Heian literature emerges not simply in sexual object-choice among humans but also across ethnic or species boundaries, with rebirth signifying a queer trope for its capacity to transform gender, status, mobility, and existence itself.⁴⁰ Remarkable here is the way a Buddhist worldview fundamental to Heian texts informs a style of posthumanist queer reading beyond a Western modern queer theoretical frame of reference. Readings like these, advanced by Japanese scholars like Kawazoe and Kimura, enrich my project's conceptual framework.

QUEER'S STAKES AND ORIENTATIONS

This delineation of relevant strains of inquiry in Anglophone and Japanese studies of premodern Japanese literature begs the question of what a rethinking along queer theoretical lines would entail: What resources would it require, and what critical habits might it produce, unsettle, or redress? How should we understand the stakes and conceptual, historical, and political orientation of *queer*? Such a rich concept deserves a multifaceted response. My goal in this and subsequent sections is therefore to clarify which concepts and tendencies circulating in the interface between Heian literary studies and Anglophone queer studies I find most useful.

Claudia Freccero argues that "all textuality, when subjected to close reading, can be said to be queer" in order to resist the term's "reification into nominal status designating an entity, an identity, a thing, and allow it to continue its outlaw work as a verb and sometimes an adjective."[41] I appreciate Freccero's stress on the term's verbal resonance but am wary of widening the term's scope to include "all textuality." More useful is her claim that the "indeterminacy of the queer . . . may in fact constitute its usefulness as a deconstructive anti-identitarian and political practice."[42] Analyzing the nature of this indeterminacy is a priority, and I find more fruitful the deconstructive anti-identitarian strain of queer theory than the activist one.

My own use of "queer" as a figure of indeterminacy is strategic: I hope to spark discussion about the concept's meanings and uses among scholars, trained respectively in queer studies and premodern Japanese studies, who tend not to share archives or conversations.[43] This is a modest hope for transdisciplinary exchange. Even so, such hope might nonetheless signify as queer insofar as it recalls Elizabeth Dinshaw's notion of a queer historical impulse, which she describes as "an impulse toward making connections across time between . . . lives, texts, and other cultural phenomena left out of sexual categories back then and . . . those left out of current sexual categories now. Such an impulse extends the resources for self- and community building into even the distant past."[44] I hope this study expands that impulse and, in time, makes it more sustainable.

The political practice that motivates *A Proximate Remove* involves assessing the politics of disciplinary formation and reproduction within both the Heian text and the contemporary university. My goal is to perform readings that make *queer* both desirable and viable as a textual approach within studies of premodern Japanese texts, ideally in a fashion that erodes some of the discipline's enduring positivism and conservatism. Taking a genealogical approach, I chart discontinuities pervading prevailing senses of what's viable historically, politically, and pedagogically. In its verbal mode, "to queer" is to rework established patterns. I therefore deploy the concept as a way to rethink notions of desire, relationality, feeling, knowledge, and learning.

As the subsequent chapter demonstrates, thematizing *The Tale of Genji*'s portrayals of feeling in terms of emotion, sentimentality, and romance has a checkered history of appraisals that have frequently oversimplified the text. Hence, much English-language discourse and some Japanese commentary continued from the late nineteenth century until the linguistic turn of the late 1970s to cast *Genji* in alternately rhapsodizing, moralizing, or patronizing reductions.[45] Such responses were fueled by geopolitical contestations in which Heian literature as a paragon of Japanese civilization was cast as exceptionally aesthetic and romantically lush. In the late nineteenth and early twentieth centuries, this characterization supported arguments for Japan's cultural sophistication being on par with that of Western nations, while in the post–World War II and Cold War periods it helped hawk Japan's humanism and apolitical (i.e., non-Communist) harmlessness. Hence, sentimentality and effete sensibility consistently overshadowed the narrative's tenor of systemic violence, not to mention its undesirable sensibilities and affections. Historicizing this containment strategy targeted at premodern Japanese texts invites comparison with corollaries such as those described by Alan Sinfield and Deborah Nelson in U.S. Cold War culture.[46]

To queer intimacy and loss is to question the normative structures—like privacy, propriety, or property ownership—that encompass them.[47] Gesture and affect matter as embodiments of these questions at differing scales. Gesture becomes a site to interpret the reverberations of disparate stimuli as they stir bodily motion; affect helps consider such movements in a granular register. I build on work like Mitamura Masako's *Genji monogatari kankaku no ronri* (*The Tale of Genji*: A logic of sensation, 1996), which bases its readings in protagonists' sensorial experiences to consider how sensation attunes us to interpretive potentials beyond standard critiques of imperial authority. Although scholarship in this vein did not label itself as queer, its explorations of the conceptual possibilities of phenomenology and *shintairon* (embodiment criticism) suggest conceptual congruities with queer commentary. I also engage Sara Ahmed's queer reading of Merleau-Ponty's phenomenology to assess the critical purchase it holds for rethinking *Genji*'s depictions of spatial practices. *A Proximate Remove* incorporates and extends these approaches to theorize the text's portrayals of intimacy and loss.

One way I do this is by reading between Japanese- and English-language accounts of phenomenological and affective modes of encounter. I take a cue from Matsui Kenji's *Genji monogatari no seikatsu sekai* (*The Tale of Genji*'s lifeworld, 2000), in which Matsui theorizes *Genji*'s depictions through Husserl's phenomenological notion of collective intersubjective perception of the lived world. Matsui's project shares a sensibility with Kathleen Stewart's *Ordinary Affects* (2007), another reference point for my own text. Through theorizing what Stewart conceptualizes as the potential that animates the ordinary, I delineate the affective dimensions in *Genji* of experiencing intimacy and loss in their most inconsequential guises.[48] In this regard, my investigation echoes feminist and queer studies' turn toward the everyday as a critical site.[49] Still, I stress how the quotidian is conditioned by overt stratifications like patriarchal and status hierarchies. For instance, mid-Heian courtship, with all its flirtations and infractions, represents an ordinary girded by arrangements that disproportionately disadvantage women. The emperor system and its reproduction of imperial authority underwrote this unfair arrangement as part and parcel of women's and men's pursuits of pleasure, distraction, sex, security, and intimacy. Thus the world of the inconsequential everyday possesses intimate ties to prevailing discriminatory structures. My analyses focus on status and gender asymmetries to delineate the processes of subjection and orientation— institutionally and in the realm of individual sensory experience. Affect in particular becomes a concept through which to consider the gnarled, disorganizing capacities of intimacy and loss in a more capillary register, offering a means, like *queer*, to unravel normativity.

Nonetheless, given queer theory's basis in civil rights struggles around sexuality and citizenship, readers familiar with queer studies will note my project's disinterest in lauding subversion or *anti* stances. According to Annamarie Jagose, antinormativity has played a formative role in animating and organizing queer concerns, "enshrined as the signature value of a newly emergent activist and academic movement."[50] But as the field has progressed, as Robyn Wiegman and Elizabeth A. Wilson note, "mak[ing] normativity queer theory's axiomatic foe" now seems questionable.[51] Anglophone queer studies scholars have thus recently taken up the task of interrogating this conceptual keystone to rethink the history and future of queer theory and activism.

This move itself exemplifies queer critique in its willingness to displace a constitutive component of its disciplinary identity, making the term *queer*, in Judith Butler's account, "remain that which is in the present, never fully owned, but always and only redeployed, twisted, queered from a prior usage and in the direction of urgent and expanding political purposes."[52] With similar skepticism, my interest in queer doesn't rest in its historical allegiance to *anti*. Instead, I'm more compelled methodologically by its adjacency to reparative gestures less bound to identitarian struggles, not for lack of solidarity, but rather because such ongoing campaigns' motivating assumptions and aims—about identity, autonomy, privacy, capacities for action, citizenship, justice—don't fit my ancient Japanese objects well.

For one thing, queer as a sexual or more broadly behavioral designation based in typical modern understandings of antinormativity doesn't pan out in a premodern Japanese context. To mention just two prominent examples briefly, socially normalized and codified practices such as male love (*nanshoku*) between samurai during the Edo period (1603–1867) and a tradition of male-male sexual relations among Buddhist clergy and temple attendants especially from the thirteenth century onward complicate if not invalidate accounts of sexual normativity bound to religious and legal prohibitions on sodomy. (We could add the absence of mandated religious confession and less draconian attitudes toward polyamory and matrimonial relations as other relevant variances from Western societies.) Indeed, *nanshoku*'s banality as a basic social fact and salient feature of institutional life announces a marked divergence from studies of sexuality in medieval Western cultures. The analytical impetus differs because there is less to expose on this score, especially in the early modern period. Sex does not become *the* secret coveted by the repressive mechanisms Michel Foucault diagnoses.[53] This lessens the need for and appeal of a symptomatic or paranoid hermeneutic, sapping their payoff. Hence, same-sex relations (among men at least) mostly figure as biographical truism, not as juicy fodder to be pried from the closet.

Queer critique does not merely oppose norms but also energizes doubt through its disinclination toward hasty foreclosure. Consequently, far more promising than a hunt for queer epitomes of antinormative resistance is queering as a mode of revising critical attention. Through this revision, queering can transition from mere critique to fashion a critical commitment to styles of thriving that are out of sync with dominant routines. Here, José Muñoz's utopian ambitions for the term stand out: "Queerness is a structuring and educated mode of desiring that allows us to see and feel beyond the quagmire of the present. . . . Queerness is a longing that propels us onward, beyond romances of the negative and toiling in the present."[54]

For Muñoz, just occupying the site of objection isn't enough. He tilts the vector of queer forward, using its dissenting spirit as a springboard to imagine enhanced futures. Its status as a "crusading slogan" and matters of gender identification or activism aside, queering questions inherited sensibilities to pursue renewed capacities for thinking, relating, and living.[55] Such questioning rehearses an "educated mode of desiring" that transcends current constraints. Thus to queer is to rethink prevailing tendencies and become more attuned to, more educated about, and more desirous of better alternatives—for approaching *Genji* and for engaging vital questions beyond the text.

In the case of *Genji* specifically, a queer intervention informed by Muñoz's framing would entail looking past the text's "romances of the negative": the doomed relationships Genji seeks out in melancholic pursuit of substitutes for his dead mother and lost status. What Muñoz suggests would also mean forgoing the negative conceptual baggage inherited from non-Heian times and places. Doing so would entail deemphasizing themes of pessimism or lack in our analyses to read in more reparative ways. Case in point: Genji's exile to Suma, despite the dispossession and toil it entails, could also be read in terms of the comfort it lends and the educational insight exile offers into a mode of artistic creation not circumscribed by the immediate demands of courtship or reproducing an aristocratic social order.

CONCEPTUAL SYNTAX

With a fuller sense of this terrain in mind, I'll now parse the book's title to map relationships between its guiding concepts.

Proximate

adjective

1 (esp. of a cause of something) closest in relationship; immediate: *that storm was the proximate cause of damage to it.*

• closest in space or time: *the failure of the proximate military power to lend assistance.*

2 nearly accurate; approximate: *he would try to change her speech into proximate ladylikeness.*[56]

As a concept, proximity prods thought. The definitions above highlight two broad senses of the word: (1) a degree of immediacy and (2) a gap in accuracy or fidelity between proximate phenomena. The example phrases mention "damage," "failure," "military power," and a push toward "ladylikeness." The implied violence, capacity for structural failure, and pressure to comply with gender norms all issue from a destabilizing impulse that spatiotemporal closeness transmits.

Proximate connotes connection but needn't denote a particular vector or orientation. In this regard, it shares some of the appeal of *beside*, which, according to Eve Sedgwick, "permits a spacious agnosticism about several of the linear logics that enforce dualistic thinking: noncontradiction or the law of the excluded middle, cause versus effect, subject versus object."[57] There is potential energy in proximity that has yet to acquire purpose: "*Beside* comprises a wide range of desiring, identifying, representing, repelling, paralleling, differentiating, rivaling, leaning, twisting, mimicking, withdrawing, attracting, aggressing, warping, and other relations."[58]

The book's title hinges on visual and aural affinities between the phrase *a proximate* and the word *approximate* because I want to stress questions of inflection from the start. Meaning and stakes shift according to how one opts to emphasize the gap before *proximate*. Whereas *a proximate* pronounces spatial separation, *approximate* makes us doubt the fidelity or depth of that discrepancy. Both permutations undermine the detachment of *remove*; both versions make us wary of the intervals they open. *Approximate* in verb form ventures outward, reaching to mime or reproduce a model referent. To approximate is to aspire in some way, desiring closeness or even equivalence with an ideal such that that ideal encases the (queer) aspirant. As Sara Ahmed points out, "The aspiration to ideals of conduct that is central to the reproduction of heteronormativity has been called, quite understandably, a form of assimilation."[59]

But these aspirational desires to approximate, incorporate, or assimilate can blur boundaries; as Lauren Berlant notes, "Intimacy only rarely makes sense of things."[60] Does the act of approximation ultimately simulate or dissimulate? Can everybody hit the mark with an equal shot at success? And what are the emotional, material, and relational costs of coinciding—for the subject, the object, the social body whose strictures magnify the stakes of meeting guidelines—especially where success implies an inability to differentiate between entities that overlap? The process of approximation smuggles with it plenty of anxious energy.

Moreover, *approximate* raises the specter of attrition, reminding us that something always goes missing (or gets taken) in the effort to aspire. Hence in the realm of social life, Berlant observes, it becomes "hard not to see lying about everywhere the detritus and the amputations that come from attempts to fit into the fold; meanwhile, a lot of world-building energy atrophies."[61] Berlant foregrounds the paradoxical nature of aspiring by formulating "cruel optimism," which "names a relation of attachment to compromised conditions of possibility."[62]

An analytical move I find compelling is that cruel optimism includes both banal and obsessive affections—phenomena occurring at varying scales—in its interpretive scope. Berlant's formulation also assists my inquiry by positing "proximity to the scene of desire/attraction" as a vital aspect of the subject's (un)conscious calculations concerning how to invest in the world.[63] I'm interested in such deliberate or unwitting adjustments in *Genji* as a function of spatiotemporal distance and as activated by desires whose full force or significance are incalculable. Epistemologically, uncertainty abiding despite or because of closeness to the attracting scene complicates evaluations of feelings' truth or magnitude. Proximity thus becomes part of theorizing desire and sensation in ways that complicate implications for the subject's life prospects.

We can read cruel optimism's manifestations in impulsive or tactical calibrations of how to maneuver in relation to one's past, present, and future commitments. *Genji* shows these maneuvers to be saturated by intimacies and losses large and small. Indeed, Genji himself is a figure of fraught thriving; he often embodies cruel optimism incarnate. His and other protagonists' desire to thrive, even as attachment to ideals of worldly success impair thriving, requires a reckoning with intimacy and loss that reads as queer in its unrelenting contradiction.

Remove

Remove resonates in several registers, too. It anticipates the "loss" of the book's subtitle, albeit with a more active valence. *Remove* marks displacements large and small, concrete and abstract. For example, it should be understood against a Heian backdrop marred by the escalating seizure of women's landholding rights.[64] But it can also signify the barest wedge of space between courtiers as they merrily share a carriage (see chapter 3); exile's understated devastation (see chapter 4); or the mournful echoes emanating from musical mementos (see chapter 5).

The wary distance connoted by *remove* lends productive friction when juxtaposed against *proximate*: as one term pulls close, the other peels away. As a verb phrase, *to approximate remove* means to fabricate an impression of distance, especially when the subject is drawn closer than it can comfortably sustain. Bad breakup aftermath comes to mind, as do instances when Genji assumes a connoisseurial stance toward incense, calligraphy, and dead or living women. Here, distance connotes prudence, poise, and insulation—a circumspect or less vulnerable vantage. This occurs when Genji is attacked by a spirit and acts tough to quell the turmoil of his emotions and environs—only to ultimately flee the scene in shambles, rescued by a lesser man (see chapter 2).

Such gestures try to tame the disorganization wrought by death and other losses. One might have to fake it till they make it, playing brave until grief abates. In classical psychoanalysis, this simulation animates Freud's account of mourning.[65] In Freud's narration, the work of mourning is symbolized by a child's repetition compulsion to master his mother's absence through manipulating a proxy object. The object's rhythmic removal from sight, followed by its return, mitigates the loss, transposing it tangibly nearer until it approximates what's absent. This nearness, vibrating along a spectrum of affects and object relations, carries phenomenological implications for other subjects and objects.

Queering

My readings of *Genji* demonstrate the irreducibility of queerness to matters linked exclusively or primarily to sexuality, as *queer* entails a far broader array of relations. The following chapter delineates the historical specificity, conceptual implications, and methodological promise of *queer* and *queering*. Suffice it to say for now that the terms mark a desire to question the formation of dominant, normative logics governing the embodied experience of space, time, and feeling. To queer is to nudge these logics' viability into doubt and to propose alternate modes of dwelling in the world. In *Genji*'s case, these logics include the workings of aristocratic patriarchy and imperial succession, and the affections that nourish both.

Often, these affections sprout along a homosocial continuum. *Homosocial* both describes the aristocratic Heian sphere in which *Genji* was composed and designates a rich subgenre of relations that it treats in compelling ways. As Sedgwick has outlined in her seminal study of homosocial desire, *Between Men*, homosocial relationships needn't include sexual contact but may be characterized by relations that are contiguous with the sexual, such as rivalry, mentorship, paternalism, misogyny, and care. For Sedgwick, "[*homosocial*] is applied to such activities as 'male bonding,' which may, as in our society, be characterized by intense homophobia, fear and hatred of homosexuality. To draw the 'homosocial' back into the orbit of 'desire,' of the potentially erotic, then, is to hypothesize the potential unbrokenness of a continuum between homosocial and homosexual."[66] While eroticism does not necessarily tinge these relations in *Genji*, Sedgwick's notion highlights desire's propensity to affect social impulses in ways irreducible to identity or libido alone.

Among the many ideas Sedgwick presents, three stand out as potentially useful for thematic reading. First is her observation that female characters situated between men—often an ostensible love interest for whom the men compete—

function as conduits for male protagonists' erotic desire for each other. These female characters' presence helps conceal the homosexuality that would threaten the patriarchy. Second is the de-eroticization of male-male relationships through homosocial bonding, which preserves patriarchy by letting men uphold each other's interests. And third is the idea of desire being "strongly mimetic in that rivalry to *be* (or best) the other is just as strong as heterosexual desire."[67] Readers familiar with scenes of Genji's more or less rivalrous relationships with characters such as Tō no Chūjō, Kashiwagi, Suzaku, Koremitsu, or his own father and son can appreciate how homosocial desire animates their interactions and thus might enrich our interpretations.

At a more meta-discursive level, Sedgwick's formulation proves valuable in its ability to bypass the binary heterosexual/homosexual categories organizing modern social relationships. As Gustav Heldt explains, because "there is no way for us to determine, in any given exchange between two men, whether or not the emotions expressed are informed by their relationship as lovers, as friends, or as patron and client . . . Eve Sedgwick's category of male homosocial desire is a particularly apt way of describing the expression of longing between men in Heian poetry."[68] Simultaneously, however, what can potentially make it less helpful is its basis in premises of agency, repression, and subversion that don't apply to a Heian context, where male-male sexuality isn't as threatening or prohibited. Thus, a notion of homosociality can help illustrate Heian literary texts while not mapping neatly onto them.

Such an impasse presents an opportunity for a mutual revision whereby Heian literature might alter the terms of queer theory, not just the other way around. After all, it isn't just that Heian specialists need queer theory but that queer theory also needs Heian specialists to enrich its lexicon. To give just one example, Heian texts generally don't fit the dominant narrative of prohibition, discrimination, and antinormative subversion foundational to queer studies. Although I pursue this more thoroughly in chapter 1, at a basic level, the structuring assumptions about sin, sexuality, and social cohesion operative in a postmedieval Western context simply don't apply, primarily because no comparably draconian discourse defined male-male sexual practices in medieval Japan. For William LaFleur, *medieval* denotes "that epoch during which the basic intellectual problems, the most authoritative texts and resources, and the central symbols were all Buddhist."[69] Thus, in contrast to Judeo-Christian dogma, a Buddhist worldview did not ascribe a similar contempt to male-male sexuality, with male-female relations actually being marked as more sinful for their contribution to suffering through biological reproduction.

As one scholar notes, "There is no compulsory hetero-sexuality in Heian Japan; there is, however, a politics of reproduction that emphasizes hetero-sexual gamesmanship to get a well-born girl, and ensure the perpetuation of power and privilege through progeny."[70] Removing the linchpin of prohibitions on sodomy enshrined in Western contexts poses some problems for traditional queer theory: How should we discuss the concept of "queer" devoid of a compulsory heterosexuality against which it might be defined? How should we interpret homoeroticism when male-male sexuality does not prove threatening per se? And furthermore, what happens to our conventional ideas of resistance or gender politics when we realize how ill-suited notions of desire, gender, or agency can be to this context? As Pandey frames the issue, "Underlying modern conceptions of agency is the assumption that behind every act there is the presence of an autonomous individual, who has the innate desire to strike out against the norms of her society. What if we were to let go of this anachronistic assumption, and were to decouple agency from liberal thought?"[71]

One consequence of this decoupling would be a need to rethink any notion of politics as it related to literary study. Ideally, this letting go could also mean loosening our grip on habits of paranoid reading that feel most productive and familiar, but that might also overshadow other, less legible alternatives. As Sedgwick wrote in acknowledging such a method's limitations, "To apply a hermeneutics of suspicion is, I believe, widely understood to be a mandatory injunction rather than a possibility among other possibilities."[72] One benefit of performing queer readings of Heian literature is the noninjunction to explore other possibilities outside the purview assumed by a queer studies reared on paranoid readings of post-Victorian Western texts. An aspect of queering discussed in the following chapter recognizes homosociality as linked to a host of other questions without overemphasizing it as an analytic crutch. Hence, queering takes up homosociality as just one, albeit important, facet of a wider relational landscape.

Intimacy

Intimacy is trickier. It can be queer regardless of whether or not sexual relations occur. It shares *proximate*'s ambit but implies more. *Intimate* denotes not just close but deep or thick as well; think "intimate knowledge" or "intimate description." It would seem to presume mutual assent between subjects. But intimacy possesses spectral qualities that insinuate the workings of nonsovereign agency.[73] While it connotes a closeness, that closeness may not always coincide with actual physical proximity or consciousness—or reality, for that matter. Throughout *Genji*, characters imagine a bond to be intimate irrespective of the object's recognition or consent.

In Lauren Berlant's formulation, "Intimacy builds worlds; it creates spaces and usurps places meant for other kinds of relation. Its potential failure to stabilize closeness always haunts its persistent activity, making the very attachments deemed to buttress 'a life' seem in a state of constant if latent vulnerability."[74] With its wayward leanings, intimacy can travel without our blessing, ripen without our knowledge, and fashion tenuous linkages according to a provisional will of its own, "for intimacy refers to more than that which takes place within the purview of institutions, the state, and an ideal of publicness. What if we discerned it within more mobile processes of attachment? . . . It can be portable, unattached to a con-crete space: a drive that creates spaces around it through practices."[75] Intimacy proves more evasive or porous than authority prefers. Here, I think of the "intimate public sphere" and the queer counterpublics congealing—if only provisionally—within and against it.[76]

Although Berlant's notion is developed in relation to a modern Western regime wherein compulsory heterosexuality and a hegemonic discourse of family val-ues exert outsize influence on how intimacy is framed, it still proves useful for Heian literary studies. Specifically, her emphasis on the instability of intimate rela-tions, their ungovernable mobility, and their ability to produce alternative spaces through provisional practices jibes with earlier cited features of Heian literary cul-ture noted by Kawazoe, Kimura, and Heldt. Their work dismantles a notion of sexual identity to focus instead on textual performances whose "failure to stabilize closeness always haunts its persistent activity," in Berlant's terms.

This formulation fits within a longer queer theoretical lineage of recuperating the productive value of failure in social relations, as represented by scholars such as Heather Love, José Esteban Muñoz, and Judith Halberstam.[77] But note here that this destabilizing failure is played out through various forms of social intercourse that, as Kimura reminds us, can often seem nonproductive, depending on their distance from the site of biological reproduction of aristocratic progeny and privi-lege. Whereas Heldt's analysis demonstrates how "the indeterminacies enabled by court poetry . . . could simultaneously affirm social hierarchies *and* suspend them as the occasion (or intended audience) required," what Berlant's formulation adds to Heian literary scholars' insights is the accent not on just alternative forms of social praxis or blurring the public/private boundary but on intimacy's capacity to usurp existing spaces, create new spaces, and even build worlds.[78]

Much queer studies scholarship on intimacy extends a feminist insistence on the overlap between private and public life, whereby personal decisions constitute political acts. Catalyzed by the AIDS crisis, this scholarship also narrates personal accounts of intimacy as a refusal to conceal sexual relationships demonized as abnormal and as a commitment to affirming the legitimacy of queer desires, erotic practices, sociality, and claims to equal rights. As Sara Ahmed notes, "Loss implies the acknowledgement of the desirability of what was once had. . . . As such, the failure to recognize queer loss as loss is also a failure to recognize queer relation-ships as significant bonds, or that queer lives are lives worth living."[79] To affirm queer intimacy was thus to assert a humanity heteronormative mandates denied by degrading the viability of other forms of human relation. In the wake of this affirmation, queer theory has moved to consider other types of relation removed from the strictly human.[80]

Intimacy comes to mind as a relationship between two people—lovers, friends, rivals. But it also rustles in connections between human subjects and inanimate objects, as Matsui Kenji demonstrates in *The Tale of Genji's Lifeworld*. In *Genji*, these objects include artisanal paper, a rival suitor's calligraphic lines, ocean air, scented robes, and a perished companion's cherished bamboo flute. Sometimes, these intimate objects serve as keepsake proxies for absent human owners, but they also furnish palpable occasions to reorient of one's sense of loss.

Less narcissistic and anthropocentric relationships exist, too. As Mel Y. Chen explains, there are innumerable points at which intimacy operates past the threshold of human subjectivity per se:

> When physically copresent with others, I ingest them. . . . There is nothing fanciful about this. I am ingesting their exhaled air, their sloughed skin, and the skin of the tables, chairs, and carpet of our shared room. The myth that we all cherish of our neatly contained individuality, our separateness, is shattered. We are bundles of molecules that are ever-moving and bonding with other molecules that move from other subjects and objects. In fact, the lines we draw between the living and the non-living, between subject and object are now up for question and revision. We are constantly intimate with each other, with nonhuman animals, with furniture, with chemical elements in ways we may have never realized.[81]

The Tale of Genji prefigures this account of subdermal, interspecies, and (toxic?) chemical intimacies with its own permeating traces. After all, presence can be difficult to pin down in *Genji*, especially when possessing spirits prowl the mundane realm to trouble the boundary between embodied subjects, to say nothing of any partition divorcing the immaterial from the concrete (see chapters 2 and 5). Hovering somewhere between lurid nightmares and ribbons of incense, these spirits infiltrate *Genji*'s built spaces and human bodies both, spurring some relationships while truncating others. As Kaoru Hayashi notes, "Spirit possession . . . represents a site in which the past, bodies, and emotions tend to be salient, vulnerably revealed and narrated. By sharing these moments and spaces, the participants deepen their sense of mutuality of being and experience the formation and reinforcement of kinship."[82] Although kinship in *Genji* is a thoroughly vexed enterprise, Hayashi's accent on spirit possession's role in deepening a sense of mutuality highlights an encounter where the porosity of temporal, spatial, and corporeal boundaries allows intimacy to assume unanticipated guises.

My readings theorize this encounter, influenced by Takahashi Tōru's theories of a spectral, roving narrational presence and by Chen's work on animacy.[83] Chen's formulation extends the possibilities of Takahashi's focus on narration not bound by a single embodied subject position. A benefit of this extension is having to take seriously a far broader, less anthropocentric range of interactions that undermine firm notions of what it means to possess or be possessed, as not just spirit possession but other less dramatic forms of contact blur what it means to exist or to lose oneself—or another.

Loss

Next comes *loss*, the gravest term of the lot. Although I have discussed the aesthetic, performative facets of mortality elsewhere, *A Proximate Remove* takes up death as just one point along a gamut of deprivations deserving our attention.[84] As David L. Eng and Alexander Kazanjian explain, "'Loss' names what is apprehended by discourses and practices of mourning, melancholia, nostalgia, sadness, trauma, and depression."[85] Eng and Kazanjian's volume focuses on twentieth-century experiences of loss (e.g., war, globalization, AIDS), reading them primarily through the frame of melancholia, joining a broader set of psychoanalytic and poststructuralist critiques that address mourning and melancholia as main avenues for theorizing queer loss.[86]

Freud's classic psychoanalytic account describes mourning as "the reaction to the loss of a loved person, or to the loss of some abstraction which has taken the place of one, such as one's country, liberty, an ideal, and so on."[87] His description emphasizes how loss of a loved object can damage the mourner's self-regard and, by extension, impoverish their sense of the wider world. Although the work of mourning "proceeds to demand that all libido shall be withdrawn from its attachments to that object," he acknowledges that "this opposition can be so intense that a turning away from reality takes place and a clinging to the object through the medium of hallucinatory wishful psychosis."[88] Despite being less central to the book than explicitly queer approaches, Freud's account of mourning schematizes the workings of adoration, substitution, and attachment in ways that prove helpful across the ensuing chapters' readings of intimacy and loss. In particular, confronting the destabilizing effects of being torn between desired attachment and demanded withdrawal characterizes how the unsettling adjacency of proximate removes are experienced in the *Genji* narrative.

Not all loss is final or even tragic, however. Part of my argument about privation, exile, and disorientation concerns characters that get lost, becoming displaced from familiar channels and losing a sense of where their pursuits will lead. Such circumstances call for the more challenging realization that tenderness may not merely involve sexual desire but also entail the mourning of other lost possibilities—not just concrete objects. Importantly, psychoanalytic accounts of loss can stress its productive aftermath, where indulging "hallucinatory wishful psychosis" might be read less pejoratively as an imagining of paths past suffering. This creative practice of working through can include crafting attachments—manic or otherwise—to new objects; a burgeoning creative impulse aimed at sublimating inner emptiness through artistic externalization; and the desire to reorient and build toward different spaces than before.[89] In Genji's case, the primal traumatic loss of his mother generates an extraordinary sensitivity to the phenomenal world we might read as queer. Loss, for whatever pain it might cause, can also bring unexpected joys, such as when losing out on a female lover galvanizes ties between two men (see chapter 3) or when exile emboldens male friendship (see chapter 4). In this, I take cues from Elizabeth Freeman's turn away from queer studies' darker emphasis on grief and loss. Her approach tempers that melancholic fixation toward something less grim and less overdetermined by the "capaciousness of meaning" melancholia grants Eng and Kazanjian.⁹⁰

That said, *Genji* broadcasts that there's still plenty of grieving to be done. In the narrative's very first chapter, for example, we observe how loss and textual mediation enfold. Genji's father, the Kiritsubo Emperor, loses his beloved wife. This death sends him reeling in effeminizing grief as he seeks solace, ensconced in the women's quarters, poring over pictures and poems like "The Song of Everlasting Sorrow."⁹¹ He forfeits masculinity and imperial authority with this escapist relocation. This aesthetic mourning practice also connects him to an imagined male homosocial community of cultural workers whose art helps ease his pain. This trope of seeking consolation through an intertextual practice of identification is mirrored later in the *Sarashina Diary* (*Sarashina nikki*, ca. 1060), when the narrator soothes her grief at losing intimates by sinking irrevocably into the realm *Genji* renders.⁹² Both examples reveal textual mediation to be vital to the work of mourning, as it can help distance bereavement's brutal reality, providing simulations that distract or console mourners.

The disorienting imprint of loss interweaves its aesthetic, spatial, and affective dimensions. This multimodal assemblage can take the form of sublimation, as when Genji assuages the pain of exile through intensively painting the stark landscape surrounding him at Suma (see chapter 4). Consolation can also prove elusive, as when Yūgiri samples the musical instruments his dead friend abandoned in an attempt to restore traces of a vacant tone (see chapter 5). Music fails to soothe his grief, but it fails in ways that manage to resonate, if not repair. Both examples show protagonists negotiating loss, trying to mediate and mitigate its pain across sensory registers.

The chapters that follow chart such efforts to confront and reshape loss, efforts that alter the spatiotemporal contours of intimate relationships among subjects, objects, and the mediating presences through which they touch. I use the term *mediating presence* deliberately to denote the ethereal echo produced when breath leaves the barrel of a haunted flute, as well as the unnerving thingness of murky, crumbling mansions as spirits stalk the halls. Divulging the ubiquity of loss, these apparitions rend bodies and buildings with their voracious entrances and exits—snatching consciousness, security, or human lives.

Loss unsettles and refigures relationships, be they aesthetic, spatial, or interpersonal. Certain bonds are ostensibly severed only to be revived in altered form, such as when Genji surrogates his mother's absence through proxies like his stepmother, Fujitsubo, and her niece, Murasaki. Loss also rescales spatial proportions and investments, as when exile displaces Genji from the Capital, intensifying his receptivity to the oceanic vista and the seamen encircling him. While scenes in *Genji* centering on human death provide the most memorable examples of loss, other absences and relinquishments also deserve to be worked through. Despite death's prevalence in the narrative, however, it is crucial to acknowledge loss as grounding the potential for *having*—not as totalized possession, but as a gesture toward sustaining, however briefly, intervals of living that deprivation can't eclipse. Indeed, the modest aspiration to have, to grasp for a desired life amid haunting loss or intimacy, can itself signify as queer.

ITINERARY

Methodologically, to queer intimacy and loss is to question those notions without an epistemological imperative to eradicate uncertainty. Therefore, the readings advanced here take on an interrogative posture: they refract established logics to reorient our critical relation to them and expand inquiry. Each of the book's five chapters focuses on a different setting and medium but asks the same basic question: How should we understand the spatiotemporal contours of *Genji*'s portrayals of intimacy and loss, and how might we theorize them as queer? By asking this guiding question in different contexts, each chapter maps how loss and intimacy are queered according to the spaces and moments in which they transpire. Each chapter focuses on a different setting and medium: (1) premodern Japanese notions of queerness and the geopolitical context of *Genji*'s modern reception; (2) the walled aisles of a crumbling house and courtship poetry; (3) fraying hedges and a lapsed household's servants; (4) paintings and intertextual poems assembled in exile; and (5) the echo of musical instruments beside a pillar in a haunted room. Combined, the chapters' readings theorize from varied perspectives how intimacy and loss suffuse and elicit queer gestures—spatiotemporally, aesthetically, and affectively.

Finally, a word about the rationale for choosing certain *Genji* chapters over others. Chapters 2 through 5 of this book each focus on a single chapter from the *Tale of Genji*. Although the issues I discuss surface throughout *Genji*'s fifty-four chapters, "Yūgao," "Suetsumuhana," "Suma," and "Yokobue" have been selected specifically for two reasons: (1) because they foreground in particularly concentrated fashion the sensorial reverberations of intimacy and loss, making them well-suited to a phenomenological analysis; and (2) because they do this within a context of portraying how male or female homosocial desire can imply eroticism while also suggesting other modes of affection, social relation, or connection with the phenomenal world irreducible to lusts for political power or sexual contact. This intersection makes them fascinating and particularly ripe for queer reading.

Chapter 1, "Translation Fantasies and False Flags: Desiring and Misreading Queerness in Premodern Japan," assesses the critical purchase and potential pitfalls of *queer* for reading Heian texts. I discuss what the concept of queering comes to mean in the project conceptually, historically, and methodologically. My goal is to estrange *queer* by accenting its discursive discontinuities. By first framing the foreignness of the modern term and then moving into *Genji* by considering how *queer* might translate into a specifically Heian context, I complicate our vernacular sense of the term by charting its cultural assumptions and blind spots. In the process, I stress elements that infuse and confuse modern, non-Japanese understandings of premodern Japanese sexuality and textuality, to say nothing of our overt and covert desires toward them as objects of knowledge.

My main question here is, What can we learn by theorizing the history of *Genji*'s translation, reception, and disciplinary location as queer? My critical genealogy begins by historicizing queer theoretical contributions, premodern Japanese discourses on sexuality and nonsexual queerness, and *Genji*'s reception, attentive to the discontinuities and contestations that animate them. In each of these contexts, questions of translation—including terminological distinctions, sexual and moral taxonomies, and cross-cultural appropriations—become crucial. These questions involve discourses of modernity, sexuality, and the formation of Japanese studies as an academic discipline in the wake of World War II. Consequently, I argue that the question of *The Tale of Genji*'s queerness cannot be addressed without considering the geopolitical and disciplinary conditions under which *Genji* becomes desirable as an object of cultural knowledge—and pleasure—in scholarly and middlebrow popular imaginations.

Chapter 2, "Chivalry in Shambles: Fabricating Manhood amid Architectural Disrepair," asks, How should we understand the relationship between masculinity and built-space? I read the "Yūgao" chapter to examine how Genji's tragic tryst in a rundown residence produces queer affinities when conventional heroism collapses. I argue that the architectural setting's disintegrating borders allow Genji to be emasculated as supernatural forces infiltrate the estate. Relying on his male servant, Genji tries to redress emasculation and rebuild his self-regard after losing both his pride and his woman. I theorize Genji's melancholic, visceral destabilization as queer.

Chapter 3, "Going through the Motions: Half-Hearted Courtship and the Topology of Queer Shame," asks, How should we understand the social structures of feeling marshaled to discipline queer subjects? Having lost Yūgao, Genji searches for new women to repress the humiliation he suffered in the haunted house. This leads him to the mysterious princess Suetsumuhana. Genji is not alone in his pursuit, and Tō no Chūjō trails him to the woman's untended residence. Consequently, at "a concealed spot where only the splintered fragments of a see-through fence remained, Genji found another man who'd been standing there the whole time."[93] This chapter examines the peripheral sites where such encounters occur to theorize how frustrated romantic desire sustains male and female homosociality. Even as the reclusive Suetsumuhana becomes a conduit augmenting Genji and Tō no Chūjō's connection, her outmoded wardrobe, dilapidated residence, and reluctance to devote herself to courtship rituals mark her as a queer figure who short-circuits the Heian marriage machine. I recuperate her queerness as a generatively unsettling mode of inhabiting an unforgiving system.

Chapter 4, "Queer Affections in Exile: Textual Mediation and Exposure at Suma Shore," bridges the book's concerns about spatial practices and how loss is mediated aesthetically. I argue that intimacy plays out on two levels. First, it emerges as a practice of intertextual homosociality. For Genji, banishment to Suma induces a desire for closeness with the infamous men who have preceded him in exile and evokes an archive of poetic and pictorial references that help orient him. Second, Genji experiences intimacy in exile through an unprecedented degree of physical and emotional exposure to both the natural elements and other men's gazes. This exposure stirs homoeroticism while exceeding it with a radical susceptibility that amplifies the affective intensity of his political dislocation and his disaffection with aristocratic mores.

Chapter 4, "From Harsh Stare to Reverberant Caress: Queer Timbres of Mourning in 'The Flute,'" considers sound and touch in order to theorize the reverberance of queer gestures. I theorize the work of mourning as a practice of discerning resonance to reorient attachments. I foreground a queer erotics of mediating loss orally, aurally, and haptically as the mourning Yūgiri performs elapses between caresses and musical echoes. I argue that Kashiwagi's passing produces timbres of loss that should be discerned within the context of a homosocial intimacy shared with Yūgiri.

The conclusion, "Learning from Loss," revisits *Genji*'s depictions of intimacy and loss to identify lessons that seem pedagogically promising. I synthesize reparative readings from the preceding chapters to outline how a queer critical sensibility might complicate—and *enrich*—our approach to teaching, if not living. Moreover, I consider the benefits of feeling our way past expertise to explore the promise of other, less anchored approaches toward knowing.

Ultimately, the goal is to perform readings that transform our sense of what *queer* and *Genji* might promise when apprehended in intimate juxtaposition to one another. The chapters revisit themes of queerness, distance, and loss in various intersecting arrangements, mapping their permutations. Although I move through *Genji* according to its chronological chapter sequence, my hope is that, like *The Tale of Genji* itself, my own chapters convey a cadence without carving a telos.

1

Translation Fantasies and False Flags

Desiring and Misreading Queerness in Premodern Japan

SUSPECT TURNS OF PHRASE

Consider the following excerpt from *The Tale of Genji,* which recounts a scene in which an exiled Genji is visited at Suma's shore by his closest male friend and rival:

While the awful tedium of Suma wore on and on for Genji, Tō no Chūjō was made Consultant, laden with society's formidable acclaim due to his excellent character. But without Genji, the world felt woefully lifeless, and he missed him every moment, until he made up his mind—*What does it matter if word gets out and they charge me with crimes?*—and sped to Suma without warning. Upon laying eyes on Genji, tears of both delight and sorrow spilled forth. Genji's residence had an unspeakably Chinese air. Besides its surroundings being of the sort one would wish to paint, the crudeness of the woven bamboo fence encircling the house, its stone stairs, and the pine pillars was enchantingly exotic. Resembling a mountain peasant, Genji wore gathered trousers, with a charcoal-green hunting cloak atop a robe not of forbidden crimson but licensed rose with yellow overtones; his unassuming fashion was deliberately rustic, and looking at him, one couldn't help but smile at Genji's stunning beauty.

The furnishings he used were also bare-bones, and his exposed room let anyone peer right in. . . . Tō no Chūjō sang a bit of "Asuka Well," and between laughing and crying, the men shared tales of the past months. Since they talked on without end, I couldn't possibly recount everything they discussed, or even fragments of it. They didn't sleep, and instead traded Chinese poems through the night until dawn came. Although he'd said he cared nothing of the scandal that might erupt should he visit Genji, Tō no Chūjō nevertheless grew anxious at the thought of rumors of his exploits spreading and thus cut his trip short to hurry home, only heightening Genji's heartache. . . .

Both the men shed tears. Each of them seemed to regret having to part so soon. In the dim glimmer of sunrise, a line of geese crossed the sky. . . . Saying, "Take this to remember me by," Tō no Chūjō gave Genji among other things an exceptional flute of some fame, though they made no keepsakes of anything that might elicit people's censure. Slowly but surely the sun rose, and with a restive heart beating, Tō no Chūjō glanced back again and again as he hastily set off; watching him leave, Genji looked all the more bereft.[1]

How should we interpret these parting glances? Like the characters, we find ourselves deposited in a queer place. As daybreak quickens pulses, these bitter-sweet pivots heighten our perception. In exile, Genji dazzles, more radiant than ever in his impeccably rustic garb. With rank and privilege stripped, he lives more simply now, frequenting a room that lets passersby peer in past pine pillars and stone steps, through bamboo fencing whose taut weave belies the man wilting within.

Language falters at this site. This fragile setting's sheer exposure urges reticence as one man plots to meet another. The narrator herself conspires, preserving privacy by concealing the extent of all the men shared that night in lieu of sleeping. Stimulated by Suma's ocean air and unchecked view, they trade verses of Chinese poetry through the night, an exchange evoking intercourse.

Overcome by longing, Tō no Chūjō has thrown caution to the wind and paid an illicit visit to his banished companion. But fear of the rumors that might stain his reputation should he linger too long at Genji's side makes him abridge his stay. Dawn dissolves their night together; the men part as geese in flight remind them of the arrows leading home. Such strict lines chafe at a time like this, since this exilic interval lends reprieve from courtly protocol, allowing them to savor one another's presence beyond the Capital's purview.

During their fleeting reunion the men indulge in conversation, wine, songs, poems, and "flutes." Each medium accentuates associations layered to assuage the sense of loss that plagues them both. Pleasures accrue along the coarse shoreline, coaxing the companions away from brooding and toward windswept revelry. In the end, however, hints of stigma mar their secret seaside tryst. And we're left to wonder what more they might have shared, had shame not spoiled their makeshift harbor.

. . .

But not so fast. I've performed an evocative reading of this scene from *The Tale of Genji*. To be sure, all the tender innuendo I've teased out loiters there in the original's lines. But such a premodern portrayal of male-male affection also reveals our own proximate remove from the scene—"removed" because a millennium has passed, the characters are Japanese, and the scene is fictional; "proximate" because we'd like to think we know what true love (or at least sexual tension) looks like. My own account draws from a sensuous sensibility infusing the text. Yet I'm also cognizant of my own propensity to read—and potentially misread—the men's reunion through a lens conditioned by twenty-first-century conceptions of (homo)sexual orientation, identity, and politics. Such notions can help divulge textual subtleties, but they also draw our focus away from facets of the text that prove less sexual, less fashionable, or less legibly subversive—more queer, in other words. So we might want to pause, pivot, and retract our reverie a bit.

How does such a scene become legible from our vantage? How do its rhetorical gestures come to feel foreign or familiar? How does it affirm or unsettle our capacity to evaluate textual possibilities—as menacing or promising? These questions sketch aspects of what we might recognize as "queer," in a manner Eve Sedgwick theorizes in her essay "Paranoid Reading and Reparative Reading" (2003). When Sedgwick catalogs the hazards of paranoid reading—with its penchant for negative anticipation, strong theories, and rapacious hypothesizing—she faults a machismo that animates close reading's commitment to unveiling. As J. Keith Vincent explains, "On the one hand, paranoid queer theory offered a set of analytical tools to expose the mechanisms of homophobia. This felt empowering and energizing, and often it led to crucial critical insights. But it also bred a kind of hypervigilance. . . . Occupying such a position, over the long haul especially, can become the opposite of empowering."[2]

If, in Sedgwick's words, "paranoia places its faith in exposure," then we should beware that faith's fundamentalist leanings.[3] Habitually unquestioned, and even upheld as a badge of disciplinary expertise or a will to mastery, this paranoid faith in exposure can overshadow phenomena less scintillating than sex acts already stigmatized far in advance. By contrast, reading in a nonparanoid mode doesn't covet predetermined transgressions but is instead attuned "exquisitely to a heartbeat of contingency."[4] In Ellis Hanson's interpretation, "Reparative reading focuses not on the exposure of political outrages that we already know about but rather on the process of reconstructing a sustainable life in their wake."[5]

In this sense, *A Proximate Remove*'s readings generally lean more toward the reparative than the paranoid end of an interpretive spectrum. Their driving objective is not to ferret out hidden traces of power's dastardly machinations. Nevertheless, my look to examples of homosocial and potentially sexual relations is deliberate. Why do this, especially when my stated goal is to foreground the breadth of queer reading beyond concerns about sexuality? The answer relates to a methodological distinction between merely disclosing sexual secrets and opening interpretive possibilities.

In other words, within the context of performing queer readings, a provisional recourse to paranoia can function as a way to pivot toward reparative alternatives. We can mine the potential for misunderstanding precisely at moments in *Genji* signaling male-male eroticism, reading against the grain to interrupt knee-jerk interpretations and complicate the salience of sexuality. These scenes offer the opportunity to read with enhanced precision and therefore theorize more carefully. In returning to scenes where what seems like homoeroticism grabs the spotlight, the point is not to sensationalize such instances. Rather, it is to leverage them to generate insights that invite deeper inquiry not just into gender relations but also into how characters perform a more sustainable relation to various facets of their world—human, living, or otherwise.

Against a routine of paranoid reading, a more reparative apprehension—not unlike the questioning pivots performed as Genji's companion left the seashore—emerges to suggest more desirable, less totalizing methods of critical departure. Throughout this book, I emphasize and develop this apprehensive tendency as a basis for queer reading—an approach that maintains a proximate remove from demands for interpretive closure.

This chapter takes as its point of departure the notion of a false flag—an ultimately deceptive sign whose prominence and familiarity tempt us into misreading it—which we witness in the off-target assumptions about men's intimacy examined briefly in the scene above. The chapter performs two tasks. First, it maps the discourses that have framed dominant notions of sexuality in premodern Japan, with an eye toward highlighting their ideological underpinnings and their discontinuities. Since the book pivots on queering, I detail what this concept comes to mean in the project conceptually, politically, historically, and methodologically. I frame the foreignness of the modern English and Japanese term and then move into *Genji*, considering how *queer* might translate into a Heian context. I hope to estrange our sense of the term by articulating its cultural assumptions and potential blind spots. Ultimately, I recommend its energizing possibilities for reading *Genji*, proposing methods that encourage readers to rethink how to engage the text.

QUESTIONS OF INFLECTION: NOTES TOWARD A PROVISIONAL DEFINITION OF *QUEER*

What do I mean by "queer gestures"? I don't mean sex acts. Nor do I mean acts that connote sexual contact. But we'll begin provisionally with sexuality, if only to denaturalize it before long. Sex and sexuality matter more for the historical provenance of *queer* than for the term's conceptual potential. We should note that *kuia* (queer) in Japanese exists as a loan word, written in katakana, the script used for imported items and concepts, like *tabako* (tobacco/cigarettes) and *feminizumu* (feminism). This detail highlights the centrality of translation—lexically, politically, culturally, conceptually—when trying to discern the contours of the term and figure out which aspects might coincide neatly between source term and translation, and which aspects might not.[6] From a linguistic standpoint, *queer* in a Japanese context is also interesting to consider beside a modern term like "same-sex love" (*dōseiai*), a gloss for homosexuality gradually superimposed on the long-established tradition of "male-male eroticism" (*nanshoku*). Neither of these terms denotes the range that *queer* indexes.[7]

These issues become especially pronounced when minding the gap between, say, a popular, twenty-first-century, U.S.-centered understanding of the term and an aristocratic Japanese context from a millennium past. With that in mind, let's consider the question of *queer*'s current connection to other categories:

> In many ways, "queer" and "gay/lesbian" are overlapping terms; but some of their implications are very different. A lot of gay and lesbian politics, for example, accepts the concept of sexual orientation without questioning it in any way. Yet, exerting any pressure at all on sexual orientation, you see that its elements are potentially quite heterogeneous.
>
> . . . That's one of the things "queer" can refer to: the open mesh of possibilities, gaps, overlaps, dissonances and resonances, lapses and excesses of meaning when the constituent elements of anyone's gender, or anyone's sexuality aren't made (or can't be made) to signify monolithically.[8]

Eve Sedgwick's explanation accentuates the dissonance between *queer* as an identity or political category and *queer* as the radical inability of such categories to account fully for the possibilities proliferating in their vicinity. She stresses how *queer* coincides with the "nondualist theoretical tendencies" of her work, and, writing in 2000, observes that "a lot of the most important recent work around 'queer' expands the term along dimensions that cannot be reduced to gender and sexuality at all."[9] This observation correlates to her axiomatic assertion ten years prior that "it is unrealistic to expect a close, textured analysis of same-sex relations through an optic calibrated in the first place to the coarser stigmata of gender difference."[10] Insofar as Sedgwick's primary concern is to generate nuanced readings, she recommends that *queer* not be beholden to gender and sexuality. For, as she puts it, "'Queer,' to me, refers to a politics that values the ways in which meanings and institutions can be at loose ends with each other, crossing all kinds of boundaries rather than reinforcing them. What if the most productive junctures weren't the ones where *everything means the same thing?*"[11] I find Sedgwick's distinctions helpful for avoiding a circumscribed sense of *queer*'s meanings. Her emphasis in the quotations above cast *queer* not as a category of sexuality or identity politics but rather as a question of emphasis: a question of where and how one might exert interpretive pressure toward "productive junctures" where meanings seem to surge, lapse, or skew.

These motions evoke the *gesture* of "queer gesture." Two senses of the term compel me. One comes from Stephen Barber and David Clark, who read Sedgwick's work alongside Foucault's and posit that if queerness manifests "a 'moment,' it is also then a force; or rather it is a crossing of temporality with force."[12] This "crossing" suggests an instantiation whose direction, provenance, intention, or magnitude may be indiscernible, even as it is still perceived or felt. *Gesture* registers this figuration's vibration across time and space. The term also appeals to me for its bodily overtones.

The second sense of *gesture* I'm fond of comes from José Esteban Muñoz, who leverages the concept to undercut constrictive notions of evidence. Explaining that "queerness has an especially vexed relationship to evidence," he writes, "The key to queering evidence . . . is by suturing it to the concept of ephemera. Think of ephemera as trace, the remains, the things that are left, hanging in the air like a rumor."[13] I confess that I appreciate this phrasing in part because rumor is the lifeblood of Heian tales like *Genji*. But beyond that, this emphasis on ephemera complicates any sense of a stable archive by introducing a corporeal potentiality that precludes textual closure. He continues, "So much can be located in the gesture. Gesture . . . signals a refusal of a certain kind of finitude."[14] If *finitude* connotes certitude, rectitude, and pretensions toward objectivity, then *gesture*'s refusal of it—however gentle—forgoes these stabs at finality in favor of less conclusive routes. An epistemology attuned to *gesture*'s capacious surplus—wherein "so much can be located"—would lend more interpretive leeway than rubrics bent on hard facts. This gesture toward *queer*'s breadth opens up a wider range of possible questions regarding subjectivity, discipline, and method.

In this nonteleological vein, the account of *queer* I find most useful comes from Sara Ahmed's *Queer Phenomenology: Orientations, Objects, Others*, where she describes the term this way:

> I have been using "queer" in at least two senses, and I have at times slid from one sense to the other. First, I have used "queer" as a way of describing what is "oblique" or "off line." . . . Second, I have used queer to discuss specific sexual practices. Queer in this sense would refer to those who practice nonnormative sexualities, which as we know involves a personal and social commitment to living in an oblique world, or in a world that has an oblique angle in relation to that which is given. . . . I think it is important to retain both meanings of the word queer. . . . This means recalling what makes specific sexualities describable as queer in the first place: that is, that they are seen as odd, bent, twisted. In a way, if we return to the root of the word "queer" (from the Greek for cross, oblique, adverse) we can see that the word itself "twists," with a twist that allows us to move between sexual and social registers, without flattening them or reducing them to a single line. Although this approach risks losing the specificity of queer as a commitment to a life of sexual deviation, it also sustains the significance of "deviation" in what makes queer lives queer. To make things queer is certainly to disturb the order of things.[15]

Ahmed's stress on the "oblique" angles at which queer phenomena and subjects orient themselves toward the world accommodates sexual and nonsexual relations alike. Her generous framing of the term allows for more explicit commitments incongruous with normative social practices, but it does so without mandating their direction or degree of force. Sidestepping such reductions, her formulation lets *queer* name a spectrum of deviation, unshackled from sexual identity. Most compelling is how Ahmed's gloss underscores the term's debt to deviation in a way that lets us transpose its propensity to "disturb the order of things" to contexts outside the exclusive province of continental philosophy or contemporary Western society.

This capacity for disturbance could issue from multiple sectors. For example, we could posit that all the violence and intrigue *Genji* recounts emerges as an effect of Genji's mother's death. To be sure, this maternal absence triggers chains of surrogation for which the tale is famous. But this displacement and the status damage it deals also mark Genji as deficient from the outset—even as his aberrant beauty and talent signify superabundance. Genji is too good for this world. He deserves the throne but is denied it; he can near it, but never occupy it.

This proximate remove from the seat of power makes for a precarious positionality that parallels what Ahmed identifies as one of phenomenology's queer dislocations. She develops her notion of queerness in relation to a disorientation Maurice Merleau-Ponty explains as involving not just "the intellectual experience of disorder, but the vital experience of giddiness and nausea, which is the awareness of our contingency, and the horror with which it fills us."[16] How should we understand this disorganizing yet invigorating awareness of contingency—the embodied experience of uncertainty, apprehension, and vulnerability—in relation to *Genji*? This notion of a visceral estrangement seems especially valuable to carry forward as we delineate *Genji*'s queer position amid competing disciplinary desires.

POSITIONING *GENJI*, POSITIONING DISCIPLINES

A Proximate Remove intervenes between the disciplines of premodern Japanese literary studies and queer studies. Its orientation owes much to the work of Kawazoe Fusae and Kimura Saeko on the one hand and that of Eve Sedgwick and Sara Ahmed on the other. For now, let's position this project within two contiguous contexts: discourse on Heian literature in general and *The Tale of Genji* in particular. Regarding the first context, Michael Bourdaghs explains,

> Early Western studies of Japanese culture tended to stress the aesthetic beauty of Japanese art and literature, to the neglect of its intellectual or political content. Politics and abstract theory were supposed to be the domains of Western modernity; Japan was assigned the task of producing pretty pictures and lyrical poems. . . . This version of Japanese studies was created largely in the early Cold War period and was complicit with the need in the United States to transform the image of Japan from that of a treacherous enemy to a benevolent Asian ally.[17]

Of all the periods of Japanese history, the Heian era was most subject to "the task of producing pretty pictures and lyrical poems," and *The Tale of Genji* outshone all other cultural products when it came to eulogizing loveliness.

Within this context, we should consider the longstanding perception of *Genji* having cachet as the truest repository of traditional Japanese feeling. Formalized by the nativist scholar Motoori Norinaga (1730–1801), this belief trafficked in an essentialist discourse designed to elevate an affective susceptibility to natural

phenomena unique to the Japanese people above a stiff neo-Confucian rational-
ism imported from the continent. This spongy discourse hoped to also elevate
the discipline of "national learning" (*kokugaku*). According to Tomiko Yoda,
"Norinaga saw in [*The Tale of Genji*]—which revolves around amorous affairs of
characters who appeared effete, sentimental, and weak from his contemporaries'
viewpoint—the most exemplary exploration of fleeting, ever-changing, and yet
irrepressible human emotions."[18]

Some late-nineteenth- and early-twentieth-century critics were influenced by
Norinaga's thesis but feared that *Genji* might in fact be too feminine to lead the
charge for Japanese cultural eminence, especially given the butch image this new
military power sought to flaunt on the international stage. For example, cultural
ambassador Suematsu Kenchō (1855–1920), who first translated parts of *Genji* for a
British audience in 1882, wrote, "Society lost sight, to a great extent, of true morality, and the effeminacy of the people constituted the chief feature of the age." Even
less charitably, Christian evangelist Uchimura Kanzō declared in 1894, "*The Tale of
Genji* might have left beautiful language in Japan, but what has the *Genji* ever done
to raise the moral spirit of Japan? Far from doing nothing, the *Genji* has made us
effeminate cowards. I would like to exterminate such *bungaku* [literature] from
our ranks!"[19]

Uchimura and other dogmatists bought and peddled a phobic logic of
chauvinist ideology that energized discourses of Japanese modernity.[20] For these
prudish nationalists, *Genji* posed a problem for being an iconic Japanese text that
not only depicted episodes of what they deemed overindulgent emotionalism
and sexual deviance but also impugned the imperial line's mythic sanctity. The
tale was squishy, salacious, and seditious at the same time. The trick thus became
how to tout *Genji* as a classic of world literature and a symbol of Japanese cultural preeminence without drawing unwanted attention to these more suspect elements. Obscuring its true status as a *monogatari* (tale, narrative) to promote its
distinction as the world's first novel had the following consequence: it boosted
Genji's profile within an international arena in which the sophistication of cultural products coded for native intelligence while domesticating the tale's queer
aspects. Similarly, highlighting the narrative's sensitivity to flora and fauna, cycli-
cal seasonal flows, pathos, and true (read "sincerely heterosexual") love helped
make *Genji* more legible along sanctioned lines, as a saccharine romance.

In effect, these emphases helped eclipse the text's portrayal of queerer facets
like homoeroticism, spirit possession, sexual violence, and imperial illegitimacy.
Deployment of a sentimentality that drew inspiration from Norinaga's nativist
faith in *Genji*'s lavish feeling served as a containment strategy for disagreeable
elements that eventually chafed Cold War imperatives. Alongside this faith flourished a desire to view *Genji* as a romance and to focus on its heterosexual pairings
and triangles, a proclivity I see as part of a broader geopolitical scheme according
to which Japan was installed as subordinate to the United States. In this context,

the incessant emphasis on Heian literature's diaphanous aura and cultish aestheticism became a tactic to exoticize and thus marginalize this cornerstone of modern Japanese cultural forms. Labeling the Heian society *Genji* immortalized as effete thus served as a way to pronounce it benign and subdue the text's potential incursions into territory thought unseemly within a postwar democratizing mission to rebuild Japan in harmless humanistic terms.

With the departure of U.S. Occupation forces and much of the draconian censorship apparatus abetting the occupation, however, scholars could increasingly criticize institutions. Although much of this criticism lambasted the ultranationalism most closely associated with recent wartime mobilization, it also accompanied critical reflection on the much longer discursive history sustaining the Japanese imperial mythos. The emperor system made for an ideal target as both a structure operative in contemporary life and as an object of rhetorical analysis.[21] As structuralist and poststructuralist readings of premodern Japanese literature proliferated after the late 1970s, led largely by those scholars affiliated with the Narrative Research Group (*monogatari kenkyūkai*), interpretations more critical of dominant political institutions also gained steam.[22]

These new approaches to the politics of language, history, and embodiment affected premodern literary scholarship profoundly. On one level, they stripped much of the belletristic luster from them. On another level, they scrutinized canonical works to delineate their complicity with accepted narratives of sovereignty's integrity. This background helps us understand the privileged position *Genji* enjoyed not just as an icon of Japanese cultural identity but also as a valuable implement with which to probe chinks in the emperor system's armor. In many ways, the same queer aspects lambasted by those on the far right decades earlier became by the 1980s welcome fodder for leftist scholars' deconstructive interventions.

ESTRANGING *HOMOSEXUAL*: HEIAN DISCOURSE AND CONTEXTS FOR A QUEER *GENJI*

We now return to the question of how to approach *The Tale of Genji* as a queer text, albeit from a different angle. How should we contextualize the narrative to do so, and what historical and conceptual expectations would we need to revise to accommodate this reorientation? One way to start would be to foreground how *Genji* consistently accents the imperial line's susceptibility to misfire and deviation, thereby exposing the myriad flaws of patriarchy in its most enshrined forms and gesturing toward nonnormative alternatives. Given the predominance of this patriarchal system, we could proceed by complicating our understanding of the relation between homosexuality and homosociality during Heian times to develop a sense of what *queer* might offer our analyses.

As Sedgwick has formulated, *homosocial* refers to a range of same-sex relations, primarily but not exclusively between men, such as competition, friendship, mentorship, or seduction. *Homosocial* is contiguous but not synonymous with *homoerotic*.[23] As a frame within which queer gestures can materialize, homosociality sketches a span of possibilities and practices more intricate than intercourse. Indeed, part of the challenge in reading *Genji's* scenes of homosocial intimacy comes in interpreting gestures such that their erotic potential can be acknowledged without flattening other features of their queer terrain beneath the banner of "homosexuality."

The scare quotes defamiliarize the term *homosexuality* and help refine its distinction from *queer* in a Heian context. I would therefore follow Gregory Pflugfelder's usage of *male-male sexuality* instead of *homosexuality* because, "inhabitants of the Japanese archipelago before the [nineteenth] century did not usually draw a conceptual link between male-male and female-female forms of erotic behavior. Thus, to adopt the term 'homosexuality,' which implies an inherent connection between the two, is to accept uncritically the effects of a discursive process whose very emergence demands historical accounting."[24] We therefore need to unpack the terminological limitations of *homosexuality* in a Heian context before addressing questions of queerness in depth.

To contextualize *Genji's* queerness within a broader cultural milieu, it helps to zoom out and consider other Heian texts whose themes and features cast the narrative's singular intervention into relief. One such text is *Taiki* (1136–55), a diary written by the courtier Fujiwara Yorinaga (1120–56). Keeping in mind that this text was written a century after *Genji*, we should be wary of retrospectively projecting late Heian ideas about male-male sexuality onto a mid-Heian literary text. Moreover, we also need to note the differences in script, style, documentary impulse, and political sensibility between the gender-specific genres of men's *kanbun* diaries, women's *kana* diaries, and women's fictional narratives. That said, *Taiki* nevertheless complicates our non-Heian understandings of what *homosexual* or *queer* could or should mean.

Specifically, Yorinaga's text documents dozens of sexual affairs with men, but it does so in a manner that has led many scholars to interpret them as a kind of diplomacy. That is to say, Yorinaga's text does not reveal some truth of his sexual identity. Rather, the style of aristocratic promiscuity *Taiki* chronicles queers *homosexual* by calling the very notion of a stable sexual identity into question. Yorinaga's diary shows that during the later Heian period, at least, sex between men of his status was customary, with a lack of stigma. As Paul Schalow points out,

Yorinaga was not unique, of course, in his choice of male sexual partners; records from the period show that the Emperors Shirakawa, Toba, and Go-Shirakawa, as well as Yorinaga's father Tadazane, and many, many others, also formed similar relationships. What is perhaps most interesting about Yorinaga's self-narrative is that it reveals male-male sexual alliances as part of his political and personal repertoire, which included all of the other ways the Fujiwara Regents traditionally deployed and expanded their power at court, such as marrying his adoptive daughter to an emperor and promoting the fortunes of his three sons.[25]

TRANSLATION FANTASIES AND FALSE FLAGS   41

While the fact of male-male sex was conventional, then, the sheer frequency and systematic mercenary thrust with which Yorinaga pursued his affairs stand out. This leads scholars to read in *Taiki* definitive evidence of Yorinaga's strategic consciousness regarding the political utility of sex with powerful men.

Kimura Saeko's work on premodern Japanese sexuality and its portrayals in medieval literature prove especially illuminating in this context:

> Unlike the capitalist system, the system of sexuality of the court regency aimed at the production of power rather than simply children, with women arranged hierarchically with polygamous marital practices. It was not all women, but only women of high birth who were expected to bear children. Women were divided into two categories: those who carried out "productive sex" and those who carried out "non-productive sex." "Productive sex" was appropriate for the legitimate wives, who could reproduce not only children but also the political power of their father through the children.
>
> Interestingly, the system of sexuality does not relinquish relations including "non-productive sex" but maintains them within the system. To consolidate a lineage and limit its legitimate heirs, all illegitimate relations were categorized as "non-productive." In a sense, "non-productive" relations can be seen as overlapping with homosexual relations. An example of this is the case of the retired emperor, who was shifted out of power and away from sexual reproduction to avoid producing further heirs. Whether he had homosexual ties to other monks within the monastery or heterosexual affairs with female attendants, these were both positioned as acts of "non-productive sex." . . . Similarly, homosexual relations could be seen as power-"productive" without being procreative.[26]

By schematizing how status, procreative capacity, and power intersect, Kimura helps us see what *queer* might signify in a Heian context. Her description complements the *Taiki* author's assumptions regarding sex between men as a nonprocreative but power-productive vehicle for social climbing and for maintaining advantageous political alliances. If out of habit we apply a modern Western notion of queerness, aglow with its subversive valence, to "homosexual activity," we fail to acknowledge that "homosexual" relations among high-ranking men did not necessarily contest dominant Heian ideologies. Quite the contrary, in fact, since such male-male sexual relations were often deployed to supplement the gains sought through fathering or adopting legitimate heirs. Fujiwara Yorinaga's practice of adopting several high-ranking nobles' daughters while concurrently having sex with several affiliates of the powerful Kayama-in and Kujō factions exemplifies this tack.[27] Whatever pleasure Yorinaga records, his male-male sexual affairs are not mere expressions of sexual identity or preference; rather, they evidence how shrewdly he hedged his political bets.[28]

Thus Ōishi Mikito asks us to think about late Heian male-male sexual networks in terms of their political value, with sexual conquest representing a kind of diplomacy. The goal of these male-male sexual affairs for courtiers like Fujiwara Yorinaga was to take political initiative and shore up coalitions that had to be secured through channels other than marriage alone. Ōishi asserts that for men of

Yorinaga's standing, exploiting this network was not just about indulging pleasure but also about capitalizing on political opportunities granted by his homosocial milieu. And he suggests that in Yorinaga's particular case, this strategy had more to do with ensuring his daughter's protection and success than with chasing individual glory.[29]

The capitalist logic of the nuclear family that casts a massive shadow over our modern consciousness fails to account for these Heian dynamics—even if concerns with sustaining patriarchal power and inheritance infuse both logics. As Gomi Fumihiko puts it in his discussion of *Taiki*, "Given the close relationship between sex and political power, using a modern perspective to deal with these phenomena becomes a misreading."[30] *Taiki* suggests the appeal of a tactical male-male sexuality that was not *queer* in the vernacular sense of *nonheterosexual*. Instead, Yorinaga's strategy of building political relationships through sexual affairs with other men should be read as a checklist of moves designed to redress queerness, where *queerness* names the precarious context of constant insecurity or threat of dispossession by rivals. In this regard, the social context becomes queerer as political exigencies mount for aristocrats in Heian's waning decades.

If, following Ahmed's revision of Merleau-Ponty's notion of disorientation, we view queerness as being bound to instability, then strategic male-male sexual affairs cement the political alliances that promise to militate against risk. Male-male sexual relations among Heian aristocrats figure as a kind of buffer against the brutally territorial networks of political violence—which claimed Yorinaga's life in the Hōgen Rebellion (1156). Hence in his case, we might posit queerness as being synonymous with the precarity that characterized Heian court life. This queerness *as* precarity led Yorinaga to place a premium on male-male sex as a means of minimizing political vulnerability, and as a normative route to improving his life prospects. Crucially, male-male affairs played out *alongside* heterosexual marriage politics, as a welcome supplement to the grander procreative strategy of producing children with powerfully connected wives. While there is no need to erect a firm boundary between sexual pleasure and political advantage, it appears that male-male sex was, for Yorinaga, aimed more toward securing political advantage than indulging pleasure for its own sake. His mentions of pleasure and fondness for certain partners are vastly overshadowed by an emphasis on how the encounters fortified his authority as Minister of the Left. Sex between men of this class might thus be said to stem less from passion than from a comprehension of the perils pervading court life.

As we've seen, *Taiki* helps estrange our expectations toward Heian notions of sexuality, politics, and their textual representation. Moving to the context of Heian fiction, we're reminded that *queer* is not synonymous with *homosexual* or *strange*, though instances of male-male eroticism or asexual strangeness can be read as queer. One literary touchstone often invoked to discuss medieval notions of what we might refer to as queerness is *Torikaebaya monogatari* (*The Changelings*, ca.

1080; revised in the late twelfth century). In this story, a sister and her half-brother are raised as a boy and a girl, respectively; after assuming adult roles at court as a courtier and a gentlewoman, they later adopt gender identities that coincide with their biological sex. Instructively, the story seems to have been more remarkable for its portrayal of the siblings' ability to pass as normal than for the gap it divulges between their sex and gender per se. As Gregory Pflugfelder points out,

> From the point of view of the central characters and the tale's early audience, what was significant about Himegimi and Wakagimi's predicament was that it was un-usual—that it set the siblings apart from the rest of society. This sense is conveyed by the word *yozukazu* (literally, "not adhering to the ways of the world"), which re-curs throughout the text, and similar phrases such as *yo ni nizu* [unworldly], *hito ni tagau* [uncommon, literally "against (the ways of) people"], and *rei nashi* [unheard of, unprecedented]. By differing from normative expectations, individuals might be perceived as "strange," a realm demarcated by such frequently occurring adjectives as *ayashi, asamashi*, and *mezurashi*.[31]

Although *The Changelings* was written after *The Tale of Genji*, both the rhetoric of strangeness and an unconcern with anything we might recognize as sexual iden-tity are consonant with the earlier Heian narrative. Notably, *Genji* trains attention on the main protagonist's momentous birth by discussing its anomalous nature, akin to that in *The Changelings*. Throughout the first chapter, we find phrases like "unexampled affection" (*onkokorobae no taguhi naki*) to describe the Kiritsubo Emperor's love for Genji's low-status mother, and "unworldly lustrous jewel of a son" (*yo ni naku kiyoranaru tama no onokomiko*). In the same vein, the narrator comments that Genji's beauty and temperament were "so singularly uncommon" (*arigataku medurashiki made*) that he seemed "so astonishing people couldn't believe their eyes" (*asamashiki made me wo odorokashitamahu*).[32] These features mark him as outside normal human parameters of expectation in ways that might qualify as queer.

For, as Kimura Saeko notes in "The Queer Desire of Court Tales," which focuses on the events of narratives such as *Hamamatsu Chūnagon monogatari* (*The Tale of Middle Counselor Hamamatsu*, ca. 1064) and *The Changelings*, queer desire in Heian literature is affirmed as it plays out not just in terms of sexual object-choice among humans but also across boundaries of ethnicity or even species.[33] She sug-gests, moreover, that in Heian narratives like these, rebirth represents a queer trope insofar as it involves not just changes in gender but in social station and mobility, too.[34] In this sense, queer elements constitute a pervasive, abiding facet of Heian literary production. Kimura's analysis is also suggestive for its reading against the prevailing misogyny of Heian Buddhist practice. Most significantly, by recuperating aspirations for rebirth and for improved circumstances more broadly as queer desires, her interpretation posits queer potentiality as a constitutive con-dition of life itself.[35] I find such transformative notions of a queer potential com-pelling, not least of all for how they highlight phenomena traditionally overlooked by Anglophone queer commentary, offering new objects and subjects through which to transform it.

Kimura's 2014 article represents an improvement over earlier scholarship that sought to pathologize the mutability *The Changelings* showcases. As Pflugfelder notes about dominant twentieth-century treatments of the same narrative, "From a modernist perspective, the tale's central characters were no longer the victims of a strange fate, but had become case histories that could be classified according to a 'scientific' taxonomy of psychosexual dysfunctions."[36] The tendency to categorize a medieval tale in this fashion stems from a presentist—if not homophobic—impulse to detain queer phenomena within a heterosexual/homosexual binary. Queerness would thus become more legible within a modern idiom and less taxing for modern scholars to appraise. Even as we might laud the desire to illuminate the tale's shifting gender dynamics, aligning the breadth of its events to "homosexuality" truncates complexities queer might preserve. For the story's main value "may lie not in its validation of Japan's 'homosexual' past, but rather in its destabilization of all fixed positions of gender and sexuality."[37]

Escaping this homosexualist rut can be hard. This difficulty derives from our modern inheritance of terms and stances toward sexuality whose naturalized status tempts us to domesticate earlier, more diverse practices, identifications, and experiences related but not reducible to homosexuality in particular—or even to sexuality in general, as David Halperin notes.[38] Halperin employs Foucault's genealogical method of delineating concepts' discursive emergence; his approach offers two useful elements.[39] First, the genealogical approach he advances helps in interrogating the provenance of some modern evaluations' nationalistic and homophobic spin on *The Tale of Genji*. Second, Halperin offers a list that helps situate premodern practices operative beyond "homosexuality's" limited scope: "The four pre-homosexual categories of male sex and gender deviance that I have identified so far can be described, very provisionally, as categories of (1) effeminacy, (2) paederasty or 'active' sodomy, (3) friendship or male love, and (4) passivity or inversion."[40]

Halperin's framework helps describe a range of gestures in *Genji* that might be read as queer. For although *Genji* does not concentrate on homosexual acts—especially if viewed from the perspective of later medieval and early modern literature—it nevertheless depicts scenes that fall under the first three headings. For example, effeminacy appears in the text when the narrator says: "Atop layers of downy white gowns, Genji wore only the basic unembellished robe in nonchalant fashion, its cord a touch unfastened, and looked so gorgeous reclining beside a pillar in the lamplight that one wished to view him as a woman."[41] This description also shows how a feminizing Heian rhetoric buoyed Genji's allure among male and female protagonists alike. We see an example of Halperin's second category when Genji opts to spend the night with Utsusemi's younger brother: "[Genji had] the page boy lie down alongside him. Since the boy was so cheerily appreciative of Genji's youthful tenderness, it's said that Genji found him considerably sweeter than his cold-hearted sister."[42] This encounter implies a pederastic rapport. Genji's relationships with Koremitsu, his servant and "breast brother" (the two nursed together), and with Tō no Chūjō signify different status-determined variants of devoted male friendship. And although "passivity or inversion" in the strict sexual sense Halperin names in his fourth category is not depicted, we might glimpse its symbolic silhouette in Genji's relinquishment of authority to his son, Yūgiri, as Genji hangs his head and languishes in grief over Murasaki's passing.[43]

LOST IN TRANSLATION: ON AFFECT, EMOTION, AND REPRESSING *GENJI'S* QUEERNESS

Here we should consider worldly phenomena whose contact with bodies exceeds a subject's evaluative or emotional response. This analytical move leads us toward a subtler sense of protagonists' bodily contact, susceptibility, and investment—in other words, along a continuum from gesture toward affect. Affect deserves exploring, especially at moments when simplification to a psychological denominator doesn't suffice. As we'll see, portrayals that accentuate intimacy and loss revel in such moments. Moreover, these portrayals let us read bodily response at an interstitial register, between the poles of posture and psyche marking subjective experience's extremities. Within this interval, a contemporary reader's affective sensitivity affords more flexibility in responding to our objects of interpretation, as Brian Massumi notes:

> Affect is autonomous to the degree to which it escapes confinement in the particular body whose vitality, or potential for interaction, it is. Formed, qualified, situated perceptions and cognitions fulfilling functions of actual connection or blockage are the capture and closure of affect. Emotion is the most intense (most contracted) expression of that capture—and of the fact that something has always and again escaped. Something remains un-actualized, inseparable from but unassimilable to any particular, functionally anchored perspective.[44]

Massumi's emphasis on affect's "escap[ing] confinement" is compelling; herein courses its potential for formulating more flexible engagements with the mercurial phenomena orbiting *Genji*'s portrayals of loss and intimacy. It is helpful to think of affect as that which remains fugitive from full consciousness and doesn't calcify into a predetermined pattern. In its evasion of capture or fixity, affect becomes a concept through which to link vital energies to aesthetic mediation in explicitly bodily terms, and an idea against which to leverage criticism of emotion's hold over analyses of Heian literary and visual culture.

We should make a distinction between affect and emotion here, especially given the facile connections traditionally made by commentators and scholars, Japanese and otherwise, from the late eighteenth century up through the Cold War between Heian literature and the emotional delicacy it is presumed to exude. Due in part to female authors' prominence during the Heian period, studies of Heian literature since the Edo period have been marked by a tendency to take a heightened emotionality and effeminacy for granted. Tomiko Yoda criticizes this powerfully structuring rhetoric of effeminacy, showing that it influenced national learning discourse in the eighteenth century and consequently informed the development of the discipline of Heian literary studies in the twentieth.[45]

Interlocutors succeeding Norinaga regularly truncate affect's spectrum, forcing replete, often hard to parse impressions into narrower emotional rubrics. Modern presumptions can buttress these reductive appraisals, purposely or inadvertently purging sensations that diverge from ideologies of virtue, beauty, and sophistication. Unlike the more vehement Meiji spokesmen itching to exterminate effeminate literature like *Genji*, Virginia Woolf, writing in 1925, takes a polemical tack but orients it in a less chauvinistically moralizing direction. She identifies with the female writer on the basis of a more "adult," nonmasculine sensibility, where "some element of horror, of terror, of sordidity, some root of experience has been removed from the Eastern worlds so that crudeness is impossible and coarseness out of the question, but with it too has gone some vigour, some richness, some maturity of the human spirit, failing which the gold is silvered and the wine mixed with water."[46] Woolf's notion, informed by Arthur Waley's translation, huddles around a well-worn Orientalist impression of languorous delicacy. In underscoring *Genji*'s sophistication, Woolf cleanses its "sordidity" and the powerful, if coarse, affects of horror and terror accompanying it.

We should acknowledge that this rosy view of Heian literature didn't take hold solely among modern Western aesthetes, for as Janet Goff explains, "[*Genji*'s] appeal as a source of inspiration and allusion was perhaps greatest . . . from the late twelfth to the sixteenth century, when the court was in an advanced state of decline. Writers and critics living in a chaotic world cherished *Genji* because, to them, it epitomized the ideal, aristocratic way of life for which they yearned."[47] In a similar vein, John Walter de Gruchy identifies the appeal of *Genji* for Europeans in the wake of World War I: "Waley's *Genji* might be called a romantic escape in prose from the aftershock of war and what Lafcadio Hearn called the 'monstrous machine-world of Western life.'"[48] Furthermore, de Gruchy underscores that "for Waley personally, the *Genji* was a release into a realm of aestheticism, and the depiction of a depoliticized, aristocratic world of delicate manners and highly cultivated aesthetic tastes was 'fortuitously consonant with the ideals of Bloomsbury.'"[49]

Similarly, Donald Keene "savor[ed] the details again. I contrasted the world of *The Tale of Genji* with my own. In the book, antagonism never degenerated into violence, and there were no wars."[50] Yet, aligned as it is with the preceding examples' pacifist preference, Keene's account complicates our picture, standing out moreover for how it links this nonviolent emphasis to *Genji*'s portrayal of an attractive style of masculinity:

> The hero, Genji, unlike the heroes of European epics, was not described as a man of muscle, capable of lifting a boulder that not ten men could lift, or as a warrior who could single-handedly slay masses of the enemy. Nor, though he had many love affairs, was Genji interested (like Don Juan) merely in adding names to the list of women he had conquered. . . . I turned to [the text] as a refuge from all I hated in the world around me.[51]

Genji embodies an alternative to the brand of heroic masculinity Keene knows from Western ancient myths and early modern romances. The appealing ideal Genji encapsulates should be read in contrast to Western literary archetypes, the warmongering of World War II, and the macho U.S. military context in which Keene found himself not long after discovering *Genji* in autumn of 1940.[52] Genji's appeal suggests a queer identification, one grounded in antisocial reclusion and an antiwar politics. Recalling Keene's fondness for *Genji*, de Gruchy reminds us that "Waley clearly found in *The Tale* much of what he wanted to find there, and he used it as a surrogate for his own repressed voice. At the same time, Waley's *Genji* was a challenge to the narrow moral restrictions of that society, offering a vision of alternative sexual identities and sexual practices as a natural part of a sophisticated and civilized culture."[53] In this reading, Waley's translation is conditioned by discourses of Bloomsbury aesthetics and Japonisme even as it operates at odds with post-Victorian mores regulating morality and sexuality. In Edward Seidensticker's warily reverential estimation, Waley "embroiders marvelously," "amplifying and embroidering" throughout his rendition.[54] We might glimpse in this embroidery traces of a queer quality in *Genji*, one that was not fabricated outright by Waley but rather merely accentuated and expanded.

Elsewhere, one finds a trope of emphasizing the emotionality or sensitivity of Heian literature to valorize its apolitical nature. For example, Arthur Waley's 1928 introduction to Sei Shōnagon's *Pillow Book* (*Makura no sōshi*, 1002) casts the literature of the mid-Heian period as "purely aesthetic."[55] Similarly, historian George Sansom's 1962 account characterizes Heian culture as "almost entirely aesthetic" and "even in its emptiest follies . . . moved by considerations of refinement and governed by a rule of taste."[56] Although Ivan Morris's explication of the Heian "Cult of Beauty" presents more nuance than Waley's or Sansom's notion of the epoch as governed by a rule of taste, it maintains its general tenor.[57] In this context, "Heian" epitomized an anodyne aesthetic realm, often to the exclusion of potential threats posed by political readings.

Here, the historical moment in which Sansom's and Morris's texts were written— the early 1960s—matters, for this insistence on aestheticism indexed an ideology of reading apolitically within the discipline of U.S. Japanese studies that was aligned with a Cold War paradigm of knowledge production. This program sought ideological containment of undesirable (read communist) sentiment. As H. Richard Okada explains, "Sansom's statement forms part of a larger postwar effort to construct a peaceful cultured nation that . . . served to counteract both the image of imperialist aggressor in the Second World War and the hold that Marxism had among the intelligentsia."[58]

These investments in a strategically delimited Heian aestheticism recall Massumi's description of the "confinement" and "functionally anchored perspective" a discourse of emotion demands. I am drawn to read his account of bodily processes in terms of its implications for bodies of scholarship. Specifically, the rhetoric of emotion, bound to serviceable notions of femininity or apolitical essentialism, deadens interpretive possibilities. As Norma Field asserts, "Indeed, the principal consequence of [Norinaga's] monochromatic drenching of the *Genji* in *aware* [sensitivity to poignancy] is the effacement of animating tensions."[59] Hence to rescue affect from emotion's clutches requires a shift of critical sensibility and a tolerance of animating intensities less legible than the shallow love, jealousy, or sadness with which Heian protagonists have customarily been stamped. This is not to say these emotions don't matter but rather to suggest that recourse to an analytic of emotion proves too coarse a metric for grasping the intricacies of Heian textuality. As an interpretive trope, emotion—especially as subsumed by *aware*—blocks more texturally rich forms of creative critical engagement that ensue when we pivot to affect.

Furthermore, translation can exacerbate this tendency even as it helps readers access a text like *Genji*, such as when, according to Earl Miner, "[Seidensticker's] clarity [in his 1976 translation of *Genji*] has the effect of smoothing out the original. . . . It eliminate[s] much of the sudden shifting, the easy grading of tone from the disturbing to the sensitive, from serious to sexual, from bantering to moral."[60] Miner's insight highlights a consequence of translating for the sake of making a Heian narrative like *Genji* legible, palatable, and enjoyable to postwar American readers: effacing the richly affective texture of the original text. Masao Miyoshi echoes Miner's critique, insisting that the "clarity of modern ironic vision" Seidensticker imposes distorts the original:

> The point is that the reader of the original doesn't know precisely where, for instance, a quotation begins or ends, and I suspect no Heian reader really cared. Mr. Seidensticker's version cleanses all such ambiguities, and turns the tale into a modern Western novel (or romance), unavoidably changing the nature of the Heian sensibility. . . . The original Genji, I repeat, flows and drifts. At every turn, the stream of narrative opens up an unexpected perspective which also revises what has come before.[61]

Miyoshi's description of a subtle intermingling intimates an interactive susceptibility to the mundane phenomena reminiscent of Massumi's account of affect. Also worth mentioning, in light of our discussion of effacements and the suppression of animating tensions, is Miyoshi's emphasis on how *Genji*'s characteristic flow has been severed for the sake of intelligibility. For some readers, this flowing sensibility, along with a tempered vulgarity, signifies a "triumph of Lady Murasaki's feminine sensibility."[62] However, I consider this linguistic drift as embodying a queer gesture, not simply in its disinterest in overtly specifying boundaries between characters and settings but also because of the way, "at every turn, the stream of narrative opens up an unexpected perspective which also revises what has come before." This recursive, revisionary tendency of *Genji*'s prose speaks to a queerness postwar translators like Seidensticker sought to straighten, not embrace. Resolving such tensions spares the reader the "taxing and arduous" task of having to keep alert for unfamiliar details like "subtle shifts in honorific level."[63] Thus, Seidensticker declares that "the Western tradition requires that fictional characters have solid, unshakeable names" in order to stave off "great confusion" and "unreadability."[64]

One wonders, though, what else was at stake in stressing such solidity. Put another way, it seems important to consider the historical conditions under which a contempt for subtle shifts in tone or title, and an aversion to presenting readers with a challenging experience, emerged. For his part, Seidensticker locates himself away from Tanizaki Jun'ichirō's "musical vagueness" and "nearer [Yosano] Akiko and Waley": "Akiko is a crisp, no-nonsense Waley sort, bringing matters into a clearer and more businesslike world."[65] We might note that this "businesslike world" is also, in the 1977 of Seidensticker's writing, very much a Cold War world. Whatever queerness Waley's early twentieth-century translations magnified in the tale flared as egregious from the retrospective standpoint of the late 1970s. Indeed, the very prevalence of the "sudden shifting" Miner notes might have mobilized the translator's drive to flatten and partition "the easy grading of tone," effectively deadening a queer energy deemed unseemly according to a Cold War era paradigm aimed at trumpeting classical Japanese literature's unambiguous virtues.

Although the question of censorship was not nearly as pertinent with Heian texts as it was with works of twentieth-century literature, we should nonetheless consider anticommunism's capacity to influence cultural producers like translators of Japanese literature. Here, Christina Klein's notions of the global imaginaries of containment and integration help contextualize *Genji*'s translation for middlebrow readers of English. Building on Alan Nadel's idea of "containment culture," Klein writes that "the global imaginary of containment also translated anticommunism into a structure of feeling and a set of social and cultural practices that could be lived at the level of everyday life."[66] According to Klein, this logic of containment "enforced 'conformity' everywhere" and rendered deviance in all its forms— sexual, political, behavioral—a source of anxiety and an object of investigation."[67] I would suggest that within the context of this containment culture, *Genji*'s rhetorical contours could be flattened to fit the structures of feeling most agreeable to a Cold War middlebrow readership. Questions of *Genji*'s potential "sexual, political, behavioral" deviance notwithstanding, the text needed to be straightened to reach this readership most pleasurably, efficiently, and profitably. Seidensticker notes that "a decision was early reached, upon consultation with Mr. Harold Strauss of Alfred A. Knopf, Inc., that the annotation must be minimal" for his translation of *Genji*, presumably to make the text less forbidding for a popular audience. On his score, it bears considering how the global imaginary of containment functioned in tandem with what Klein calls the global imaginary of integration, which "constructed a world in which differences could be bridged and transcended."[68]

In assessing the influence of the intertwined imaginaries of containment and integration, we can understand the work of translating Heian literature during the Cold War as working on both fronts simultaneously: stifling the expression of unsavory textual elements to help usher ancient, aesthetically palatable, and politically benign foreign stories smoothly into middlebrow American consciousness. By the time of Royall Tyler's 2001 translation, the geopolitical terrain had shifted once more, and a post–Cold War sensibility—in scholarship and publishing—seemed more amenable to reviving some of Waley's queerer rhythms, and those of the original, which cared little for stark clarities and "solid, unshakeable names." In Tyler's view, "The original readers of *Genji* were in no hurry, and they appreciated a rich, copious work that required them to come forward, as it were, to meet it halfway, in a process of fully engaged listening or reading. I therefore hoped to draw the modern reader into something like that kind of active engagement. Among other things, I translated long sentences into long sentences, and I preserved the discretion and decorum of the narration."[69] This solicitation of an undiluted engagement through a deliberate retention of *Genji*'s texture sets the stage for a potentially unsettling and energizing textual encounter I would posit as queer.

ASSESSING AFFECT'S CRITICAL PURCHASE FOR *GENJI*

Given translation's fraught history, how should we bridge the gap between premodern Japanese theories of affect and their Western counterparts? Norinaga's valorization of *Genji*'s overflowing feeling helps us in this task. As Tomiko Yoda elucidates, in distilling Genji's essence to *mono no aware*, or "capacity to feel and be moved by the things and events in the world," his "discussion of affect keeps turning to the shadowy realms of the human heart: the desire that crests against the prohibition, temptations that arise despite one's better judgment, and the ambivalence and vulnerability that haunt even sage priests and fearless warriors." Yoda explains that Norinaga "deployed [femininity] as the signifier of uncensored, true feelings," which "escape the control of regulatory principles and rigid articulation—ever changing, multilayered, and often conflicted."[70] Norinaga's emphasis on the feminine lets him exempt feeling from the masculine, Confucian codes he resisted for being too prescriptive and unfaithful to the realities of human experience. Instead of categories of action, virtue, and vice schematized by these codes, he advocates a more complex, "incessantly shifting" notion of feeling irreducible to the rigidities of emotional rubrics. His opinions anticipate those of present-day theorists who stress affect's mercurial phenomenological qualities.

Lauren Berlant, for example, describes affect as "the body's active presence to the intensities of the present" or, after Silvan Tomkins, as "the biological portion of emotion."[71] So, it is not just a feeling of sadness but sagging shoulders or strained breaths that register impacts past intellection's surface. The *Illustrated Handscrolls of The Tale of Genji* (*Genji monogatari emaki*, ca. 1160) give at least one example of this. Whereas the angular stylization of the majority of the scrolls' paintings can make it difficult to ascribe distinct affective states to specific bodily postures, the "Wakamurasaki" painting of an ill, mourning Genji visiting a mountain healer offers a notable exception. Genji sits to the right, with a downcast expression. The parallelism of the two men's opposing figures underscores his malaise, with Genji's position starkly contrasting the ascetic's straight-backed posture. Genji "was suffering from a recurrent fever," but just before that he was "prone to spells of vacant melancholy" following his lover's death.[72] The illness of mourning precipitates physical ailment as Genji's posture registers his anguish through a gloomy face and softened spine.[73]

Blood rushing to cheeks, the dilation of pupils, or a watering mouth also evince affective swells and shifts. Berlant's and Tomkins's characterizations of the "body's active presence" evokes episodes in *Genji* when "the Left had one more turn [in the picture contest's final round], and when the Suma scrolls appeared, the Acting Counselor's heart beat fast"; or when Murasaki crumples at a glimpse of a powerful letter: "In the City his letters aroused strong feelings in most of those who read them. [Murasaki] lay down at once, grieving and yearning, and she would not rise again."[74] I want to be wary of positing a transcultural, transhistorical entity. And yet, insofar as it represents the biological portion of emotion, affect implies a sensory apparatus operating below or beyond the cognitive level of cultural mediation.

Therefore, while the same gestures can signify different things in different cultural contexts, we nonetheless notice transcultural overlap. For example, consider the loss of appetite Genji's father experiences in mourning: "He only went through the motions of breaking his fast and took no greater interest in his midday meal, until all who served him grieved to see his state"; or Murasaki's shift in posture on being touched by her grandmother's tearful concern for her: "[Murasaki's grandmother] wept so bitterly that the watching Genji felt a wave of sorrow, too. Child though she was, the little girl observed the nun gravely, then looked down and hung her head."[75] As a final example, consider the following:

It was therefore only in the secrecy of his own heart that [Genji] sighed and thought, Ah, how short a life he was destined to live! His tears threatened to fall like rain while he pondered the fragility of life, but he stealthily wiped them away because the character of the day forbade them, and he hummed to himself, "I have long known the sorrows of silent thought. . . . One or two of [Onna San no Miya's] women must know what happened. How I wish she would understand me! But no, to her I probably look like a fool. Never mind my own part in this, though—I feel sorrier for her than for me." Genji's face betrayed none of these thoughts. . . . Pity and regret drove the affront from Genji's heart, and he burst into tears.[76]

This passage helps delineate the contiguity affect shares with emotion and highlights the insufficiency of any facile notion of "sadness" to account for the complexity of feeling's embodiment. Here, Genji is beset by a vexing cluster of affects that he tries—and fails—to master through the deliberate exertion of conscious will. Genji hates Kashiwagi for cuckolding him and fathering a son with one of his wives. This hatred only swells as Genji enters the public context of mourning Kashiwagi, thus the secret sighing, issued out of Genji's frustration that he must suppress his anger in this space.

This passage stands out for its description of the tension between affect and emotion's codified public display. To show sadness in this context requires adherence to mores. Genji's sorrow curdles, out of sync with the style of melancholy most mourners practice. His tears mustn't fall too freely lest he betray some hint of outrage: "There were tears in his eyes, and his tone was bitter."[77] While Genji's "face betrayed none of these thoughts," his sighs, hums, and tears tell a different story, as the sheer pressure of trying to regulate his emotions only detonates a mass of affects. Such episodes suggest how sensitive we must be when interpreting *Genji*'s depictions of sensitivity. For indeed, this scene gives a sense of how Genji closets his true feelings even as he expresses sympathy.

THE PLACE AND ROLE OF SHAME

Examples of affects include joy, excitement, arousal, disgust, anger, fear, disorientation, or shame. Shame discharges an affective force omnipresent in *The Tale of Genji*. For those familiar with the historical trajectory of queer theory, emphasis on shame here will seem familiar.[78] But given the historical and cultural distance between Heian and Western traditions, the persistence of shame's circulation in *Genji* stands out.

Shame roils early as discredit surrounding Genji's maternal background, and as dismay at the necessity to ascribe Genji the rank of something other than crown prince. Indeed, this book's chapters each articulate venues for reading shame: it reappears when Genji crumples in an unlit aisle, emasculated by the wraith that kills his potential wife, Yūgao (chapter 2); it invades appraisals of Suetsumuhana's seeming disaffection as devotees to normative romance chasten her for not loving like they wish her to (chapter 3); it returns at Suma, as Genji learns to swallow his disgrace beside the sea (chapter 4); and Yūgiri feels it when he fails to play the perished Kashiwagi's flute adeptly (chapter 5).

In all of these cases, albeit to varying degrees, shame serves a purpose. It pulls characters together, binding them to places and states of being they often long to escape. Self-reproach fastens subjects to a social order that, while it might not have their best interests at heart, still lends something to rely on as they navigate loss. We also recognize shame's social utility within an ideological regime of romance geared toward ensuring heterosexual reproduction. The compulsory vector of this system attempts to suppress any aberrant body opting for other lines of allegiance. These tensions suggest a link between structures of judgment and queer modes of moving astray.

Recalling the modern homophobic and imperialist condemnations of *Genji* helps us recognize the potent workings of shame both outside the text and within it. For indeed, we can safely assume that what upset prudish commentators so much in that turn-of-the-twentieth-century moment was based in a fear of *Genji* outing some perversity of Japanese culture. *Genji*'s supposed effeminacy and unabashed portrayal of the imperial bloodline's corruption stood to invalidate the myths of national patriarchy and integrity central to Japan's modernization and militarization. During a period when proving the civilized might of one's nation seemed paramount, *Genji* stuffed Japan between a rock and a soft place. On the one hand, the text's heft and intricacy let it be championed as a masterpiece "novel" on par with any Western exemplars; on the other hand, it struck its Japanese spokesmen as womanish and depraved. Much to their chagrin, if not outright horror, *Genji* could expose to Western nations a sexual secret whose status as damningly regressive had itself only recently congealed with the avid incorporation of Western paradigms. Cast as homosexual—which was more embarrassing than being portrayed as merely effete—this secret was one discourses including sexology, psychology, social Darwinism, and literary criticism sped to repress.

Cognizant of *The Tale of Genji*'s shameful propensity to serve as a queer icon of Japanese culture, on the one hand, and its heavy thematic investment in shame as a rhetorical vehicle, on the other, we can approach shame from a different angle. Namely, we can bypass any moralizing bent and focus instead on how bodies register shame as part of their linkage to their social environment and also consider how such bodies become serviceable to ideological designs. It becomes helpful to acknowledge a link between shame and queerness, but also to decouple them to consider interpretive possibilities for *queer* outside a moralizing framework.

QUESTIONING ORIGIN THROUGH QUEER TEMPORALITIES

With the preceding conceptual and historical background under our belts, the question now becomes, How might we activate those insights in more direct and sustained relation to *Genji*? One way to read *The Tale of Genji* as queer is to note how the narrative itself begins by posing a question, in passing: "In which reign was it . . . ?" (*idure no ohontoki ni ka?*). In Royall Tyler's popular 2001 translation, the opening reads, "In a certain reign (whose can it have been?) someone of no very great rank, among all his Majesty's Consorts and Intimates, enjoyed exceptional favor."[79] This inaugurating rhetorical maneuver posits a posture of proximate remove from Murasaki Shikibu's own historical moment and political circumstances. For the narrator to mention offhand that she cannot seem to recall when the fiction's events occurred circumvents censure from those who might recognize too much overlap with actual events at court. But in feigning ignorance, the coy opening also questions the very nature of temporality's relation to imperial ownership: Perhaps the very notion of time being emperors' property deserves rethinking? Furthermore, the question twists imperial succession's vector, loosening linearity's hold on narration. A coy implication emerges: that regnal time has been naturalized as sovereign does not mean it must frame how all stories start or end. "Emperors may own eras, but I can't be troubled to remember which of them owned this one," the narrator hints, "and whose reign it was in fact matters far less than the story I'm about to share." Whatever claim an emperor may have had on this era fades before an endeavor to recount less official, more enthralling episodes.

Genji's opening line reads as queer for its nonchalant insistence on the speculative and for its circumspect detachment from a sanctioned temporal sequence. Moreover, its elliptical retrospection performs a world-building gesture by establishing a narrational frame proximate to yet removed from any designated imperial schema. These altered relations to time ally the eleventh-century tale with a repertoire of current queer temporal critiques—formulations in which *queer* denotes temporal orientations resistant to normative time. For example, Judith Halberstam criticizes "a middle class logic of reproductive temporality" wherein "long periods of stability are considered to be desirable."[80] In such a frame, she continues, "queer time perhaps emerges most spectacularly, at the end of the twentieth century, from within those gay communities whose horizons of possibility have been severely diminished by the AIDS epidemic."[81] Similarly, José Muñoz rejects the oppressive present imposed by straight time to champion a queer aesthetic's possession of "blueprints and schemata of a forward-dawning futurity."[82] This puts him at strict odds with Lee Edelman's antirelational formulation of queer as being antithetical to the heteronormative tyranny of "reproductive futurism."[83] In harnessing the indeterminacy of *queer*, Carla Freccero invokes anachronism as a temporal process constituting queer time to read "against history" and thus "counter to the imperative . . . to respect the directional flow of temporality, the notion that time is composed of contiguous and interrelated joined segments that are also sequential."[84] Freccero's conception, which "proceed[s] otherwise than according to a presumed logic of cause and effect . . . and otherwise than according to the 'done-ness' of the past,'" develops a notion of spectral temporality in which the affective past haunts the present.[85] Moving from an early modern European to a medieval European context, Carolyn Dinshaw forgoes the ghostly metaphor but still stresses disquiet in the temporal theme of asynchrony: "different time frames or temporal systems colliding in a single moment of *now*."[86] And for Elizabeth Freeman, these collisions proliferate as queer fragmentations of "homogeneous empty time" that materialize as "asynchrony, anachronism, anastrophe, belatedness, compression, delay, ellipsis, flashback, . . . repetition," and more.[87] Additionally, she helpfully articulates the concept of temporal drag, "a counter-genealogical practice of archiving culture's throwaway objects" to extract usable pasts.[88]

Many of these formulations resonate with spatiotemporal features of the queer scenic moments in *Genji* to which I alluded earlier. Among these formulations of queer temporality, it is worth noting those of Carla Freccero, Carolyn Dinshaw, and Heather Love for their focus on the problem of queer historicity and the desires surrounding it. These include, respectively, desires to do justice to the past that haunts the present; desires to mine nonmodern orientations to recognize the temporal heterogeneity of "now"; and a desire to embrace the vexing "backwardness" of historical queer figures routinely dismissed from idealistic considerations of modern queer identity.[89] In all three cases, the authors argue against barriers between premodernity and modernity to underscore the value of reckoning with the occasionally unsavory insights gained from confronting earlier sensibilities. Beyond their usefulness in reading *Genji*, I appreciate these critiques for their worldly refusal to relegate the nonmodern to an inferior position within contemporary debates.

Similarly, in raising doubts about the nature of temporal codification, *Genji*'s opening lines also pose questions of proximity, status, and desires oriented toward the past or future. As Masao Miyoshi insists, "The original *Genji* . . . flows and drifts. At every turn, the stream of narrative opens up an unexpected perspective which also revises what has come before. The subject of a verb is often unknown, then is revealed, then is lost again; the narrator blends with characters, who also intermingle with each other and with their environments."[90] This rhetorical strategy of the text enacts a queer gesture in its flowing revision of earlier perspectives, and it dissolves partitions between characters and settings to produce vertiginous senses of proximity between them.

At another level, within the close-knit world of Heian nobility, the gentlewoman narrating voice can take for granted her affinity with readers. Hence she relies on the aristocratic audience's shared social consciousness to trust they'll catch the critiques nonetheless. By framing the tale as removed from the early eleventh century in which Murasaki Shikibu was writing, this narrator allays some readers' suspicion. And yet, the very need to nudge the narrative away from their present attests to how well it translates to their own historical moment. Thus the initial question's insinuation of remove in fact betrays the proximity of the tale's insights to the tacit truths of Heian life.

FROM TRANSGRESSION TO DEVIATION:
GENJI'S QUEER CONCEPTION

To understand better how *Genji* animates queer reading, we should consider how the text's initial interrogative gesture opens up other avenues of questioning—not just normative timelines but also social norms around imperial succession and the transgressions that threaten it. Here, I would like to question the dominance of transgression as a lens for interpreting *Genji*. Instead, I would propose a move toward deviation, recuperated for its spatiotemporal implications as a positive term that avoids the reifying associations *transgression* tends to carry.

Scholars have generally used the language of transgression, sin, and taboo to characterize a foundational motif introduced in the narrative's first chapter. Such language is used most frequently to discuss Genji's affair with his stepmother, Fujitsubo, and, as Fujii Sadakazu has shown, to mark his desires as deviant from the perspective of a time when incest taboo prevailed.[91] For Norma Field, "incest as transgressive love becomes indispensable" to complicating the trope of prophecy in the narrative and creating fictional interest, and she notes that "incest provides an ideal ground for the play of the mutuality of the political and the erotic, as well as of the sacred and profane, the mythic and the fictional."[92] She is disinterested in interpretations that posit the violation, which disrupts imperial succession, as being transgressive in terms that are either primarily political or primarily sexual. Field's reading of these realms as entwined complicates our understanding by avoiding moralizing claims.

In a slightly different manner, Haruo Shirane has taken up transgression as a major theme in the text, inaugurating his analysis with a section titled "Kingship and Transgression" and ending the first chapter with "Transgression and Renewal." This frame posits Genji's incestuous affair as a convention of the "exile of the young noble" trope; his transgression of a normative kingship becomes an obstacle that must be overcome to allow him a "renewal" that will lead him back to courtly glory.[93] Although the narrative certainly references a banishment/return motif, this trope should not be read in a teleological fashion that locates renewal at a pole opposite transgression, or as its implied outcome. Doing so presumes a normative paradigm in which "transgression" names acts that ultimately just affirm the preexisting Heian order.

Rather than read transgression as the negative entity against which this order positively defines itself, it might be better to focus on how what is deemed transgressive activates new possibilities without merely reinscribing what has already existed. This might allow for more of a departure from the discourses of sexual and political norms bound to the emperor system. A queer reading could instead interpret the transgression discourse—in *Genji* and in its criticism—as an occasion to theorize how boundaries between licit and illicit desires, actions, or styles of sociality were constructed. As Keith Vincent notes, "The queer critique of norms is thus not a call to rid the world of norms and liberate sex, but to understand how norms function and how to institute new and different ones that do less harm and more good in the world."[94]

Thus a queer reading might take a rhetoric of transgression as a prompt to regard the very category of transgression with skepticism, if not abandon it altogether. Therefore, I'd like to question how the frame of transgression, while helpful in some respects, might overdetermine our readings, compromising our ability to acknowledge alternatives. Emending this interpretive habit could involve using other potentially less rigid concepts, like deviation, which references a norm without necessarily announcing how the departure from it will travel or where it will land.

This returns us to questioning *Genji*'s own queer point of departure. In terms of status, the narrator's demure caution bespeaks her own distance from the imperial seat, since greater closeness to it would lessen the need for equivocation or apology. We might posit that Murasaki Shikibu's own middle-ranking status as an empress's tutor allowed her a privileged yet precarious perspective on Heian society. With regard to the backdrop *Genji* establishes, for the emperor (Genji's father) to favor someone of no very great rank (Genji's mother) to a degree exceeding her station spells peril. The "exceptional favor" lavished on Genji's mother diverges dangerously from convention. The emperor's desire for a woman beyond the perimeters of precedent and aristocratic expectation sites an intimacy his nearest courtly peers despise and fear as aberrant and misguided—threatening in ways that summon pejorative modern valences of *queer*.

With this status-skewed devotion in mind, we can extend our reading of *Genji* as a queer text by considering the particular overlap it proposes between deviation and deviance, key terms in early studies of gay sexuality.[95] (Such studies might note, with relish, that in this particular case, the Kiritsubo Emperor's behavior registers as sexually deviant precisely in its *hetero*sexual capacity, producing an heir half-tainted by lower birth and thereby undercutting a monopoly on aristocratic privilege.) The queerness I explore spans these terms to delineate instances where adherence to established routines wavers. *Genji*'s critical potency emanates from its insistence on sensitizing readers to the deviations from prevailing mores that recur at Heian society's highest tier. It is a text invested in elaborating the dramas of misalignment, from infinitesimally subtle to realm-shaking. Its dedication to interrogating these nonnormative formations and gestures orients it along a queer continuum.

We can begin mapping this continuum in the narrative's very first chapter. Here, the inordinate interest Genji's father takes in the boy's lower-ranking mother sets the stage for a slew of incongruities to come, Genji's birth among them:

> The physiognomist was dumbstruck and made many a disconcerted nod. "I foresee him becoming father of this land, someone destined to ascend to the Monarch's unequaled station; when I envision him in that mold, chaos and anguish seem to loom. When I foresee him becoming a bastion of the court, a figure who upholds this entire realm under heaven, the prophecy deviates unmistakably once more."

The Emperor, who had according to his own wise impression using the native Yamato method of physiognomy thus far not named his son a Prince, deemed that the foreign diviner had been truly insightful to advise along the same lines. Thus he reckoned—*Since even my own reign's fate is quite uncertain*—that rather than letting the child float through the world alone, deprived of backing from his mother's side, he might manage to indeed support him all the more and afford him an auspicious future by having him serve as a commoner instead; hence he made the boy study the myriad paths of politics ever more in earnest. Given how exceedingly gifted the boy was, it was really regrettable to make him but a commoner, but since if he became a Prince everyone would surely suspect his ambitions, once consultation with one ac-complished in the ways of astrology pronounced the same conclusion as his own, His Majesty made up his mind: it would be best to make him a Genji.[96]

Genji's birth poses problems from day one. Fears of suffering and disorder over-run whatever hope the child inspires. His very existence exceeds reason. Hence he perplexes onlookers and draws suspicion. The tale's inaugural omen derives from a status warfare endemic to Heian courtly life. And indeed, Genji's queer characterization here derives not from his sexuality or gender but from the dis-concerting mismatch between his questionable maternal pedigree and his capacity for greatness. Genji's mien, as read by experts and laymen alike, radiates such that all recognize his imperial potential. However, his lack of strong maternal back-ing makes it impossible for him to secure the future he deserves. At this incipient stage, he lacks the endorsement needed to anchor his claim and is thus displaced from a future of official rule by the faction that harassed his mother to death so as to promote their own heir. So Genji is made a commoner, a privileged one, but demoted nonetheless. This positions him as an oblique figure whose circum-stances of being blocked from the throne despite his sovereign caliber confirm the hardships of factional strife.

We must remember how critical this framing trope is for the *Genji* narra-tive and for our sense of Genji as a queer figure. For indeed, the legacy of Genji's inaugurating dispossessions erupt in his unstoppable drive to fashion intimate rela-tionships to remedy that primal maternal, material loss through a range of com-pensatory affections and affiliations. Genji's queerness revolves ultimately around his dispossession. The fracturing blow he suffers in losing his mother and being passed over as heir apparent hurls him into a tailspin littered with encounters with men and women through whom Genji might draw closer to a solace neighboring imperial glory. It is Genji's deeply felt sense of contingency that sets the stage for his searching—and at times desperate—attempts at interpersonal closeness.

This is not to pathologize Genji's relationships, nor is it to undercut their sig-nificance by highlighting how factors beyond conscious intention shape their paths. Instead, I want to notice how Genji's fundamental status anxiety tilts his tendencies toward the social actors most likely to grant him advantage—regardless of their sex.[97] Genji's own inclination might be said to morph with the playing field's contours. So we see him with men like Tō no Chūjō or Kashiwagi and notice that he experiences moments of heightened desire, envy, or resentment. The quick shifts that occur stem from a relentless contingency plaguing Genji's life, which frames the sense of threat or tactical opportunity Genji fathoms in women and men alike.

Genji often practices an expedient promiscuity. Consequently, gender roles and sexual preference can matter less than strategic worth. Happenstance or karmic relationships aside, these assignations get subordinated to a political calculation, one whose propensity for error only betrays Genji's own provisional status. Genji's frequent repositionings, then, should not be interpreted as confusion or mindless gallantry. To the contrary, they read more convincingly as often flawed but earnest calibrations designed to inch him closer to his (rightful?) throne. The world's supply of cruel lessons helps Genji hedge his bets in a game he rightly suspects is rigged to bleed him dry.

To be sure, all the hyperbolic hand-wringing around Genji's birth is premised on his biological sex; had he been female, the stakes would plummet because women were effectively barred from rulership by this point. Nevertheless, this backdrop frames a set of dislocations and deviations that expand our sense of how queerness might signify within the narrative, allowing us to read Genji as a queer figure long before questions of sexuality arise. Sexual activity matters, but mainly as the primary means for maintaining patriarchal privilege. Heterosexual reproduction is hence taken for granted within *The Tale of Genji*'s aristocratic milieu as a vehicle for attaining or preserving the good life—over and above the lives of one's rivals, and ideally over the course of countless generations.

This reproductive paradigm grounds our capacity to theorize Genji as a queer figure. Indeed, one striking difference between him and other male protagonists is that for all his sexual activity, Genji fathers only three children (only two of whom can be acknowledged), while the more normative Tō no Chūjō and Yūgiri both have houses full of them, making Genji's lack of fecundity seem queerer by comparison.[98] And yet biological and social reproduction only get us so far, especially given Genji's shifting gender presentations. Here, we recall Kawazoe Fusae's arguments about Genji's androgyny demonstrating the futility of defining him in terms of sexual preference or identity.[99] Similarly, taking a cue from the work of scholars such as Yoshikai Naoto, Tateishi Hikaru argues that Genji's androgynous beauty is tied to the danger he summons as an outlier and semimagical figure of imperial descent.[100] Yoshikai explains the characters exhibiting "male beauty" (*danseibi*) as emerging during a period when earlier heroic archetypes are gradually assimilated to fit more refined Heian aristocratic paradigms.[101] By contrast, Tateishi focuses more on the trope of androgyny in *Genji* and earlier sources to delineate how gendered traits such as manliness and its softer variants play into Heian courtly society's function. Highlighting the link between eroticism and imperial power, specifically, Tateishi stresses the implications of the phrase "one longed to see him as a woman" (*onna nite mitatematsuramahoshi*), which is used with regard to Genji, primarily, and his illicit son, Emperor Reizei. Given the numinous aura his androgyny emits, men's "wish to view [Genji] a woman" not only expresses a kind of same-sex desire toward Genji; it marks moreover a desire to attenuate whatever political threats Genji might pose.

Tateishi's observations help us understand possible relationships between a nonexclusive gender identification and the political system within which Genji operates. For one thing, androgyny can be taken as an index of a kind of queerness that goes hand in hand with a gossamer boundary between Genji's ability to fascinate and his violation of imperial protocol. In this sense, androgyny marks Genji as a seductive figure whose presence energizes a space of anxious doubt all the more threatening for its capacity to upend the reigning social order. Indeed, it turns out that those concerns about the realm's fate are well-founded, for by secretly fathering a son with his stepmother, Fujitsubo, Genji severs sanctioned imperial succession to interpose his own heir as emperor. We could, following the lead of Meiji-era nationalist discourse, read this predicament as perverse. But why not read it as a queering of the symbolic core around which other family schemas are arrayed?

Before androgyny and pseudo-incest enter the picture, Genji's queerness is to an overwhelming degree structured not by sexuality but by an apocalyptic mismatch of status positions between his birth parents: "Even in China had society been upended and calamity ensued exactly due to things like this," cautions the narrator in reference to Yang Guifei's incendiary beauty.[102] This sets the ideal schema of succession askew, as Genji's birth ruptures what should have stayed an undisputed telos. Furthermore, his features foretell a career not as "future pillar of the court and support of all the realm" but as something less steadfast.[103] Genji's rise must therefore wend slantwise to an official arc. So the sages shake their heads at the incongruity and ambiguity he presents, the calamity he heralds, confused and disappointed that this dazzling child supposed to assure faith in the future fails to ratify their hope.

We should consider this disappointment's implications. On this point, Lee Edelman's assertion that children symbolize within modern society the heterosexual ideal of "reproductive futurism" also proves useful in considering all the promise and threat Genji symbolizes. The terms of reproductive futurism "impose an ideological limit on political discourse as such, preserving in the process the absolute privilege of heteronormativity by rendering unthinkable, by casting outside the political domain, the possibility of a queer resistance to this organizing principle of communal relations."[104] For Edelman, the child is deployed to direct energy away from present desires and toward the future well-being of innocent children as part of an agenda to vilify homosexuals and the perceived decadence of their daily lives. The child "remains the perpetual horizon of every acknowledged politics, the fantasmatic beneficiary of every political intervention."[105] Within this context and against this horizon's narrowing of the sphere of political action, "queerness names the side of those *not* fighting for the children, the side outside the consensus by which all politics confirms the absolute value of reproductive futurism."[106]

Based as it is not on sexuality but rather on Genji's mother's rank, the discrimination Genji faces does not coincide neatly with the bourgeois capitalist context Edelman has in mind. Yet despite the historical gulf separating modern American and precapitalist Japanese society, the specter of reproductive futurism manages to haunt the latter to its core. Granted, the context of Heian marriage politics finds no easy equivalent in contemporary American society. But one aspect of the disparate systems that translates well is their shared insistence on the reproduction of progeny who will inherit the future. In fact, the desperate measures taken by Heian nobles to ensure the success of their family line—including exile and outright murder—represent a brand of reproductive futurism whose stakes far outweigh those of their Western counterpart, mainly due to the indispensable role of heirs in extending an actual aristocratic family bloodline, as opposed to a more amorphous symbolic hope for a prosperity promised by capitalism. Indeed, Genji himself becomes both the victim and the purveyor of such violent ambitions. Concern about the fate of Genji's father's career as emperor only magnifies these stakes, "since even my own reign's fate is quite uncertain." Mounting anxiety about imperial succession makes Genji's already extraordinary birth all the more untimely given this anticipated regnal brevity. Alongside Genji's lack of maternal backing, this factor helps explain the antagonism he faces, since the more powerful Kokiden faction would be all the more keen to install their own heir if it seemed that the sitting emperor would cede the throne soon.

The distressing uncertainty that binds the potential consequences of Genji's birth evokes Judith Halberstam's description of queer time's ramifications: "'Queer' refers to nonnormative logics and organizations of community, sexual identity, embodiment, and activity in space and time. 'Queer time' is a term for those specific models of temporality that emerge within postmodernism once one leaves the temporal frames of bourgeois reproduction and family, longevity, risk/safety, and inheritance."[107] Halberstam's tethering of *queer* to a host of "nonnormative logics" highlights common elements that bridge divergent histories. Bracketing the phrases "within postmodernism" or "bourgeois," we can nonetheless acknowledge Heian courtly society's own distinct yet related—and often more vicious—commitments to reproduction, longevity, safety, and inheritance, all of whose conflicts striate *Genji*'s worldview and constrict Genji's available sphere of action. These investments aspire to an inevitability that would subdue the inexorable contingency imbuing them.

Yet in light of Halberstam's framing, we can read the narrative's opening as conjuring forth a queer time: a span in which conforming to the timelines of Heian politics needn't apply. Through this invocation, readers are summoned to leave the temporal frames of Heian social reproduction and regnal time in favor of an altered, adjacent temporality where predominant logics don't rule. As protagonists and readers are invited into an interval removed from such restrictive frames, they ideally come to encounter *Genji*'s world in a less hurried fashion whereby aristocratic society's commitments can be questioned more readily. The text's invocation of a queer temporality means this encounter can emerge as a more provisional unfolding present that, in being unscripted by a normative telos, is consequently less hidebound and unaligned with any outcome known in advance.

Genji's conception occurs in the midst of this queer time. His birth embodies a queer event that triggers waves of unease about the integrity of hierarchy, familial reproduction, and inheritance confronted when a gorgeous outlier comes to steal some faction's hard-won spot. Insofar as his ambiguous destiny does not neatly reinscribe the "perpetual horizon" of reproductive futurism Edelman outlines, Genji's untimely presence prefigures a looming failure of the social. Indeed, the recourse to catastrophic precedents in China seeks to stabilize the unnerving sense of anticipation surrounding this social collapse by tying Genji's unpredictably unfolding queer time to a predetermined historical referent. The anxieties unleashed around the epicenter of Genji's birth index the capacity of one anomalous child to detonate an entire realm. These fears engender the necropolitical violence that was routinized as part and parcel of the Heian reproductive regime, including the violence that kills Genji's mother, two of his lovers, and makes him crush the cuckold Kashiwagi, too.

Deviation intersects deviance at this cruel juncture to make Genji, in Michael Moon's phrasing, "precociously acquainted with grief."[108] The Heian backdrop of factional violence against which *Genji* unfolds authorizes brutality on behalf of the noble child. Following Edelman's logic, the system's queer potential would seem to be weakened by this violence insofar as it endorsed a reproductive futurism. Despite this, the Heian system's callous bent is telling: it evinces a desire to repress contingencies that threaten aspirations to secure the future through one's progeny. These contingencies stem at least in part from what Edelman calls "the possibility of a queer resistance to this organizing principle of communal relations."[109]

In this vein, and in opposition to a normative organizing principle of communal relations within the Heian court, Genji's emergence marks a deviation that sets the narrative in motion by nudging succession's equilibrium off-line. This inaugural deviation not only provokes subsequent ones, it actually *necessitates* deviance— represented through spirit possession, cuckoldry, and secret heirs—to quell these divergences. If nothing else, this pattern makes for good fiction. But furthermore, such fiction teaches us how hard it is to condemn or pinpoint deviance when it flourishes in such systemic fashion. And indeed, this might be one of *Genji*'s most profound lessons.

Akin to *deviation*, *deviance* denotes moral judgments that can seem at odds with the more radical critical work performed by the narrative—namely, the critical project of exposing the contingent, fictional character of prevailing myths of inviolable imperial heritage. Where the propensity for noble bloodlines to veer astray was so ample, this Heian text relates the societal response to Genji's affair with his stepmother, the Imperial Consort, as a crime of sexual deviance laced with treasonous potential. His impropriety diverts the imperial line as his own vexed birth was augured to do, prying it further out of joint as he fathers an emperor from his commoner's station. Genji swerves out of bounds, queering this most sacred of family trees with an illicit desire whose consummation wreaks more havoc than gay sex ever could.[110]

With this queer reading of *Genji*'s conception underway, we now enter more thoroughgoing engagements with a series of key moments in the narrative. The following chapter examines an especially dramatic instance in which intimacy and loss merge for an adolescent Genji, as his shattering experience of losing a lover to spirit possession sends him reeling toward his servant.

2

Chivalry in Shambles

Fabricating Manhood amid Architectural Disrepair

How should we understand the relationship between gendered intimacy, loss, and built-space? Here, I read the "Yūgao" chapter to examine how Genji's tragic tryst with Yūgao in a rundown residence opens the door for masculinity to be questioned and queer relations to take center stage. Conventional chivalry collapses at this site. With *chivalry*, I shorthand masculine ideals typified by mid-Heian literary tropes of courtiers' expansive mobility, industrious "sexual appetite" (*irogonomi*), and material or martial wherewithal to support or defend women and property, all of which are destabilized in *Genji*. The residence's disintegrating borders allow Genji to be emasculated as supernatural forces infiltrate the estate. This drama unfolds after Genji ushers Yūgao, his new love interest, to a deserted mansion, hoping to seduce her. He gets to play tough in this eerie estate, but its disrepair invites violence that fractures Genji's facade. Genji has been favoring Yūgao over Rokujō, and on dreaming of Rokujō, a spirit seeps through rafters to murder Yūgao. Genji fails as protector and is left defeated in a heap on the floor. But here, his faithful manservant Koremitsu swoops to the rescue, literally lending a shoulder to cry on as Genji attempts to redress emasculation and rebuild his shattered self-regard in the wake of losing both his pride and his woman.

In this chapter, I highlight scenes where the assertion of hegemonic masculinity falters alongside a host of homosocial affinities and homoerotic undertones that sustain it. I examine the slide between these, informed by Eve Sedgwick's account of male homosociality, which posits "the potential unbrokenness of a continuum between homosocial and homosexual."[1] Male intimacy in "Yūgao" becomes less about erotic pleasure and more about the male bonding needed to preserve the gap between rehearsing an idealized erotic masculinity and keeping certain intimate relations at bay.

64

I argue that Genji's relationships with Yūgao, Rokujō, and Koremitsu show how the breaching of architectural boundaries can reshape intimate relations along queer lines. The dilapidated site hosts a spirit possession that de-eroticizes the female object of desire, as this encounter repulses Genji to fuel forms of caretaking and susceptibility left unrealized elsewhere. I demonstrate that the porosity of this site sets a straightforward romantic vector adrift, skimming the vicinity of homo-erotic desire but without lodging there. This departure from ideal courtship stokes a form of male-male intimacy forged in the rubble of failed chivalry and fatal loss. Accentuating the phenomenological facets of this embodied experience of failure, I read this scenario as queer insofar as characters grapple with a disabling, disori-enting contingency in veering between the materialities of vengeful apparition and abject corpse.

SETTING THE SCENE: KOREMITSU'S SERVICE AND THE EXPANSION OF EERIE SPACE

We learn early in the "Yūgao" chapter that "there wasn't a single person, even those catching merely a glimpse of him, whose heart didn't pause on Genji. See-ing this radiance that surrounded him, men of every station, even down to the rough-hewn woodcutter, wished, *I'd love to have my dearest daughter attend him*; while there wasn't a man who, despite being lowly, didn't keenly consider send-ing a sister he thought promising into Genji's service."[2] This detail reminds us of Genji's irresistible charms—notably by emphasizing men's desire rather than that of the potentially interested daughters or sisters themselves. This rhetorical twist highlights a triangular framework wherein Genji's beauty rouses men to secure connections to him through their female kin. That the men fall along a spectrum of status positions underscores the breadth of Genji's allure.

Besides giving a sense of the erotic (and inevitably political) desires men have for Genji, this description also anticipates his deepening homosocial relationship with Koremitsu. Koremitsu serves as faithful retainer and intermediary for Genji's affairs with women. Following orders, Koremitsu reconnoiters Yūgao's residence through a fence and then "report[s] in wonderful detail what he'd ascertained": "I really can't fathom who that woman is. I certainly get the impression she's doing her best to keep hidden from everyone. Her women pass humdrum days. . . . Although I could only faintly make it out, her face indeed suggests she's quite alluring."[3] Koremitsu thus paves the way for Genji's exploits with this reputed beauty.[4]

Koremitsu's desire to please Genji mounts: "Koremitsu smiled as he talked on, noticing how very eager Genji was to know more. 'My own romancing of a woman there proceeds as planned, and I've left no nook unmapped in scouting the residence. They think their secret so well hidden, but . . .'"[5] In courting one of the women of Yūgao's house, Koremitsu subordinates heterosexual desires he might have to his desire to please his lord. Here, Gustav Heldt's insights regarding the fluidity of *tomo* (friend/follower) and *kimi* (milord/my love) in Heian court poetry seem apt: "Desire in such cases is the expression not so much of a sexed identity as of a relationship determined by power differentials."[6]

Koremitsu marshals his newfound knowledge to titillate Genji. Koremitsu's tone both solicits affirmation ("Please commend my courtship skills!") and is haughty, with a misogynistic tinge ("Those ladies think they're so clever!"), as he tries to impress and enthrall Genji with a display of juicy knowledge. The intelligence Koremitsu gathers on the women coaxes Genji closer to him. Genji asks to "peek through that fence" himself, determined to gain firsthand the knowledge his retainer has conveyed verbally.[7] Koremitsu thus transfers Genji into the dominant position of courting Yūgao, first visually, and then physically, by smuggling him into her residence: "Pondering the condition of where Yūgao was living for the time being at least, Genji thought, 'She must represent exactly that lower grade Tō no Chūjō derided. What if within it were an unexpectedly enticing find?' Koremitsu, who hated the thought of veering even slightly from his lord's wishes, mustered his own sweeping courtship knowledge, arriving after much roving back and forth at a plan to usher Genji into the house."[8]

Yūgao's "lower grade" intrigues Genji and suggests that she would be delighted to have him woo her. Notably, this detail, based on the disrepair of Yūgao's dwelling, cites the "Rainy Night Discussion" from two chapters earlier in the narrative. In that conversation, Tō no Chūjō explained, "The girl unknown to the world, the surprisingly alluring one shut away alone in some rundown house overgrown with creepers, this is exactly who's boundlessly intriguing. *How did she ever end up that way?* you wonder, since it strays from expectation, captivating you with curiosity."[9] Tō no Chūjō himself had in fact previously considered venturing a relationship with Yūgao.

Considering the "Rainy Night Discussion," we should remember that this "elegant locker-room discussion on the varieties of women available to young aristocrats," in Norma Field's terms, itself represents a primal scene of male homosocial exchange whose heterosexual eroticism stirs homoerotic desires among the men: "Rain had been dribbling the whole humdrum day, showering softly into evening. . . . Over supple white gowns, Genji wore only a dress cloak, donned with a casual disregard, its cord slightly unfastened, and his lamplit silhouette as he reclined there against a pillar was so sublime that one wanted to see him as a woman."[10]

A discovery I made in translating this passage and comparing Seidensticker's rendering to the original Japanese merits mention here. To revisit a point I argued in chapter 1, Seidensticker's version actively avoids homoerotic language and even fabricates a means to deflect the suggestiveness of the original. Seidensticker appears to have redacted details that—from the vantage of the 1970s—were deemed too queer to include. He writes, "Because it was very warm, [Genji] loosened his dress, and they thought him even handsomer. . . . The Minister came to pay his respects. Seeing Genji thus in dishabille, he made his greetings from behind a conveniently placed curtain."[11] "Conveniently placed" indeed: there is no mention of "supple white gowns" (*shiroki ongoromodomo no nayoyokanarau ni*), a "lamplit silhouette of Genji reclining against a pillar" (*sohifushitamaheru onhokage*), or, crucially, "that one wanted to see Genji as a woman" (*onna nite mitatematsuramahoshi*). These phrases are remarkable for the selectivity of their omission. Part of the weirdness here comes from the odd interposition of summer warmth as a rationale for Genji's seductive appearance; it comes out of nowhere in Seidensticker's rendition. This recourse to hot weather dampens the scene's eroticism by reducing Genji's alluring exposure to mere pragmatism (the heat is to blame for his appearance!), making desire between men less discernable and scuttling the queer potential liable to surface when articulating textural particularities of clothing and gesture.

In short, Seidensticker drains the eroticism from this charged scene of homosocial exchange. Stranger still is the interposition of a "conveniently placed curtain" to cordon from view a "Genji thus in dishabille." Indeed, this curtain's appearance is utterly too convenient; I find no trace of it in the original Japanese of this passage. The jarring recourse to French here— perhaps to cushion the scenario's risqué tenor with foreign flourish?—flags an uncharacteristic excess in his translation. Consequently, the curtain appears out of thin air as an overcompensating architectural concoction designed to neutralize the presence of homoerotic arousal by shielding protagonists and hapless readers from Genji's wiles. In this regard, Seidensticker's Cold War translation reads as phobic toward the Heian text's queer tenor.

The androgyny foregrounded by the phrase "wanted to see him as a woman" is complex, partly because it lacks an explicit subject, making it possible to translate the desiring entity as a general *one* or as the more localizably concrete *they*, referring to the men sharing the steamy chamber with Genji as they gossip. Rajyashree Pandey further enhances our sense of this scene's implications:

> The fact that the text does not specify whether it is the viewer who wishes to be a woman or whether he or she wishes to see Genji as a woman points to the fluid and interchangeable nature of "male" and "female" here. The scenes in which the men around Genji express their erotic feelings are perhaps best read not as manifestations of homosexual desire but rather as culturally available performance stances in which the tropes of *otoko* and *onna* . . . could be playfully manipulated by the male protagonists of the text, irrespective of their physical sexual attributes.[12]

Pandey's insight disallows an oversimplified recourse to gender categories as indicative of sexual preference. She even argues that the performative nature of desire itself makes locating its bodily origin or destination futile.

Meanwhile, the provocative phrase nonetheless highlights an erotic potential infusing homosocial competition between the men as they vie for varied distinctive ladies. Paul Schalow observes that "with the rainy-night scene, the friends embark on a sexual rivalry that dominates the next several chapters of the tale, covering the entire span of their youth."¹³ Tsutamura Tomohiko stresses further that even though Genji and Tō no Chūjō are brothers-in-law, their true bond comes from their exchanges of women; Yūgao's purpose in the narrative is to serve as shared property binding Genji to Tō no Chūjō.¹⁴ And for Dote Shiori, that Genji learns of Yūgao's death before Tō no Chūjō signals Genji's growing dominance over him.¹⁵

But the status gap between male hunter and female prey attests to Genji's opportunism. This detail betrays the fragility of Genji's masculinity through his disinterest in more formidable, securely situated women. For his part, Koremitsu now moves to phase two of his oblique form of courting Genji: using his "own sweeping courtship knowledge" (*onore mo kumanaki sukigokoro nite*) to convey Genji closer to the secluded woman Genji hopes will exceed his modest expectations. Interactions like these help us problematize an idealized chivalry flaunted in texts like *Tales of Ise*, which *Genji* inherits and retools. By reducing Genji's sphere of movement, magnifying his dependence on other men, and highlighting his inability to seduce securely and successfully, the tale undercuts literary conventions of male heroism.

The secrecy suffusing this narrative juncture helps build drama by stressing status boundaries that might be blurred as the men conspire: "Unable to deduce for sure that this woman was who he sought, Genji didn't announce his own name, going to terrible lengths to play down his true station and pursuing her with such exceptional vigor that Koremitsu saw that Genji would surely be thought foolish, and thus gave up his own horse, dismounting to walk alongside his lord. Koremitsu lamented, 'How perilous it would be the moment they discovered the great lover making his way contemptibly on foot!'"¹⁶

Genji's disguise conceals standard markers of rank to situate him more on par with the vassal shadowing him. Within this pocket of secrecy, the men's bond tightens, and Koremitsu garners a space to offer his horse and walk beside Genji, not out of mere duty but out of an admiration for Genji's "exceptional vigor" (*reinarazu oritachi arikitamahu ha*). Koremitsu's capacity to identify with "the great lover" and indispose himself to augment Genji's appearance in women's eyes suggests a developing intimacy between the men premised on, yet not reducible to, servitude alone. For instance, Furuta Masayuki notes that because of Koremitsu's link to Genji through Koremitsu's mother, who nursed both boys, another kind of familial relation can achieve glory surreptitiously, via Koremitsu's efforts to assist Genji's imperial ambitions.¹⁷

This intimacy, manifested through Koremitsu's efforts to assist Genji's infiltration, allows Genji to carry Yūgao off to the deserted spot where his manhood will be tested. Before Genji arrives there, however, he is taxed in a more trivial fashion. He makes a preliminary visit to Yūgao's residence, where, "On the eighth month's fifteenth night, Genji was amazed by the appearance of a dwelling the likes of which he'd never seen, as boundless moonlight came flooding through countless crevices in the plank-built house, filling every cranny."[18] The structural porosity of the shabby house allows not just excess light but also excess sound inside:

> Yūgao felt quite mortified by the incessant clamor of folks rising and leaving to carry out their pathetic daily business. One reckons the place's impression would surely have made someone aiming to display a fancy countenance want to melt right into the earth. Louder than thunder roared the deafening clunk, clunk of a treadle mortar whose sound seemed to pound their pillow until [Genji] realized this was exactly what "shameless racket" meant. Clueless as to what was making the echoes entering his ears, he merely heard a baffling, loathsome noisemaking; it was nothing but a nonstop raucous muddle.
>
> The sound of snowy robes being drubbed at the fulling block drifting faintly toward him from this way and that, the cries of geese in flight—these joined an assortment of surrounding sounds to amass a poignancy difficult to subdue. . . . The hiss and hum of myriad insects intermixed. And for Genji, who had only rarely heard even a cricket in the wall, this mishmash of singing grazing his ears nearly made for a wholly peculiar sensation. Even as he pondered how [Yūgao] might take more care to boost her outer appeal a tad, Genji still desired to see her unconstrained. "Come along, let's go spend the night cozily at some nearby spot. Meeting only here like this has really taken its toll."[19]

In this radically permeable space, Genji is simultaneously fascinated and annoyed by the "bizarre novelty" of its cacophony. Genji is vexed by the noise because of its variety and volume, but also because of its dislocating potency. He cannot discern the referent for some sounds; others pummel identifiably at his pillow block; still others percolate, dispersed, in the sky or garden, echoing toward him from all sides. This onslaught makes Genji feel exposed and on edge. He lacks the means to seal the physical and aural membrane of the house or to manage the "incessant clamor" of those coarse neighbors going about "their pathetic daily business." This unnerving excess provokes Genji to seek less distracting, less constricting surroundings, wherein he could orient himself more stably to woo Yūgao. The vexing noise around him makes Genji take a more forceful tone with his female associate. In analyzing Genji's conversations with female characters, Murayama Maki observes that with the middle-ranking Yūgao, Genji uses the command form unusually often.[20] This suggests that his invitation to spend the night elsewhere reads as an order aimed at someone he views as subordinate, marking the affair as initially empowering for Genji.

However, Genji gets far more than he bargained for in switching to a far less bustling, less constrained locale. The new site is similarly porous, and its atmosphere grows murky. Genji tries to play brave despite his fragile constitution:

> While Genji coaxed however he could, [Yūgao] shrunk from dashing off into the unknown beneath a dithering moon, when, without warning, it was concealed

by clouds to show a stunning daybreak sky. Before daylight exposed his exploits, Genji rushed out as usual, breezily scooping Yūgao into the carriage, and Ukon also came aboard.

They reached a certain estate not far away, and, waiting for the attendant to emerge, they peered up at the dismal ferns sprawling from the decrepit gate's eaves, immeasurably dark with trees. With fog thick and dew coating all, Genji's sleeves got utterly soaked merely lifting the carriage blinds. "I've never encountered anything of this sort before," he said. "It's really something that frays the nerves, huh?" . . .

Exceedingly untamed, the abandoned garden spanned far into the distance, its ancient woods looming with a sinister air. The shrubbery close by lacked any particular appeal, and mounds of water weeds had clogged the lake, making the place all the more creepy indeed. There was what looked like a shed of some sort where someone might have lived, but that sat off at a remove behind the main house. "What an eerie place! But all the same, let's see those demons and such slip past *me*," Genji said.[21]

According to Norma Field, "From Genji's point of view, the Yūgao episode represents an excursion into foreign territory—foreign . . . for its unaristocratic realism as well as for its supernaturalism."[22] Similarly, Nakanishi Susumu notes that the eeriness of the mansion's depiction stems from Chinese references deployed to thicken the setting's mystique.[23] The desolation of the spot Genji has chosen for his tryst with Yūgao arouses as it unnerves, partially because the scene's allusions to Chinese literature—such as the moor-like expanse, where "mounds of water weeds had clogged the lake"—intensify an *irogonomi*, or "desire for ladies," who are reminiscent of Chinese beauties.[24] Various images also interlock to create a sense of a harrowing expanse of space, new to both Genji and the reader: the "abandoned garden" that "spanned far into the distance" and the "ancient woods looming with a sinister air" confront Genji with his smallness and stymied movement. Furthermore, as Ōta Yōsuke observes, descriptions of the moon throughout "Yūgao" depart markedly from other instances of lunar imagery seen in both *Genji* and other Heian literary sources in their consistently ominous associations.[25] Even as Genji puts on a show of strength in lifting Yūgao into the carriage and scoffing at demons' threats, travel to this place delivers the first truly disconcerting blow to Genji's gleaming notion of himself.

GHOSTLY INFILTRATION AND THE SCRAMBLE TO SOUND MANLY

More significant than its sinister ambience is how the locale determines gendered action as a wraith surfaces. The setting's remoteness, "unkempt and deserted garden," and "ruinous eaves" underscore a spatial permeability and lack of safety. While the setting holds promise for Genji in implying heightened privacy and the increased sexual availability of the woman he is courting, its permeability allows for disorientating infiltrations that disrupt the heterosexual masculinity he's eager to enact:

Genji passed the day with [Yūgao], chiding her one moment, then sweet-talking her the next. Gazing at the indescribably tranquil sunset sky, Genji recalled how dreadful she found the house's murky depths, so he raised the outer blinds and snuggled down beside her. They traded glances in the evening glow, and in a setting like this, Yūgao was surprised to find that despite her misgivings, she had forgotten her countless troubles; she became quite alluring as her attitude toward Genji thawed a bit. She spent all day lying there fixed beside him, seeming heartrendingly girlish in being so frightened by everything. He lowered the lattice shutters early and had the lamp brought in, complaining, "It's too cruel to bear. We've grown past our lingering res-ervations, yet at heart some hindrance still remains for you."

"What an uncanny love this is! And on Rokujō Avenue, how warped her feelings must be. Though it's tough to admit, I comprehend the ill will she no doubt harbors toward me," Genji mused, his concerns focused foremost on her. . . .

Late that evening, when Genji had fallen slightly asleep, a gorgeous woman seated herself at his pillow. "I view you as so marvelous, yet you don't think to visit me, con-veying a lackluster creature here like this and showering your affections on her. It's so stunningly callous of you . . ." she said, and Genji saw her start shaking the woman beside him awake. Jolted, Genji woke up, feeling assaulted by some unseen presence. The lamp's flame had died. Rattled, he drew his sword, laid it down, then woke up Ukon. She came to him, looking like she also had felt frightened.

"Go wake the bridgeway guard and tell him to bring a hand torch," Genji ordered.

"But how can I possibly manage, in the dark?"

"Oh, don't be such a baby!" Genji chuckled and clapped his hands. Ominous echoes answered, like voices in a mountain haunt.

No one could hear him, so they weren't coming. Meanwhile, Yūgao was shud-dering violently, and one wondered what on earth should be done. She was now drenched in sweat and seemed comatose.

"How pitiful! So frail, and prone to spend her days just staring up at the sky," Genji thought.

"I'll go and wake [the guard] myself. Getting just these hollow mountain echoes for my clapping is too galling. Wait right here with her, close," he said, dragging Ukon over. Then he went to the Western double doors and pushed them open to find that the bridgeway's light, too, had gone out. . . . The steward's son rose to heed his call.

"Fetch a hand torch. And tell my footman, 'Twang your bowstring and keep shouting without pause.' . . . How could you drop your guard to fall asleep in such an isolated place? I thought Koremitsu had come, but . . ."

"He was in your employ, but you issued no orders so he went off, saying that he would return to get you at dawn."

Genji went back in and felt his way to Yūgao. She was still laid out as before, with Ukon lying there face down beside her.

"What's all this about? Your witless cowardice is such a joke! In deserted places, things like foxes and such will try startling people with eerie little frights. I bet that's all this is. Plus with the likes of me around, there's no chance we'll be intimidated by anything like that," he said, pulling Ukon upright.

"I was only lying down like that because I feel so awfully unwell and totally per-turbed. My lady must be scared senseless all the more," she said.

Genji replied, "Sure, but why should she be?" and reached to touch Yūgao. She wasn't breathing. He shook her, but she just swayed, limp and clearly unconscious; feeling helplessly bereft, he reckoned, "As terribly childlike as she is, a spirit must've stolen her away."

Someone brought the hand torch. Ukon appeared in no condition at all to move, so Genji drew up the nearby standing curtain. "Bring it closer!" he ordered. These circumstances being unprecedented, the servant couldn't manage to approach Genji any closer, so he hesitated, stopping short of even crossing the room's threshold.

"Bring it closer already! Save the ceremony for another occasion," Genji barked. Once the torch was brought closer, he saw, right there at her pillow, the very same woman whose face he'd seen in his dream, her phantom there dimly before vanishing in a blink. *One hears of things like this in those old tales*, he thought, but despite all his astonished terror, he was so frantic wondering firstly, *What has befallen Yūgao?* that he forgot all dignity and lay beside her.

He yelped, trying to rouse her, but she grew colder by the second and had long since breathed her last. He was speechless. There was no one he could trust in to tell him how to handle this ordeal. He should have remembered that this was the type of time when a monk was precisely what one required, but despite wanting to be so tough he had a child's heart, and watching Yūgao die before his eyes devastated him. He clung to her, pleading, "Oh my love, come back to life! Don't do such a cruel thing to me!" But the body had gone cold and now became loathsome to touch.

Whereas "How dreadful!" was all Ukon could think before, all her fear and trembling gave way to a horrible frenzy of wailing. Recalling the example of a demon that had once accosted some minister in the palace's Southern Hall, Genji summoned courage to speak up.

"No, this can't be. She can't possibly have just perished like that. How blaring a voice sounds at night! Hush up!" he scolded Ukon, the whirlwind events having left him in an irksome stupor. He summoned the footman, saying, "Send my retainer straightaway to where Lord Koremitsu is lodging and tell him he must hurry back here at once."[26]

A phenomenological method becomes valuable here, because much of this scene's drama hinges on how spatial borders are manipulated to modulate physical intimacy and sensory perception jointly. Just before disaster strikes, we notice Genji raising the blinds to allow more sunset light into the room and thus comfort the timid Yūgao. Soon afterward, he lowers the lattice shutters and lights a lamp, to set the mood and to comfort himself through sex with her. This oscillation of opening and closing the room's outer wall echoes the alternating reproach and flattery of Genji's flirtation. More importantly, the actions indicate a wavering structural border that portends invasion.

To control the permeability of the room is for Genji to exercise a masculine authority premised on a capacity to police borders. Genji disposes those borders to his advantage, first for seduction and later to speed the arrival of help, when, in a claustrophobic panic, he "went to the Western double doors and pushed them open" and "drew up the nearby standing curtain." Having insisted on greater privacy and dismissed trusty men like Koremitsu, Genji himself must now perform the frantic labor of opening doors and crying for help. Indeed, as Genji yells, "Bring [the torch] closer!" we find that "the servant couldn't manage to approach Genji any closer, so he hesitated, stopping short of even crossing the room's threshold," which suggests that Genji has overdone it with his efforts to commandeer the space. The situation deteriorates because he can no longer reliably calibrate the proximity of bodies to desired effect. Men like Koremitsu and the unnamed servant might have stood guard, but their closeness to Genji's bedchamber would have also deprived him of a fuller impression of authority. The site's forbidding character encouraged delusions of grandeur—so long as the perimeter was secured.

But the trespassing spirit perforates that delusional bravery. Although Genji dreams of Rokujō just beforehand, the narrative does not specify the spirit's identity; only Genji witnesses it, and no mediums or exorcists extract its name. This ambiguity distinguishes Yūgao's spirit possession from all others in the tale, exemplifying a queerness in its unnerving indeterminacy.[27] Heterosexual dalliance in these porous quarters provokes a queer disorientation that afflicts the would-be seducer. Therefore, this spirit reads as queer in forcing courtship's failure and for the inescapable contingency it both embodies and inflicts.

Despite Genji closing the shutters, the spirit invades the tryst to plant itself at his pillow and murder the woman he prefers. The spirit revenges Genji's distance from Rokujō by forcibly projecting itself into both his bedchamber and his headspace. The visitation's violence—with all the shaking, shivering, and pouring perspiration it provokes—reads like an assault targeted to enter Genji's innermost sanctum and slit it wide. While the attack literally kills Yūgao, it symbolically castrates Genji. It deprives him of the light on which he would rely to regain his bearings and makes him lay down his sword.

Loss of speech further marks Genji's emasculation. Where he's just been shouting in panic, yelling orders to bring the hand torch—a phallic symbol of light and knowledge that might dispel the feminizing darkness—his words now wane. His status and concomitant ability to make announcements that demand subordinates' response mean nothing once the spirit descends. Genji's screams sound both extreme and feeble compared to the spirit's dreamy whisper; the sheer volume at which he now barks orders signals his descent into impotence. Similarly, the physical work that Genji does—pushing open shutters, dragging and shaking bodies—recalls the bustle at Yūgao's old house, suggesting that the status he normally maintains vis-à-vis the menials charged with such tasks has eroded.

Genji has dismissed his entourage so he might indulge his lovely fantasy all alone and at leisure. He appreciates their absence and Yūgao's "heartrendingly girlish" manner, as both make him feel like more of a man. Eerie environs scare him, but they scare his woman more, which helps to deflect his own misgivings. Where secrecy ruled the day as he arrived and sought sex, Genji now scrambles for all the light he can get. He opens doors, shutters, and curtains, exposing not only himself (and his bumbling) but also his dying lover. The murdering ghost snatches anonymity's cozy entitlements away. Hence Genji has no choice but to acknowledge his plight as akin to that of the menials beside him. He wants to unbolt the space and allow as many men as possible to close in and crowd out the solitude he felt in being beset by the apparition. This homosocial closeness will help him reorient himself, take stock, and hold court despite having fumbled his sword.

The layers of architectural and interpersonal mediation that would normally insulate this Heian noble from the vulgarities of everyday interaction evaporate amid the emasculating immediacy of spirit possession. As Kaoru Hayashi explains, "The narrator tells us how [Rokujō's] father once held high hopes for her to become an empress consort, but these plans were dashed at the very last moment as Zenbō did not ascend to the throne. Her name—a combination of the location of a non-imperial residence as well as her title as a widow—embodies her family's failed expectations and her resulting physical distance from the imperial palace."[28] Given this background, the loss of Genji's loyalty and distance from him in the Capital arguably leads Rokujō to induce other losses elsewhere, not to redress her own misfortune but to produce an artificial kinship in the sense of "misery loves company." She cannot have the romantic intimacy she desires with Genji; therefore, she foists trauma on Genji to produce an altered sort of intimacy with him through shared loss—with Yūgao serving as the conduit binding murderer to mourner.

To punish Genji for staying away from Rokujō in favor of Yūgao, the spirit hurls him too close for comfort. The spirit that alights at his pillow attacks by peeling all filters from Genji's sensory experience of the murk, depositing Genji into a state of radically de-mediated exposure to the cruel world's stimuli. Thus the narrator remarks that the victim's "body had gone cold, and now became loathsome to touch" as Genji experiences a new position and perception sensitive enough to register the shift in temperature when he "went back in and felt his way to Yūgao."

Emptied of eroticism, skin-to-skin contact with Yūgao only chills Genji's bones and elicits his screaming. This contact reads as queer in its conjoined phenomenological emphasis and a violent disorientation characterizing the strange porous space in which vision fails, touch unnerves, and sounds infest Genji's ears while his own voice rings hollow and unheeded. The spirit forces the cowed Genji to "for[get] all dignity and lay beside [Yūgao]." As Genji gropes for steadiness amid the swirling clamor, the spirit makes him first relinquish his sword and then prostrate his very body, assuming a position mimicking that of the murdered woman. This assault wickedly grants him the closeness he coveted earlier, but it simultaneously withholds fully functioning powers of proprioception and surveillance that could control that closeness.

This dislocating violence makes Genji long for the proximate removes he formerly enjoyed vis-à-vis both servants and lovers. At those manageable distances,

Genji maintained optimal authority and mystique. But this ramshackle patch of land, with its teeming weeds and rickety planks that let the icy moonlight stream through, establishes a frame inhospitable to the optimized distances Genji accepts as natural entitlements. These were distances of space and status. Despite Genji's recourse to commanding those around him, "no one could hear him, no one was coming."[29] The porous nature of the space, which so aroused Genji's interest initially, now nullifies his once commanding voice. So Genji keeps shouting, each call more desperate, as he "chuckle[s] and clap[s] his hands," praying any noise might snap the spirit's spell.

No other passage in *Genji* toggles so starkly between coaxing whispers and harsh shouts, as Genji tries to stand his ground. Not unlike Genji's earlier alternation between closed and open spaces, this modulation attests to his lacking the "faintest idea what to do now." One moment he's yelling at a servant to "bring [the torch] closer!"; the next he's remarking, "How blaring a voice sounds at night! Hush up!" Frantic hope sprouts that the torch will replace the sword, banishing shadows to restore equilibrium and lending strength. Holding the torch partially reinstates Genji's purview within an ever-encroaching aural surround in which "the pines' howling sounded like the deep woods', and a creepy bird cried with ragged caws" to "give the place a sheer horror defying description."[30]

SOMEDAY MY PRINCE WILL COME

As Genji struggles to regain his composure and his language, the cavernous house amplifies the sounds penetrating from the expansive wilds outside. At this juncture, Genji reaches the limits of his senses, and his macho façade fractures:

> The desolation held far and wide; not a single human voice sounded. As Genji's thoughts churned, "Why," he asked himself, steeped in pointless regret, "did I ever decide to spend the night in this despicable place?"
> Ukon was distraught and clutched him, shuddering like she'd surely die. *And what will become of this one*, he wondered in a daze, holding onto her. He alone had kept his wits about him, yet he hadn't the faintest idea what to do now. The flame faintly petered out, while over the screen standing at the chamber's edge, from murky corners near and far came the fitful hiss of unseen things' footfalls rasping as they stalked.[31]

The lamp goes out and Genji crumbles, feminized beside the bawling Ukon, Yūgao's breast sibling (*menotogo*). Edith Sarra explains, "This is important because it creates a symmetry: she is to Yūgao as Koremitsu is to Genji. When Genji clasps Ukon to him, the gesture also suggests a class-based disorientation: Genji is put in Koremitsu's place."[32] Note the spatial transition: where Genji wooed Yūgao at a sleeping dais, he now has been literally lowered and thrust to the aisle, where servants might sleep. The screen shields Genji, Ukon, and Yūgao's fresh corpse only in the barest sense, letting in the "fitful hiss of unseen things' footfalls." These noises confound Genji further, making him rue the absence of his man: "He felt them coming up close from behind. *If only Koremitsu would come quickly!* Genji thought. But Koremitsu's whereabouts were uncertain."[33]

Genji is unmanned as he yearns for his loyal steward to come make everything alright. Where Genji once actively governed the permeability of built-space, he has now fallen to the aisle, flanked in darkness by two women, one dead and another "shuddering like she'd surely die," not to mention the roaming specter. The chapter "Yūgao" has mined porosity for its dramatic tension: drama builds according to how architectural borders adjust apertures of perception. Now, with the spirit's entrance, bodies, too, are pried open. Genji has ceded his sword, crawled into the corridor, speechless and sightless, and is exposed to forces he can't withstand. With his senses of hearing and touch piqued by the enveloping darkness, Genji's dread and wish for rescue bud like an arousal. Formerly amused by this setting's resemblance to ancient romances, Genji now discovers himself playing the forlorn heroine. Like such a woman, for he had "hear[d] of things like this in those old tales," he awaits a hero who will quell this insufferable uncertainty. Genji's anguish recalls his mother's desperation at the Kokiden faction's hands, and for Ueno Tatsuyoshi, Yūgao's resemblance to Genji's mother explains the courtier's distress.[34]

Waiting for relief makes "the ages spent as [Koremitsu] scoured high and low for Genji until dawn broke feel as though that single night eclipsed a thousand ages."[35] This interminable span stands out, especially because Koike Seiji notes that "Yūgao's" time is narrated in a documentary style that chronicles nearly every moment of that twenty-four-hour period.[36] The trope of courtly women waiting in vain for lovers' visits is well-worn. But this interval Genji inhabits is different. Aristocratic paramours lauded in Heian literature keep mobile, pursuing new conquests and enjoying the prerogative to forgo waiting. But haunted houses gnaw that privilege down. In the "ruinous eaves" that remain, Genji has no option but to keep still, keep waiting.

Emasculation amplifies the duration he endures. A single minute unfurls exponentially as Genji's disoriented longing protracts temporality, transposing him into the feminine position of waiting for torment to end, until "finally, he heard a cock's far off crowing." In a Heian literary context, the cock's crow immediately calls to mind the trope of heterosexual lovers having to end their tryst at dawn, though we shouldn't forget the use of "dawn parting" for depictions of male-male sexual liaisons in later eras.[37]

Recontextualizing the motif of the cock's crow in this emasculating predicament queers its associations. This stock scenario has been reconfigured by the self-inflicted chaos sparked by Genji's lust for dominance through sex with a lower-status woman. Genji's inability to control the porosity of the space is what lets that heterosexual vector veer off course. Whatever type of man Genji thought himself to be before he "decide[d] to spend the night in this despicable place," he has already been flung wide of that persona as the crowing he finally hears "send[s] his thoughts reeling."[38] As his thoughts whirl, the narration shifts to Genji's perspective:

> What former life's bond could have possibly led me to risk my life facing such a trial? I know it's all my fault, payback for imprudent desires that never should have been, and now it appears this story will surely leave my example in infamy for generations to come. Try to conceal it, but one can't hide what's in the world, so it would be all anyone thought about or sought to mention, most likely from His Majesty's sanctum down to those lowlife children tossing gossip. In the end, everyone will know me as a laughingstock![39]

Disorientation and panic at being outed as a failed gallant go hand in hand. This shows that the true threat Genji fears rests with the court of public opinion. Paranoia at being outed as a coward or "fool" here means being branded unmanly, unable to keep one's wits intact and one's women safe.

ROLE REVISIONS AND THE AXES OF HEROIC DUTY

At this point, Koremitsu arrives—unforgivably late—and Genji, feeling violated, humiliated, and abandoned, becomes petulant:

> Despite feeling bitter, Genji called him in, and he was crestfallen to find, once he tried to tell Koremitsu everything, that suddenly he couldn't utter a word. Upon hearing what sounded like Koremitsu, all that had happened from start to finish trickled back to mind for Ukon, and she wept. Genji couldn't bear it either. Although he alone had kept it together, cradling her in his arms, now that Koremitsu was here he sighed with relief, and able to reckon with his sorrow, he couldn't stop sobbing for a good while. It just hurt too much.
>
> In time he calmed down and said, "Something incredibly bizarre occurred here, in this place, something more horrid than words can convey." . . . Saying this, the weeping Genji looked so very superbly lovely that Koremitsu, too, grew sad watching him and broke down bawling.
>
> After all was said and done, this was exactly the time when they needed someone mature and well versed in the world's ways, a seaman who had weathered life's storms, to rely on. But with the both of them being but callow youths, they were unspeakably out of their depth.[40]

We can view Genji's emotional responses as attesting to his depth of feeling. This aligns with the *irogonomi* sensualism epitomized by literary forebears like *The Tales of Ise*'s Ariwara no Narihira. So when Genji cries with Koremitsu, it recalls the waiting damsel motif by inverting the prototypical male position normalized by Narihira's excursions to nab provincial women.

Koremitsu's arrival grants Genji a welcome dispensation to bawl like a lady-in-waiting, a spatiotemporal interval in which to weep freely.[41] In this shared moment of intimacy, Genji becomes especially beautiful to the man who has come to rescue him. Indeed, it is the very failure to man up on Genji's part that enables such affection. The mishap makes Genji vulnerable enough to approach. In registers of both status and gender, then, Genji forfeits authority, becoming more Koremitsu's equal. Hence each man can extract comfort from tears mirrored in the other's eyes. Genji cries beside Ukon. But he cries both *for* and *with* Koremitsu, as though he'd been waiting for Koremitsu's arrival to bare his emotions.[42] Koremitsu's low status relative to Genji absolves the richer man of extra embarrassment or fear of censure. Furuta Masayuki sees this intersecting status gap and breast-brother bond between Genji and Koremitsu as framing Koremitsu as a safe foil who showcases Genji's multifaceted character by sharing in his secrets and failures to an extent that a male foil like Tō no Chūjō, as a rival of comparable status, does not.[43]

Words fail Genji again. But this time, the failure stems from disappointment in his delinquent manservant, a projection of Genji's even greater disappointment in himself. Ashamed, Genji grows less brash, no longer shouting after having dissolved into tears. Asked, "Could she somehow have been feeling unwell from the start?" Genji responds clinically: "That was not the case at all" (*saru koto mo nakaritsu*).[44] The implication is that if Yūgao had not been sick, then her death must be all the more Genji's fault. Such an admission, even tacitly, pricks Genji with more guilty feelings, making him cry again. In Koremitsu's eyes, Genji becomes beautiful once he dispenses with the formalities of rank and with butch pretensions and instead speaks on virtually equal terms. This casts Genji in a gentler light, letting empathy bloom such that Koremitsu reciprocates his wounded master's tears.

The "superb loveliness" (*ito okashige ni rautaku*) Genji displays should be conceived as resulting from transitions along two axes: one of gender and one of status. Genji's deadly failure to live up to his own personal standards of heroic masculinity, not to mention traditional literary ones, daubs him with an alluring shame, that of a brash ingénue who's caught his comeuppance and now looks with favor on the soul kind enough to not mention his folly. Although the status divide no doubt still exists between Genji and Koremitsu, Genji's mellowed tone and moist eyes allow for an interval of intimacy framed by the men's mutual commitment to secrecy regarding Genji's fall from grace. That Genji's spectacular failure would "be all anyone thought about or sought to mention, most likely from His Majesty's sanctum down to those lowlife children tossing gossip," until everyone knew him "as a laughingstock" highlights the inefficacy of rank in shielding him from ridicule by high and low alike. Hence Genji and Koremitsu both become aware of the lord's vulnerability and the vassal's resultant rise in import.

Wordlessly knighted with new duties, Koremitsu springs to action. What ensues is a scheme to remove Genji and Yūgao's corpse from the premises undetected. Koremitsu is now tasked with protecting what little remains of Genji's honor. For Miyake Saki, Genji's fears demonstrate that the Fujitsubo and Yūgao affairs are related, but where the first is seen as an incestuous sin, this one represents dis-grace. In her reading, this debacle effectively displaces penance, making Genji pay for his Fujitsubo sins with this partially divulged death scandal.[45] Despite escaping mortal danger, Genji's reputation is still at stake. So Koremitsu takes the reins, resolving to spirit himself and Genji away to a secluded temple in the Eastern Hills before anyone gets wind of the scandal.

The rescue scene displays how much Genji needs Koremitsu—for his strength, mobility, and wherewithal. The two men's roles are reversed as Koremitsu now gives Genji orders. Where he once "breezily scoop[ed] Yūgao into the carriage," Genji is now too weak to lift Yūgao's body, despite her slightness. Genji rides Koremitsu's horse, implying a demotion as he trots despondently along, outside of a carriage and thus visually unprotected by the sturdy oxcart's walls. Koremitsu is now more mobile, with an added pep in his step after having seen the body of Genji's lover directly. With his heterosexual lover gone and the status symbol carriage ceded along with her, Genji has lost much of his orientation. These two things offered anchoring points that let him locate himself within Heian society stably and with no shortage of pride. This is why he staggers so without them: "In the midst of his dismay and his breast bursting with anguish, skull aching, body feverish, he felt so miserably addled that he thought, 'This frail, I'm apt to meet a wretched end myself.'"[46] Here, Genji's condition recalls the queer disorientation Merleau-Ponty explains as involving not just "the intellectual experience of disor-der, but the vital experience of giddiness and nausea, which is the awareness of our contingency, and the horror with which it fills us."[47]

In such a sorry state, Genji needs Koremitsu more than ever. Koremitsu's loaned horse props Genji up to lend some reminder of the status hierarchy accord-ing to which he might rebuild himself. Furthermore, this gap structurally parallels the earlier occasion on which "Koremitsu saw that Genji would surely be thought foolish, and thus gave up his own horse, dismounting to walk alongside his lord. Koremitsu lamented, 'How perilous it would be the moment they discovered the great lover making his way contemptibly on foot!'" Reprising this willingness now that Genji has sunk so low matters more than it did before. In both cases, the desire to maintain some visible modicum of dignity shapes the men's spatial arrangement. Yet in this instance, staging that contrast gains special significance as the "the great lover" (kesōbito) struggles to rectify his shortfall. The physical boost Koremitsu provides by citing this earlier gesture literally helps ease Genji back into the saddle as his battered ego mends.

The spirit possession episode underscores the communal nature of sustaining masculine fantasies of sexual and spatial dominance. The trial Genji undergoes here spotlights his limits as a callow youth: "But despite wanting to be so tough he had a child's heart, and watching [Yūgao] die before his eyes devastated him." Age here signifies as a marker both of inexperience and of a certain machismo that aspires to impermeable composure. Given that Genji's staggering loss occurred in attempting to seduce Yūgao, Koremitsu works to redress that sexual humiliation with supplements like the horse and the backstage finagling to bury evidence of his lord's debacle.

This added responsibility for Genji's masculine well-being occasions new privileges that alter Koremitsu's relationship with him. For example, Genji gives Koremitsu instructions for how he would like Yūgao's funeral performed, sending him off to put things in order. However, Koremitsu no longer takes orders blindly but now takes more of a stand to offer unsolicited counsel of his own: "'What, now? No, no,' said Koremitsu, standing. 'Sir, this is not the time to overdo things.' Genji despaired to see him leave" (*tote tatsu ga, ito kanashiku obosarureba*).[48] As Koremitsu states his opinion—"standing" as he does so—Genji feels forlorn. This heartache evokes a lover's parting, reinforcing the sense that Genji has slipped into an acute dependence on Koremitsu following Yūgao's death. Koremitsu's rise denotes a shifting dynamic between the men that repositions Genji more passively, casting him as concerned with the increasingly assertive Koremitsu's attentions as the two men collude.

This new conspiratorial closeness draws suspicion: "Catching snippets of the exchange, the ladies-in-waiting wondered vaguely, *How strange! What could be happening? Genji says he can't head to the palace on account of being defiled. Still, what's with them whispering and grumbling like that?*"[49] The peanut gallery chimes in, lamenting the lowered volume that makes these men's secrets harder to discern. This intrusive curiosity frames Genji's closed-door consultation with Koremitsu as a pseudo-tryst, laced as it is with urgent groans and whispers.

Genji strives to regain equilibrium. By holding last rites for Yūgao, he aims to end—at least symbolically—the ongoing loss he feels. Genji therefore travels to attend the secret funeral, where he ends up trying to console the distraught Ukon—and to some degree himself—by assuming the paternalistic role of assured confidant. However, time is of the essence, and given the compromising circumstances, Genji mustn't tarry too long:

> Koremitsu said, "It seems the night is bound for dawn. You really need to make for home at once." Genji could only look back time and again, his breast brimming with anguish as he rode off. Along the dew-drenched route, he felt like he hadn't a clue where he was, set adrift within an abnormally dense morning fog.
>
> *She looks as she did when alive, lying there in that crimson robe of mine from when we traded ours. Whatever could our bond have been?* He mulled this over throughout his journey. Once again, Koremitsu was at his side to help, because Genji was shaky in his saddle, seeming unfit to ride, and even slid off his horse as they reached the Kamo riverbank. Woefully unhinged, Genji said, "You should probably just abandon me here in the middle of the road like this. I truly feel like there's simply no way I can make it back home," which rattled Koremitsu, who thought, *Had I been thinking straight, despite what he voiced, would I ever have let him mount up and head off on this journey?*

Getting quite anxious, Genji washed his hands in the river's water and called on the Kiyomizu Kannon for aid, but he still felt baffled, with no solution in sight. For his part, Genji girded up his loins [*shihite ongokoro wo okoshite*], in his heart beseeched the buddhas, and with whatever help he could get, managed to return to his Nijō manor.[50]

Tainted by guilt and death pollution, Genji stoops by the Kamo riverbank to perform a makeshift lustration and entreat deities. However, Koremitsu nips Genji's despondent ministrations in the bud, cutting Genji's mourning short.[51] By sending the bereaved Genji home sooner than he would have liked, Koremitsu flings him into a tailspin: "Genji could only look back time and again, his breast brimming with anguish as he rode off." By curtailing the grieving process, Koremitsu also prolongs the span of time in which Genji needs to lean on him. Given that "along the dew-drenched route, [Genji] felt like he hadn't a clue where he was, set adrift within an abnormally dense morning fog," Koremitsu's value as confidant and guide persists at a premium. For the Genji blinded by grief, Koremitsu serves as a compass, and moreover as a buffer from the desolation that threatens to engulf him. Koremitsu becomes the force that keeps him upright and moving forward through the thickening fog—toward "home" and away from the pollution of Yūgao's death that has soiled Genji.[52]

The description "dew-drenched" (*ito tsuyukeki*) suits Genji's tear-soaked journey through melancholia's "abnormally dense morning fog" (*itodoshiki asagiri*). Historicizing melancholia's gendered implications within a Western context, Juliana Schiesari reminds us that "the melancholic of the past was an accredited figure of alienation and very much desirous of accentuating *his* difference from the everyday. . . . Women have not had the same cultural tradition, one that would enable them to express feelings of disempowerment and loss in a 'non-alienated' way."[53] Schiesari's observation pertains to Genji's predicament. In Yūgao's case, and in contrast to Ukon's reaction, the female object can't be marked or mourned fully by him for fear of disgrace. This implies that for all his pain at Yūgao's death, Genji's capacity to weep and swoon as he does—even in semisecret—is still underpinned by his privilege as a high-ranking man.

As the partners in crime decamp, notice the pull exerted in opposite directions: Koremitsu's eyes are locked on the path ahead of them, while Genji can't help twisting backward repeatedly. Koremitsu takes on the task of conveying Genji away from the distressing bodies of Yūgao and Ukon and back home, away from the feminized atmosphere of death and anguish and toward the Nijō residence, where Genji might convalesce and regain his footing. Koremitsu's stabilizing presence matters vitally as Genji struggles with his precarious position. For example, when Genji slides to the ground at the Kamo River's edge—a liminal space at which water adjoins solid ground—he and Koremitsu must both try hard to keep Genji from drowning in a grief whose allusions to the "Song of Everlasting

Sorrow" augment the gravity of Yūgao's death.[54] By the same token, Genji's tumble to the roadside and his incapacity to fathom the route back to his estate mark an off-axis bearing that had in fact been brewing since his arrival at the haunted house. The emasculating haunting and death of Yūgao spur the shift.

Nonetheless, we should dwell on the question Genji poses as he recalls the material exchange of robes he made with Yūgao: "Whatever could our bond [*chigiri*] have been?" This question opens space to acknowledge more fully Koremitsu's function as a binding agent. More than any traded fabrics, Koremitsu serves as the force linking Genji and Yūgao. For even beyond the physical labors he performs to advance Genji's romantic escapades, Koremitsu also suppresses his own sexual desires for Yūgao in order to please Genji: "Koremitsu went to find them, bringing refreshments. Amused, he surmised that her looks must indeed be enough to warrant their trudging all this way. Even so, he felt miffed: *I was well on my way to winning her affections myself, but I let him have her. How big-hearted of me!*"[55]

This "big-hearted" (*kokoro hirosa yo*) concession of desire rewards momentary heterosexual abstinence with an enduring homosocial bond. Even if Genji can't recognize the answer right next to him—"He mulled this over throughout his journey. Once again, Koremitsu was at his side to help, because Genji was shaky in his saddle, seeming unfit to ride"—the narrator's mention of Koremitsu's artful generosity demonstrates the extent to which Genji's link to his female lover relies on Koremitsu's intimate assistance. This homosocial help happens adjacent to the scene of heterosexual coupling. As a chapter, then, "Yūgao" suggests that such a coupling cannot occur without the homosocial male intimacy that undergirds it. Without the concerted, if occasionally "vexing" (*mezamashiu omohiworu*), affective labor Koremitsu puts forth to keep that coupling on track, Genji's tryst would never have stood a chance.

Genji's bid to sort out the nature of his heterosexual tie to Yūgao and stabilize himself both vertically (on the horse, relative to his walking servant) and laterally (from the cremation site, relative to his Nijō residence) also depends on Koremitsu's redemptive realignments. To call these efforts "straightening" might seem to undermine the homosocial rapport Koremitsu upholds. However, we observe that it is precisely the scenario of heterosexual courtship that allows and even demands that male-male rapport's flourishing. Having sought dalliance in fairy-tale ruins, Genji now finds himself bereft: nauseated, fallen from his mount, slumped between the river and the road. His agonized admission to Koremitsu rings with a queer resonance: "I truly feel like there's simply no way I can make it back home" (*sara ni, e yukitsukumajiki kokochi namu suru*). "Home," Genji's Nijō manor, rings here as a preserve of courtier privilege, of the oblivious and untested (and thus undamaged) masculine self-image with which he initially ventured from home into the dark. "Home" centers the site of masculine dominion. It is a place where swords need not be drawn (or dropped), where a man needn't raise his voice to get things done, where torchlight is always plentiful, and where nothing moves external to the master of the house's specifications. At these queer junctures, however, the veil of aristocratic mastery falls to reveal the ample extent of servants' actual control. Perhaps most importantly, this home space does not allow Genji to get lost. It sits just south of the imperial palace on the city's grid, with its wings, gardens, and gates intact. This is why, later in the narrative, Genji "sought refuge at Nijō," because "every room at Nijō was spic-and-span, and the whole staff, men and women alike, awaited his arrival."[56] Genji can thus feel unsullied and even worshipped in his capacity as Nijō mansion's lord.

Tellingly, that masculinity does not travel well. It crumples easily once an apparition splinters his fantasy of masculine stability. In this regard, the spirit queers with the questions it poses and the relationships it reshapes. It also brings men together, slotting them into environments wherein one must rescue the other like he might a storied princess. Without this mediating phantom, Genji and Koremitsu's standard master/servant binary avoids revision. But once the phantom haunts the premises, depriving "Shining" Genji of his light and wits and sword, Koremitsu's relative stature towers as Genji sobs behind a screen.

We might read the spirit's revenge as poetic justice. It gives Genji what he wants—close contact with Yūgao—but amplifies it to a lethal degree. By murdering Yūgao, the spirit flings Rokujō's rival's ragdoll body into Genji's trembling arms. He can touch her to his heart's content now, yet the clammy cadaver, which had become "loathsome to touch," grants no pleasure. Simultaneously, the spirit's assault on Genji's bedchamber hurls him into Koremitsu's arms. Spirit possession thus transposes two ill-fated heterosexual relationships—Genji's liaisons with Yūgao and with Rokujō—into a queer register by making them the basis for dislocation and alienated sensation. Crucially, this visceral disorientation manifests queerness, but the men's increased intimacy with each other signifies only a notable outcome of this queer upheaval, not its cause. Even as the ramshackle setting recalls stereotypical *monogatari* motifs, the spirit upends these genre conventions to queer the gendered schema according to which feminine and masculine styles of experiencing space, time, and feeling cohere.

SECRECY, SERVITUDE, AND SACRIFICE

On this queer note, we observe finally that Genji's pronounced physicality in dealing with women's bodies in this chapter implies compensatory grabs at laying hands on the feminine phantom that unmans him: he "dragg[ed] Ukon over"; "went back in and felt his way to Yūgao"; "pull[ed] Ukon upright"; and "shook her, but she just swayed, limp." These gestures all mark Genji's desperate attempts to rein in a runaway apparition. He fumbles to reinstate his unquestioned rights to touch and know. Genji takes these prerogatives for granted—most visibly in the realm of sexual relations.

This expectation carries epistemological repercussions, too. For indeed, what appears to plague Genji's subjectivity most is not just the cadaver's material presence but also the fact of death's capacity to penetrate and disorganize the proprioceptive and sensual faculties. Blind ("the lamp had gone out," *ho mo kie ni keri*) and mute ("he was speechless," *ihamukatanashi*), Genji must rely on touch and hearing to locate himself amid the chaos.[57] And yet he hears and feels far too much for comfort. The pendulum swings between sensory overload and deprivation, "the whirlwind events having left him in an irksome stupor" (*ito awatatashiki ni, akiretaru kokochi shitamahu*). If the confusion Genji suffers is any indication, spirit possession undercuts heterosexual masculine fantasies of supremacy by exploiting the porosity of spatial boundaries. What began with Genji nuzzling his lady in a cozy, shuttered carriage ends with him exposed in a broken pile beside a river as that lover's body burns to ash in secret.

What was inside the preserve of polygamous heterosexual courtship has been snatched into uncharted queer territory. In being cast outdoors, past the most familiar bounds he knows, Genji careens toward Koremitsu: "Now that Koremitsu was here, he sighed with relief, and able to reckon with his sorrow he couldn't stop sobbing for a good while." The comfort Genji feels stems not just from physical closeness but also from Koremitsu's capacity to mitigate the public's knowledge of the fiasco. Koremitsu hence serves as a countering force to the spirit's queering menace. It works the crannies to pry wounds open and expose Genji to death and ridicule, but "seeing Genji in such disastrous shape made Koremitsu willing to go on and sacrifice his own life for [his lord]."[58]

Beyond coming to Genji's aid, lending him a horse, and even moving Yūgao's dead body, Koremitsu also reassures Genji by promising that he is "on the case" and that he has "no intention of leaking word of this to anyone."[59] Koremitsu even goes further, explaining, to Genji's relief, that he "altered things and told everyone, even those monks, a made-up story."[60] Koremitsu assumes a mediating role in dissimulating the truth of Genji's failures to facilitate his transition out of the emasculating mansion and back into the public eye with his name and manhood ostensibly unscathed.

This labor counteracts the queerness recounted throughout "Yūgao." Broadly speaking, it aims to neutralize the visceral contingency protagonists repeatedly confront. More specifically, Koremitsu's intimate assistance veils Genji's susceptibility to violence, allowing the Shining Prince's manly reputation as "the great lover" to persist uncompromised. Koremitsu interposes himself between Genji and "those lowlife children tossing gossip" to protect his comrade and keep him gratefully close. In this manner, Koremitsu's mediation strategically distances a woman's death to enhance his homosocial proximity to Genji. Koremitsu's labors repair Genji's ego and redress his devastating shame. His serviceable servant's body displaces the social and physical weight of Yūgao's death from Genji shoulders, becoming an invaluable vehicle through which to reintegrate the subjectivity of his lord. Through lending his body and skills of deception to Genji throughout the Yūgao adventure, Koremitsu helps the weak-willed Genji man up to rehearse an authoritative straightness.

Genji's feeling of security derives in no small part from Koremitsu's inferior status, which dampens the sense of risk Genji feels confessing his inadequacy to this man who steers his carriage. That the social distance allows for such a degree of emotional closeness reflects status and gendered boundaries whose very rigidity opens a space for anguished nobles like Genji to face their subordinates candidly, fearless of betrayal or derision. The very precariousness of the servant's position within the structure of Heian society—the looming threat of bare life on which that political schema insists—nullifies any danger attending the noble's collapse before a subordinate's eyes. The vassal's subjection is so entrenched that such intimate exposures bear no evident risk for the superior who deigns to unravel. Consequently, structures of servitude can ensure a homosocial proximity habitually oriented toward redressing or suppressing the master's devastating encounters with loss.

CONCLUSION: QUEER LINES
AND THE CONTINGENCIES OF BUILT-SPACE

For Katō Matsuji, "Koremitsu is an important character who bolsters Genji's charisma."[61] True enough, but this bolstering is itself scaffolded by a rundown residence. Ultimately, what Koremitsu's relationship with Genji demonstrates is how the breaching of architectural boundaries augments potentials for intimate relations to be remediated along queer lines. Although this queerness accompanies the homosocial intimacy between Genji and Koremitsu, it nevertheless exceeds that category—much like the roaming spirit that engulfs the desolate residence to rupture Genji's subjectivity. Here, I invoke the figure of queer lines to recall Sara Ahmed's notion of the "off-line" quality of queerness and its attendant disorientations.[62] To be sure, "Yūgao" foregrounds "the intellectual experience of disorder" of, say, Genji trying to comprehend his fate in pursuing the chapter's female protagonist. But it moreover chronicles the "vital experience of giddiness and nausea" that imprints Genji's interactions as he is forced to inhabit a debilitating "awareness of [his] contingency"—in overlapping spatial, gendered, and affective registers.[63]

The spirit's queering reworks patterns of social station and physical orientation. This queering involves role reversals as new levels of affectionate dependency crystallize between Genji and Koremitsu. It also shapes the built environment: in their dilapidation and distressing darkness, the very structures ostensibly designed to securely compartmentalize space invite deterritorializing presences that dismantle standard vectors of heterosexual romance. We're left with a transfigured terrain where visual mastery of spatial organization splinters and the disordered sensorium attests to queer energies circulating within even the most mundane settings.

The following chapter revisits some of these motifs as a new woman enters the picture and attracts the attention of Genji and his rival, Tō no Chūjō. Her entrance moves our discussion of male homosocial intimacy toward examining the function of queer embodiments within broader female networks of affective attachment that underpin Heian courtship.

Going through the Motions

Half-Hearted Courtship and the Topology
of Queer Shame

How does death queer the amorous pursuits sought in its aftermath, and how should we understand the outpouring of hope and disenchantment that ensues? After he fails to save Yūgao, Genji tries to move on, chasing new women in part to repress the humiliation he suffered in the haunted house. This leads him to a similarly remote but less foreboding residence to which he steals in hopes of bedding a mysterious princess named Suetsumuhana. As it turns out, however, Genji is not alone in his pursuit; Tō no Chūjō trails him to the woman's neglected residence. Miffed that Genji would disguise himself to go gallivanting without him, Tō no Chūjō spies his frenemy's flirtations from gaps in the woman's fraying hedges before confronting him petulantly at the manor's periphery. This chapter examines sites at which such encounters occur to understand better how queer gestures traverse the borders of built-space, thus resituating the previous chapter's discussion of masculinity's shifting landscape.

Here, especially, the narrative makes a farce of Heian romantic ideals and protocol in a manner that lends itself to queer reading. Genji and Tō no Chūjō enter a triangular relationship with Suetsumuhana in which they pursue the same inaccessible woman to intensify their ties to one another. This situation presents a classic example of the mimetic desire and competition Eve Sedgwick theorizes in *Between Men*, where men's battle in heterosexual courtship builds homosocial intimacy between them. Hence the reclusive Suetsumuhana acts as a conduit that augments Genji and Tō no Chūjō's connection. For Doris Bargen, "Courtship here is a contest between the two men that seems to bind them to each other rather than to the woman, thus leaving the kinship ties between the brothers-in-law unchanged."[1] Yet simultaneously, Suetsumuhana's outmoded wardrobe, dilapidated residence, and reluctance to devote herself to courtship rituals mark her as a queer figure who fails to snap into the Heian marriage machine. Therefore, I argue that Suetsumu-hana's very bearing and dwelling call Heian ideals into question.

Cast as hopeless when it comes to courtship, Suetsumuhana triggers shame and frustration for those connected to her, who bemoan her abstention from the system governing their aspirations. Whereas feminist readings of Genji might posit Suetsumuhana as an agentive refuser of courtship, I instead highlight her atypical disinterest in sex—a queer disposition threatening enough that it needs to be discredited by shaming her. In considering Suetsumuhana, I recuperate her queerness as a generatively unsettling mode of inhabiting a world hostile to the detachment she embodies. Less a willful stance than a hapless posture, Suetsumuhana's bearing figures a queer approach to residing otherwise within an unforgiving Heian world.

REVISING HOMOSOCIALITY IN THE TRANSITION FROM "YŪGAO" TO "SUETSUMUHANA"

The previous chapter showed both how devastating Yūgao's death was for Genji and how that devastation grounded a thriving intimacy with his servant, Koremitsu. Koremitsu still has his role to play beyond the "Yūgao" chapter. However, in "Suetsumuhana," the temperamental rapport between Genji and his brother-in-law, main friend, and rival, Tō no Chūjō, becomes the male homosocial relationship stressed most by the narrator, alongside the female homosocial rapport between Suetsumuhana and her breast-sibling (menotogo), Taifu. Although we got hints of Koremitsu's begrudging willingness to back off and let Genji court Yūgao, we also understand how the clear status difference between master and servant framed—and likely necessitated—such romantic unselfishness. But with Tō no Chūjō, things are different because of his nearly identical rank in relation to Genji, not to mention their comparable talents: "Accompanying Genji continuously in his comings and goings, Tō no Chūjō joined him day and night for both study and music, his pace nearly neck and neck against Genji's, and tagged along whatever the place, until before he knew it he could no longer maintain his inhibition, unable to conceal from him whatever heartfelt thoughts he had, and became inseparably fond of him."[2]

Doris Bargen notes that by secretly appropriating Yūgao's daughter with Tō no Chūjō, "Genji tries to repress the multifaceted relationship to Tō no Chūjō by minimizing his proximity in kinship terms."[3] However, this attempted repression can produce queer effects. Erotic objects can fluctuate within courtship's homosocial mediations to spark other forms of intimacy that might minimize the men's kinship in theory while drawing them closer in practice. Paul Schalow asserts, "If there is one great friendship in the Genji monogatari," this is it: "The exposition of their friendship has a psychological complexity that far surpasses anything seen before in the literature [of the Heian period]."[4] This "complexity" involves flirtations and fickle violences that recall Genji's machinations with women. The men's "great friendship" is also a relationship in which seductive ploys and emotional games abound, as when Genji shares his erotic correspondence. As Schalow notes,

> The text informs us that these are the least significant of Genji's love letters; the important ones Genji has put safely away. The revelation suggests that Tō no Chūjō's discovery of the letters had not been the result of Genji's carelessness but was deliberately orchestrated by him to probe and explore his friend's love life. Genji then issues a challenge to Tō no Chūjō: if you show me your love letters, I'll show you mine. The scene is highly seductive, each man drawing the other into his world of desire. The scene also reveals a certain degree of calculation in the openness Genji allows himself with Tō no Chūjō.[5]

Indeed, Genji's rivalrous friendship with Tō no Chūjō stands as an archetypal male homosocial relationship in the narrative. The two are thick as thieves, and their affection for one another swerves between animated gabbing about the frustrations of courting women and pointed combat in that same arena—with plenty of calculated openness along the way. Vying with each other for the same woman, Suetsumuhana, Genji and Tō no Chūjō adhere to a triangular pattern outlined by Sedgwick in her revision of Rene Girard's schematization of desire, in which "the choice of the beloved is determined . . . by the beloved's already being the choice of the person who has been chosen as a rival."[6] Sedgwick criticizes the schema's emphasis on the symmetrical nature of the triangular relation and inattention to the "asymmetrical," "slippery" quality of "the apportionment of forms of power that are not obviously sexual."[7] I follow Sedgwick's impulse to stress the asymmetrical features of male homosociality—such as those seen previously between Genji and Koremitsu—while acknowledging the basic configuration Girard outlines. Ultimately, the interactions transpiring within and around Suetsumuhana's deteriorating estate demonstrate the extent to which that triangular frame winds up overrun by strains of mournful and erotic longing irreducible to rivalrous love.

REDRESSING EMASCULATION BY REVISITING THE RAMSHACKLE ESTATE

Genji tries to overcome the death of Yūgao by pursuing Suetsumuhana, a princess residing in a rustic, ill-frequented estate, who has been abandoned after her father's death. This new affair gives Genji the opportunity to prove himself more competent at courting than the Yūgao tragedy displayed. According to Aileen Gatten, "The princess is less easy to fit into a set role. She is a complex character, pitiable for her gaucheries but admirable for the staunchness with which she upholds paternal admonitions. Some have wondered if she serves any purpose at all. I suspect that 'Suetsumuhana' was intended as a comic interlude after the tragic events in an earlier chapter, 'Yūgao.'"[8] This seems possible, yet Suetsumuhana's residence—"a place so terribly tumbledown and forsaken"—recalls the site where Yūgao died and effectively lets Genji try his hand again.[9] This time, he needn't fear a spirit's attack.[10] Suetsumuhana's fusty manner and her displacement from the halls of power means she poses no threat in either courtship or the factional politics that fuel it.

Suetsumuhana's appealing harmlessness stems both from her middle-tier status and her crumbling estate. She is neither too pampered nor too lowly to merit disqualification from courtship; her rank suggests that a higher-ranking courtier like Genji might take liberties with her. Her status also hints at charms belonging to the category of "the girl unknown to the world, the surprisingly alluring one shut away alone in some rundown house overgrown with creepers" who is "boundlessly intriguing."[11] Suetsumuhana's estate, with its middle gate "deplorably warped and apt to collapse [*ito itau yugamiyorobohite*]," captures Genji's imagination: "This kind of place must be just what those folks meant when they spoke of 'an old gate overgrown with creepers.'"[12] Taking in this rickety vista, Genji "went on thinking things like, *This is exactly the kind of place where sorts of poignant episodes would occur in ancient tales, but upon thinking he might make overtures toward her he grew sheepish and eased his approach, worried she'd think him too brazen."*[13] As it was with Yūgao, Genji's imagination is stoked by fictional texts that suggest the lady of the house might prove ripe prey. That the once stately house has fallen into disrepair suggests a dip in status that might let Genji snag Suetsumuhana at a discount. Although he's not had difficulty securing more elite women, Genji is motivated in part by this one's social decline, the architectural evidence of which accents her exoticism. Weakened walls and fences arouse Genji's curiosity because they promise scopic and physical access to the sexual prize ensconced within.

The boundary's flimsiness arouses the suitor's desire to penetrate the architectural membrane, a prospect all the more inviting given the way Genji's masculine ego took a recent beating at the hands of a jilted apparition. The punctured boundary trope is a well-worn Heian literary device for framing erotic exchange, chiefly in the form of *kaimami*, in which men, predominantly, derive voyeuristic pleasure from gazing at women through gaps in built or natural borders like fences or hedges.[14] Yet we should not assume this schema to be absolute, for as Doris Bargen notes, "Confronted with the ever-present possibility of being spied upon, the Heian noblewoman was thoroughly socialized to be on constant alert. . . . While scanning the physical boundaries surrounding, concealing, and protecting her, the Heian noblewoman kept an eye on her own impeccable appearance."[15] Moreover, at a meta-textual level, Edith Sarra asks, "How do we account critically for the fact that the gaze of the hero in the *kaimami* scene frequently depends on the mediation of feminine narrators and female authors? Who is looking at whom in these scenes?"[16]

Sarra's question implies a critical vantage taken by the feminine narrator in *Genji* (if not by the author herself), whose narration plays up this visual paradigm's potential for failure. For indeed, although "Suetsumuhana's" plot setup aligns superficially with *kaimami*'s gendered template, the narrative bends that frame to reroute voyeurism's typical vector:

> Likely having promised himself at another engagement elsewhere, Genji very discreetly prepared to return home. He snuck off toward the main house, thinking, *Perhaps I'll hear some sound from her!* When he approached a concealed spot where only the splintered fragments of a see-through fence remained, Genji found another man who'd been standing there the whole time. *Who could he be? Some playboy smitten with her, I bet*, he thought, adhering to the shadows as he stood there hiding. It was Tō no Chūjō.
>
> This evening, they had both departed the palace together, but once they parted paths and Genji didn't head for His Excellency's or for Nijō, Tō no Chūjō thought it odd and wondered, *Where's he off to?* trailing him to figure things out, despite having his own place to be. Since he'd come on some offbeat horse and wore an unassuming hunting cloak, Genji couldn't make out who he was. Because Tō no Chūjō had seen Genji enter this altogether unfamiliar place, he was perplexed and stood there listening to the music, eagerly waiting for when Genji emerged, about to leave. Not wanting to be recognized himself, Genji was tiptoeing away when the man neared him without warning. "The misery of your ditching me was such that I thought I'd come serve at your side, sir."[17]

The narrative drops a hint about another (presumably heterosexual) rendezvous only to reveal Tō no Chūjō as the unanticipated partner in the tryst. Genji skulks about, trying to secure the closest vantage from which to spy on "the lady within."[18] That his spot has already been taken by Tō no Chūjō implies that Tō no Chūjō has clearly been observing Genji's movements up to this point, placing Genji within a nested structure of eroticized surveillance in which he is watched closely even as he clamors for a glimpse of his heterosexual target. Doris Bargen notes that "the threat of discovery makes Genji behave like a woman sensing an unwelcome *kaimami*."[19] By adding this layer to the normative "hedge-gap spying" motif, the narrative queers the pattern of male voyeurism to accommodate a portrait of homosocial interchange.

Here, we get a sense of the *kaimami* motif's utility in stimulating readerly interest. Just as Genji "was irritated, but also found it somewhat amusing once he saw who this figure was," so too might Heian readers have grinned at the trope's transposition.[20] Despite the normalization of *kaimami* as a driving component of Heian literary courtship, part of the convention's thrill comes from its illicit character: an element of danger attends the secret peeping. Hirota Osamu explains this risk in terms of *kaimami*'s gendered criminal thrust in *Genji*. He notes that *kaimami* constitutes a social and cultural offense by which the secrets of a woman's birth and genealogy will be divulged, making her all the more vulnerable to men.[21]

For *Genji*'s Heian readers—and female ones especially—part of their enjoyment may have stemmed from being able to look on and judge such infractions from a safe remove structurally akin to that of the fictional watcher, as Edith Sarra has suggested.[22] In a less sophisticated reading, Royall Tyler argues that scenes like this actually allowed Heian female audiences reading or hearing the tale to vicariously indulge their fantasies about Genji through an eroticized male gaze:

> In short, Murasaki Shikibu could not show her audience a dizzyingly sexy Genji without assuming in the ladies present (perhaps ones far above her in rank) feelings that they could not properly admit to having. . . . Still, it would have been a shame not to describe Genji meltingly at all; and that is no doubt why, when he looks good enough to eat, we see him through the eyes of a man. Although in real life men, too, might sometimes have felt that way about a man like Genji, in the tale these male watchers seem to be a device at once decorous and titillating to save the reader's dignity and leave her perfectly free to enjoy the view.[23]

Matters of preserving decorum aside, Tyler's lavish language here deserves a queer reading all its own given the way it curiously deflects the possibility of homoerotic desire while simultaneously acknowledging the socially disorganizing propensity of Genji's "dizzyingly sexy" figure. On that same page, Tyler explains, unconvincingly, that "if these were scenes of homoerotic desire, the theme would be followed up elsewhere in the tale; but it is not. Nothing develops the repeated motif of the male watcher stirred by the sight of an informally dressed, languishing or excited Genji."[24] Indeed, the very fact that the text deploys this erotic interplay between males as "a repeated motif" should coax us to theorize it seriously instead of dismissing its implications—however dizzying they may be.

The recourse here to a rhetoric of theme to foreclose a fuller consideration of homoerotic desire recalls H. Richard Okada's critique of Japanese literary translation-commentary exploiting theme for its monological, totalizing function, which "deprives a work of its specificity and difference."[25] In the above passage, Tyler's totalizing gesture emits a homophobic tenor evoking that of the modern scholarship outlined in chapter 1. In short, Tyler's interpretation might be profitably repurposed toward a reparative reading of homosocial desire that didn't necessarily subsume male homoeroticism beneath female voyeurism and instead treated these options as just two possibilities among many.

Genji's ideal vantage has been usurped by his main rival. That the spot at the tattered fence is "sheltered" (kakure no) implies a modicum of privacy for these men's encounter even though what drew them to the site was, ostensibly, unchecked scopic access to Suetsumuhana's body. A locus of gazing that asymmetrically disposed female bodies to male surveillance morphs here into a crevice capable of hosting an unexpected rendezvous between men. The fragmented fence becomes a porous pretext that queers prevailing romantic tropes through a destabilizing closeness.

The characters' arrangement in space deserves attention. Notice that hedge spying requires an optimal aperture (wide enough to peer through but small enough that the viewer can't be seen) and distance (neither too close nor too far). In this case, the shielded remove from the women's detection grants Genji and his male companion an interval in which to meet outside the strictures of court protocols. The lure of the diminished woman has brought the men together, allowing them to sample a fresh proximity to each other. The frayed periphery enables this rapport.[26] "Standing there the whole time," Tō no Chūjō has been watching and, moreover, *waiting* for an interruption in the action. He stands within a span of time outside the official clock of court duty or the commonplace imperative to bag a lady of repute. The presence of "some playboy smitten with [Suetsumuhana]" obstructs the clear sight line Genji had expected.[27] By taking up this "sheltered spot," Tō no Chūjō interposes himself between Genji and Genji's original female object of desire. This unanticipated interference redirects Genji's curiosity: "Who could he be?"

Genji now watches the stranger who has been observing him, "adhering to the shadows as he stood there hiding."[28] The perforated fence does not merely allow "some playboy" (*sukimono*) to be "smitten by her" (*kokoro kaketaru*), it also allows Tō no Chūjō to track Genji's movements undetected. By the same token, Genji's heterosexual desire to peer more deeply into the ladies' den leads him to the periphery, whose very location and permeable nature let lust trickle more malleably toward homoerotic territory.

The pretext of staring at the lady of the house from a proximate remove lets the men enjoy even greater proximity to one another as they each expose the other's secret. Both men are disguised. Tō no Chūjō had "come on some offbeat horse and wore an unassuming hunting cloak," so "Genji couldn't make out who he was."[29] This misrecognition highlights masquerade's potential to spur encounters that drift past a heterosexual binary. Whatever errand the two men initially set out on drifts off course to mimic cruising, with Tō no Chūjō "trailing Genji to figure things out, despite having his own place to be."[30] This desire to know more of Genji's behavior beyond the confines of the palace gates leads Tō no Chūjō to change into less restrictive robes and abandon his plans so he might pursue Genji instead. Tyler's translation, "rendezvous of his own" for *ware mo yukukata aredo*, dispels the original text's ambiguity, perhaps at the cost of unduly stressing the romantic, heterosexual character of the outing. The irony here is that in trying to uncover Genji's secret courtship, Tō no Chūjō effectively winds up courting Genji.

CRUISING THE FRINGES OF COURTSHIP

Curiosity has curved Tō no Chūjō's route to a heterosexual rendezvous. Aroused as much by Genji's change of outfit and surreptitious bearing as by his own chagrin at not being invited to come with, Tō no Chūjō "eagerly lies in wait" (*shitamatsu narikeri*) until the moment is ripe to confess his intentions.[31] His exchange with Genji evokes modern cruising tropes. Replace the phrase "his own place to be" (*ware mo yukukata*) with "discotheque," and the overlap gleams, both in the buildup before Tō no Chūjō reveals himself to Genji and in Tō no Chūjō's wish to accompany him (*onokuri-tsukaumatsurituru ha*).

For high-ranking courtiers like these, visiting static ladies emplaced behind tiresome layers of hedges and shutters and screens and servants and robes occasionally loses its appeal. Suetsumuhana seems remarkably mysterious, thus Genji's secret visit. But intrigue can assume various shapes. And indeed, Genji's desire leaves other shades of longing in its wake. To be sure, the entire complex of erotic relations hinges on how distance is managed between subjects and their objects of desire. When does close become too close? And how might one resolve to close the gap with what is desired? Temporal and spatial intervals—waiting, trailing, watching another man's silhouette lilt in the saddle, wondering what's beneath his unassuming cloak—defer the pleasure of consummating contact to amplify its intensity. These deferrals thicken the plot. They also decouple alignments underpinning Heian marriage politics' routines of social reproduction. This unfastening nudges prototypical Heian literary tropes, like the hedge-gap spying or the moon-viewing motif, out of joint.

On revealing himself, "near[ing] Genji without warning" (futo yorite), Tō no Chūjō composes the following poem:

> We were side by side when as friends we took our leave from Palace Mountain.
> But now, this sixteenth night's moon shuns showing me where he'll lie.[32]

Within the poem's opening unit (morotomo ni) is embedded tomo (friend/follower), which Gustav Heldt reminds us can mediate homosocial tensions through its dual valence.[33] "[Taking] our leave," we drift away from the palace's high center and toward a lower, more liminal and hidden spot, where the "sixteenth night's moon shuns showing where he'll lie" (iru kata misenu isayohi no tsuki). As Tō no Chūjō's poem highlights, the men's awkward run-in occurs on the sixteenth night—one night after the full moon.

Whereas the fifteenth night's moon carries celebratory associations of poetic beauty, along with a magnified visibility accompanying strong moonlight, the sixteenth's offers slightly less. Waning height and brightness suits the disenchantment coating this couple's secret rendezvous. Where calibrated sight lines predominantly secure female erotic objects for gazing males, this poem laments the withdrawal of visual access to reproach Genji's concealed retreat from Tō no Chūjō. Like the sixteenth's stepchild moon, Tō no Chūjō has been left to play second fiddle to some dusty maiden.

Still, this lesser moon accentuates other possibilities. Akin to the turn away from palace protocol, this moon's incrementally softer light allows for gentler exposures. Rather than throwing everything open to view, this weaker moon shelters the object of desire sought. Moreover, "where [Genji] will lie" can be read as a metaphor for Genji's secret destination, but its language also carries erotic undertones. The moon (tsuki) can also mean in verb form to "strike" or "penetrate." The term "lie" (iru), meanwhile, denotes insertion, or entrance into the moon's home amid the clouds. Overall, the poem recalls Heldt's claim that "it is precisely the ability of poetic images to arouse desire while deferring recognition of its object that would seem to endow them with aesthetic (and erotic) interest."[34]

Hence, we witness a revelatory instant when the desiring subject dispenses with the shadows to confess his longing to the spying partner. Notice that moment of emergence at which the erotic potential of a homosocial intimacy seeps through. With his curiosity piqued by Genji's suspicious behavior and sudden departure, Tō no Chūjō seeks out his friendly rival's light, hoping to bask in it away from prying eyes. To determine where the coy moon will set is to locate where Genji will spend the night, and Tō no Chūjō insists on intercepting him there.

Genji's ambivalence at being hunted this way derives from the men's mercurial rapport as well as from embarrassment at being discovered on a night his manly charms have failed to snare the manor's mistress. Although salty, Genji does not rebuff his pseudo-suitor:

> Genji was irritated, but also found it somewhat amusing once he saw who this figure was.
>
> "How unthinkable of someone to do this!" he fumed. . . .
>
> "What would you do if someone else were to shadow you like this?" Tō no Chūjō countered, upbraiding Genji.
>
> "Truth be told, when you're out here traipsing about like this, having a guard with you is really the more appropriate thing to do. I don't want you leaving me behind. Plus, untoward things could happen with you out prowling in disguise."[35]

His rival then chides Genji by referencing the "Yūgao" debacle, and Genji responds coquettishly with a poem: *"Bathing each village alike in its radiance one longs to gaze, but who would search Mount Irusa where the roving moon enters?"*[36] Much as the patch of tattered fence delimiting Suetsumuhana's residence alters the standard heterosexual vector of voyeurism, this coy banter at "a concealed spot" along that thinning boundary speaks to such a space's capacity to host erotic poetic exchange between men. To ask "who would search Mount Irusa, where the roving moon enters?" puts to Tō no Chūjō the chiding question of why he has followed Genji in this way. The rhetorical query registers Genji's slight dismay, even as the flirty poem manifests some of the boundary testing taking place across the "Suetsu-muhana" chapter's settings more broadly. Genji's reply plays at a "look but don't touch" provision. The line "bathing each village alike in its radiance, one longs to gaze" lets the admirer ogle Genji. The poem grants visual access only to curtail its implied physical consummation, protracting the tart give and take initiated by Tō no Chūjō's pouty reprimand.

The poem encapsulates a proximate remove through which these men express desire. It establishes a disproportionate ratio between sight and touch, sparking desire for the latter with a coy deferral. The poem preserves distance between "gazing" and "setting/entering," implying an effort by Genji to police the physical boundaries of Tō no Chūjō's affections. At the same time, the men's gender and status grant them parallel degrees of mobility that make such aims difficult to achieve. The linked amusement and annoyance Genji feels stems from this difficulty. The freedom of movement both men share opens each up to pursuit and capture by the other. Neither man wants to be lonely or denied; each man has the pluck and means to prevail on his rival.

BITTERSWEET ASYMMETRIES AND FANTASIES OF DOMINATION

Tō no Chūjō announces his displeasure under the pretext of concern for Genji's safety and reputation. In truth, Genji's secret jaunt unnerves Tō no Chūjō. If he can't discover where Genji is headed or where he spends the night, then how can he ensure that his affections trump the lure of other roaming eyes? Despite being slightly higher in rank than Genji, Tō no Chūjō recommends himself as an attendant whom Genji would do well to value and keep close.[37] Tō no Chūjō's complaint makes it seem as though he would be content with Koremitsu's job, gladly willing to shed his own precious rank for the chance to gad about as Genji's sidekick.

But "it made Genji feel bitter to be discovered like this," and the reproach he suffers here strains his alliance with Tō no Chūjō.[38] This is because unlike the faithfully indentured Koremitsu, Tō no Chūjō is not beneath Genji. Therefore, Genji must cover any resentment with aplomb befitting his station; there can be no tantrum like there was with Yūgao's death. Sore feelings nevertheless surface in a grievance-airing spat and then subside as the two men untangle wishes for affectionate proximity and romantic independence.

Fences typically figure as membranes that mediate and magnify scopic pleasure. Here, however, the tattered stretch of fence intimates a queer interval insofar as its porousness dilutes heterosexual desire. With this dilution comes Genji's "adhering to the shadows as he stood there hiding" (*kage ni tsukite tachikakure-tamaheba*) as he tries and fails to gain the upper hand.[39] The border's dissolution makes it tougher to discern which man holds sway, hence the erotic subtext percolating in the moonlight poems. The poetry puns on shifting placements: being together, turning our steps away, hiding, hunting, the unseen point at which the moon enters mountains. The homoerotic tenor of these movements issues from the frayed nook where the men reveal themselves. Genji and Tō no Chūjō emerge from the bushes with renewed mutual fondness:

> Now feeling warmhearted and thus unable to part ways to visit the previously promised destinations they each had, they rode together in a single carriage along a path beneath a moon appealingly shrouded by clouds, blowing in unison on their flutes until they reached His Excellency's residence.
> They had sent no herald to ride ahead of them, so they snuck in, changing from their disguises into proper dress cloaks in an unobserved corridor. Then, pretending innocence, as though they had just now arrived, they burst into piping away on their two flutes.[40]

While the flimsy fence allows a woman to come between them, it by the same token lets the men enjoy closer contact. The concealed spot along Suetsumuhana's tattered fence provides a stretch of time and space in which to amend the men's rapport. This gap, conventionally disposed toward men's spying on women, instead hosts a renewal of male homosocial bonds.

Having outed their identities and aired their gripes, Genji and Tō no Chūjō can redouble their affection. Neither opts to leave the other's side for the sake of chasing women's hems. Instead, "unable to part ways . . . they rode together in a single carriage" (*e yukiwakaretamahazu, hitotsu kuruma ni norite*).[41] This ride in the same carriage supplies welcome levity after the skulking and bickering. In part, mourning drives Genji into another man's carriage, once he finds that a fusty woman is less available than his male companion. Besides grieving Yūgao, Genji wants to abandon the burdens of propriety and precedent to enjoy a bit of spontaneous recreation with his male friend.

Yet Edith Sarra urges us to notice the intentionality this friend displays in dragging Genji back to Tō no Chūjō's natal home: the domesticated orbit of the Sanjō mansion, where the Minister of the Left, Tō no Chūjō's father and Genji's father-in-law, resides. The deliberate swerve back to this location reads as a corrective of Genji's neglect of Aoi, Tō no Chūjō's sister. Thus the men's travel prefigures the type of maneuvers seen in the twelfth-century *Taiki*, where courtiers' homoerotic enjoyment is deployed in service of homosocial alliances secured through their daughters' or sisters' marriages.[42]

The carriage grants privacy after the double exposure of loitering outside and having one's clandestine visit divulged. Read against radiance that "bathes each village alike" (*sato wakanu kage oba*, literally "without division"), the men's new spatially enclosed encounter "beneath a moon appealingly shrouded by clouds" (*tsuki okashiki hodo ni kumo kakuretaru michi no hodo*) implies a less dominative optic.[43] Discord wanes in these quarters. Whereas they prowled around before, the carriage's enclosure now lets them live out loud. They cut loose on flutes, the phallic rods proving the perfect instruments through which to express their bliss at reaching accord.[44]

Reentering the official confines of the Minister of the Left's Sanjō mansion compels the men to dial their revelry down momentarily, before the master of the manor and some female attendants join in a scene of domestic revelry. The ludic surges at the fence and carriage abate as hierarchies of rank and gender reassert themselves within the mansion's walls. Their behavior marks the space as more constrained than the moonlit copse or carriage. As they "steal in" (*shinobi irite*), unattended by any menials who would advertise their arrival, Genji and Tō no Chūjō must abandon their rustic outfits. They reassume the perfunctory guise of "innocence" (*tsurenau*) expected within this patriarch's purview. Yet more respectable need not mean authentic: the juxtaposition of these costume changes marks them as comparable masquerades.

The primacy of the court cloak wavers once we consider how the men play after dark. Moreover, the very vastness of the mansion furnishes crannies for circumvention like "an unobserved corridor" (*hitominu rau*).[45] As Kojima Shigekazu observes, *Genji* traffics in the trope of men needing to abase themselves for courtship, hiding and seeming shabby to secure intimacy with women.[46] But this convention implies that no such requirement exists for intimacy with men, thus Genji's blithe undressing with Tō no Chūjō after they return from Suetsumuhana's fence, with barely any barrier between them.

Insistent desire for homosocial intimacy links divergent spaces—the tattered fence, the carriage, and the deserted gallery—allowing different kinds of closeness. The eroded fence tempts Genji with a better peek at the lady of the house, but the tract also lets a male admirer observe his movements from a comfortable distance. The carriage hosts the final stage of the men's tiff. After all the furtive stalking, gazing, and abrasive repartee, the two relax their guard in the carriage, allowing reconciliation through unabashed frolic on their flutes. Finally, the deserted gallery lets Genji and Tō no Chūjō dress in front of one another, hurriedly switching outfits to hide the romp enjoyed outside the palace gates. Along the arc of departure from the palace and return home to Sanjō, Tō no Chūjō and Genji run the gamut of emotions: curiosity, suspicion, dismay at being left behind, voyeuristic pleasure, anger, amusement, annoyance, and joy.

The "Suetsumuhana" chapter, whose ostensible linchpin is its titular female protagonist, in fact treats the woman and her wasting house as way stations along a more intricate elaboration of male homosocial attachments. Through touchstones like the tattered fence, the narrative foregrounds queer potentialities that fluctuate alongside prevailing patterns of conveying desire. While more than incidental to the plot, Suetsumuhana's presence becomes a medium through which Genji and Tō no Chūjō negotiate their fraught affection for each other. This mediation occurs in imaginative, textual, and spatial registers. For example, the lady's restraint unveils the imaginative space in which thoughts of bliss spill into homoerotic musing:

> The young lords remembered those notes of the zither, their thoughts lingering pleasingly on how unusual that pitiable house had seemed. Tō no Chūjō even thought, *How marvelous it would be for that quite enchantingly lovely lady, who'd likely spent all that time uncourted as the months and years piled up, to fall for him at first sight; he'd be so desperately lovesick that everyone would no doubt make a massive fuss, and his own feelings would likely make him a sloppy specimen.* Halfway irritated, he worried about the conspicuous air Genji gave off like this: *Is there any chance that guy would ever pass up such a perfect prospect?*
>
> After that, it seemed each of them was sending letters Suetsumuhana's way. Neither of them saw a reply, which bewildered and miffed them. *She's really being too callous! Someone living in a place like that should certainly profess artfully what moves them by gauging their emotions from time to time, linking all the melancholy feelings they've known to the ephemeral impressions of flora or the sky.* Her manner was solemn

[*omoshitotemo*], but still, that she'd stayed buried in herself so much this way [*ito kau amari umoretaramu*] was obnoxious and unbecoming. Tō no Chūjō smoldered more on this score than Genji.[47]

Notice here that Tō no Chūjō's desperate lovesickness (*imijiu kokorokurushiku ha*) arguably matters less than the fact that "everyone would no doubt make a massive fuss" (*hito ni mo motesawagaru bakari ya*). The explosion of gossip carries the real force; heterosexual love counts little unless one's male rival musters reasons to resent it. What Tō no Chūjō actually relishes is the delicious thought of driving Genji mad.

Genji's caprice in taking lovers prompts Tō no Chūjō to imagine a joyful future with some woman he's never met. Rather than heterosexual courtship merely serving as a vehicle for homosocial intimacy, then, this fantasy shows how the prospect of a happy heterosexual future derives directly from men's desires to surpass one another. Getting the girl is not enough; Tō no Chūjō wants the world to know, so he can rub Genji's face in it. The fantasy's excess is telling. For indeed, it seems like the passion he dreams up subsists on Genji's recognition. Identification with Genji—as bosom friend, bitter rival, and even potential lover—suffuses Tō no Chūjō's consciousness such that the folly he provokes could easily refer to the risk of falling for Genji. Such a tremulous margin lets Tō no Chūjō meander into Genji's mind: "*Is there any chance* that guy *would ever pass up such a perfect prospect?*"[48]

Putting himself in Genji's shoes gives Tō no Chūjō the boost he needs to pursue his reckless love; without Genji in mind, he'd lack the will. And yet,

> Tō no Chūjō was quite irked thinking Suetsumuhana had snubbed him. Genji came to think it tiresome that he was facing such apathy in a situation for which he lacked any deep concern, nevertheless he figured that if that Tō no Chūjō was making overtures this way, she would likely yield to the person who kept wooing her by corresponding the most. The image of the smug face she'd no doubt make upon dismissing all notion of her original suitor proved keenly oppressive.[49]

This frustration prompts the anxious exchange of letters. Once again, Tō no Chūjō's desire to win Suetsumuhana stems from an investment in his comrade's response. His concern about her tendency to stay "buried in herself so much this way" (*ito kau amari umoretaramu ha*) extends from his own penchant for baring his soul to Genji, which he fears won't be mutual. The spatial metaphor of being "buried" or "shut up" refers both to the architectural impediments thwarting the men and to the lady's indifference. More than desiring entrance to her garden, however, Tō no Chūjō aspires to burrow into Genji's confidence. Love can be cruel, though, and Genji's own frustration at being rebuffed leads him to needle his colleague. Genji's nonchalance mimics the strange silence Tō no Chūjō received writing to Suetsumuhana. In this regard, both Genji and Suetsumuhana frustrate others by withholding. Their difference, though, hinges on Genji's willingness to mislead his friend to generate some tolerable response. Lacking answers from their primary target, who lies out of reach, the men turn to each other. Genji can't make the lady want him, so he savors his comrade's irritation instead.

This tactic implies a micropolitics of disclosure wherein emotional vulnerability becomes gendered and spatialized. Compelled to confide in Genji, Tō no Chūjō "inquires woefully" (*to urehureba*) about Genji's own luck on the same romantic score.[50] In sharing like this, Tō no Chūjō misrecognizes their status-based symmetry as assuring some inclination to confess insecurity reciprocally, much like he did in the "Rainy Night" conversations. But intimacy need not assure reciprocity, and those close to us can often scar us worst. In this case, Tō no Chūjō, still humming from an adventure where he and Genji rode merrily in a carriage "now feeling warmhearted" (*amaete*) and "blowing in unison on their flutes" (*fue fukiawasete*), mistakes Genji as a confidant and shares just enough to get hurt.[51] In lieu of soothing words, Genji feigns indifference, lying that he "lacked any deep concern" about being rebuffed by Suetsumuhana. This slight nettles Tō no Chūjō. Even so, the underhanded gesture still grants Genji some candid emotional contact—something withheld from him by the baffling lady in the house.

Genji exploits an artlessness in Tō no Chūjō that he helped bolster earlier that same night. However, things have changed since Yūgao's murder. Genji's sudden switch in demeanor with Tō no Chūjō—from open to closed—feigns toughness at his friend's expense. Tō no Chūjō's masochistic willingness to be vulnerable to Genji lets Genji regain the pride he yielded in the haunted house. His newest slight reads as a recuperative maneuver. Since Genji can't recover what manhood he lost the night the spirit attacked, he rehearses hurt homosocially to mend the damaged border of his self. His dig at Tō no Chūjō thus reads as a bit of compensatory violence designed to retrospectively disown the emasculating violation he felt cowering against Yūgao's cadaver.

Breathless from their spell of fluting, Tō no Chūjō doesn't realize the extent to which he's being played. He becomes a vehicle through which Genji repairs chinks in his own armor. As such, Genji's ploy at simulating distance speaks to how badly his fragile barricade was sundered. Where the murderous apparition proved elusive to the touch, Tō no Chūjō is well within reach. Ultimately, it is this proximity that lends credence to Genji's callous efforts at distancing his friend. In his quest to nurture a semblance of sovereignty, Genji milks homosocial intimacy, subtly dominating his companion to approximate a reparative remove.

THE VICISSITUDES OF MELANCHOLIC COURTSHIP

Competition with Tō no Chūjō lets Genji rebuild his heterosexual masculinity by enacting a hyperbolic style of sexual pursuit whose dramatic arc wends smoother than that of the Yūgao scenario. But that episode haunts Genji. Consequently, Genji yields to a cattiness toward Tō no Chūjō that kicks their relationship from carefree camaraderie back into frenemy mode. Homosocial competition between the two courtiers spurs redoubled efforts at heterosexual courtship—seasoned with misogyny. Genji's interest in the mysterious woman is already taxed by her inscrutable reserve. Peeved, he remarks at one point that "it seems she's neither thoughtful nor quick-witted" (*rauraujiu, kadomekitaru kokoro ha naki nameri*).[52] Given this fading fascination with Suetsumuhana, Genji's enthusiasm for her survives only insofar as Tō no Chūjō stokes it.

However, beside this oblique arousal sit other motivating factors: "Spring and summer passed while Genji suffered from his chronic malady and his heart stayed quite continually immersed in a grief hidden from the world" (*warawayamahi wadurahitamahi, hito shirenu monoomohi no magiremo, ongokoro no ito manaki yau nite, harunatsu suginu*).[53] Coupled with his impregnation of his stepmother, Fujitsubo, Genji's failure to prevent Yūgao's death gnaws at him as he mourns secretly. This concealed loss tangles ties in his life. In Genji's connections with Tō no Chūjō and Suetsumuhana, we glimpse traces left by his lover's sudden death:

> "Truly, how I would love to settle down here with someone heartrendingly lovely to fret over and adore; I could lose myself in that to distract myself from my forbidden heartache. What a waste that what one imagines for this dwelling veers from the demeanor of the lady living here, who has nothing to recommend her [*omohuyaunaru sumika ni ahanu onarisama ha, torubeki katanashi*]," Genji thought. "Is there anyone but me who'd esteem her more? How I crave someone with whom to engage in some run-of-the mill repartee [*nadarakanaru hodo ni ahishirahamu hito mogana*], even if our connection's not especially profound."[54]

How might mourning's tenor infuse our reading of queer space? We could unpack what it means for it to be "a waste that what one imagines for this dwelling veers from the demeanor of the lady living here, who has nothing to recommend her," especially as it relates to Genji's ongoing rivalry with Tō no Chūjō, and interrogate the nature of that marginally utopic "imagined place" (*omohu yau naru sumika*).[55] Suetsumuhana doesn't match the expected mental image, and Genji wants a smoother or "flatter" (i.e., less jaggedly challenging) interaction with her, as do her gentlewomen. Bemoaning Suetsumuhana's worthlessness, Genji helps us understand Tō no Chūjō's value in distracting Genji from lingering heartache. Here, Genji seems to briefly disregard Suetsumuhana to imagine the newly discovered Murasaki, whom he seized in the narrative's previous chapter to help distract him from the "forbidden heartache" (*arumajiki monoomohi*) he feels for Fujitsubo and to postpone mourning work for Yūgao.

Genji wishes not merely to have "someone heartrendingly lovely," but also to install them in this removed locale to keep them safely to himself. Although scholars traditionally assume Genji dotes on women here, the text's language leaves open other possibilities as the phrases "not especially profound" (*ito fukakarazu to mo*) and "craved someone with whom to engage smoothly in some run-of-the mill repartee" (*nadarakanaru hodo ni ahishirahamu hito mogana*) suggest that Tō no Chūjo or Koremitsu might even fit the bill—especially given Genji's shaky

standards.[56] The demonstrated range of Genji's heterosocial and homosocial relations to this point in the narrative sustains this ambiguity.

Genji's "immersion in a grief hidden from the world" over Yūgao's death presses
him to expand his ties to the living. Heterosexual conquest supplies one arena
in which to prove himself while mourning. Genji tries time and again to breach
Suetsumuhana's defenses and colonize her overgrown terrain. This new adventure's setting offers enough resemblance to the residence in "Yūgao" to let Genji
process an emasculating grief in his own time, grazing along this site's fringes. He
even admits, "Unlike how this would play out normally in conventional society,
I'm not after all that you-know-what; what I want to do is spend some time seated
on that ramshackle veranda of hers. I feel like she's outright incomprehensible
to me."[57] Genji doesn't understand Suetsumuhana mainly because he doesn't
care to. Still, her veranda might lend some time and space to surmount loss. The
creaky veranda reminds Genji of the ruinous site where he lost Yūgao, albeit without its lethal threat. Thus, every swipe he takes at Suetsumuhana distances the
galling memory of the night he fumbled his sword.

Tō no Chūjō is mobile and resilient enough to play the dependable surrogate.
Like the spool tossed out of sight and then retrieved by the melancholic child in
Freud's paradigmatic account of mourning, Tō no Chūjō serves as Genji's manipu-
lable implement. By leaving Tō no Chūjō behind, only to encounter him again;
chiding him as a prelude to sharing a melodious carriage ride with him; and coaxing confession only to pirouette and shut it down, Genji repeatedly casts and reels,
rehearsing mastery over loss with the rhythm of unkind deeds.

Deliberate oscillation of closeness and distance enables an impression of stability and dominion to grow. Hence Genji can increasingly forsake those close to him
without fear of the deprivation their withdrawal could create. This may be why
lust matters less than wasting time at the veranda. Occupying time this way, within
such a liminal space, unconsciously evokes the Yūgao debacle while allowing a
reprieve from grief.

Genji's drive to score distant women and bully comrades mimes a repetition
compulsion aimed at denying the disorienting immediacy of loss. Whatever
shape his intimate relations take, the long moments Genji spends along ragged
borders like Suetsumuhana's fence and veranda unseat the primacy of sex as
a motive. Beyond sexual relations per se, vital here is the capacity to linger at a
remove near enough to help him handle his hidden grief and rebuild his fractured
self-regard.

SUETSUMUHANA'S GROTESQUE DISPASSION

We've seen how this melancholic exercise plays out in relation to Tō no Chūjō, who
covets Genji's companionship and esteem. However, this intimate homosocial rapport contrasts sharply with Suetsumuhana's predilection:

Despite feeling thoroughly reluctant, since she hadn't the slightest notion how to do something like talk to a person like this, Suetsumuhana went along with Taifu's coaxing this way, figuring, *She probably has some means to work things out.*

An old person resembling a wet nurse had by this time drowsily entered the gentlewomen's quarters to lie down. There were also two or three young women who were hectically dolling themselves up, feeling much eagerness to witness Genji's looks, renowned throughout society. Having changed into suitable clothing and spruced up, Suetsumuhana herself went out to meet him, without a speck of such enthusiasm [*nani no kokorogesau mo nakute ohasu*].[58]

Notice the strong comparison between old and young women here. *Kokorogesau* denotes gestures designed to curry favor or attract attention, especially those intended to make oneself attractive to a suitor. While not as blasé as the sleepy old wet nurse, Suetsumuhana nonetheless lacks her younger compatriots' exuberance in primping for Genji's arrival.

Removed from the center of court life, Suetsumuhana avoids its bustle of politics, fashion, and romantic intrigue. Having lost her father and thus his clout, too, she seems to stagnate in her aging estate, oblivious to trends directing the tastes of those closer to the action. This ignorance dates her, tarnishing her appeal:

Over an absurdly faded layer of licensed pink she added a dress gown blackened past any trace of its original hue, and for the outermost layer, a highly lustrous, fragrant coat of ebony sable pelts. Although dignified regalia in olden times, for a lady who was still young, such an outfit struck one as all too glaring and dreadfully outrageous in how ill-suited it was [*nigenau odoroodoroshiki koto*]. Nonetheless, indeed, one could see from the look of her face how much colder she'd likely be without these pelts, and Genji regarded her with pity.[59]

Here, the plural use of the color black underscores the protagonist's drab eccentricity, with the senses of vision, smell, and touch all referenced through the ponderous ensemble. Moreover, her outfit implies a grotesque and even deathly animality through the sable skins adorning her body. Genji pities Suetsumuhana for her criminally oblivious fashion sense, and her cluelessness unnerves him: "Even as he wondered, *What on earth possessed me to discover what every bit of her looked like?* She made such an extraordinarily strange sight that he just couldn't help staring at her."[60] From Genji's perspective, the narrator tells us the following:

First, her seated height was unusually tall, making her look like she had an elongated back; *Just as I thought!* Genji's spirit was broken. Next up was the thing that appeared oh so acutely flawed: her nose. His eyes landed on it at once. It brought to mind that elephant the Bodhisattva Fugen rode. It was startlingly high and drawn out, the reddened tip drooping a bit to make it astoundingly abhorrent. Her complexion was white enough to shame snow, bluish even, and her forehead was unsurprisingly broad. While all the face below it seemed to extend for a disturbingly long way. She was gaunt, so acutely skinny as to seem skeletal, and one could even notice her achingly jutting shoulders through her robe.[61]

Suetsumuhana's body is distended as though she has been stretched across a wire-thin armature; she is translucent, but daubed with gaudy patches. Her droopy nose makes her bestial—if not extraterrestrial.[62] The "overgrown old house" permits such deformations with its slack borders and the cloistering it provides. Suetsumuhana's physicality assumes something of the engrossing blend of fragility and excess displayed by her estate.

If we align our assessment with Genji's perspective, then it is easy to focus on Suetsumuhana's repugnance and forget the lady's own satisfaction with her remoteness as well as her decided lack of enthusiasm for romantic rigmarole. Whatever desire male suitors feel toward her, Suetsumuhana's contented ignorance insulates her from the volatility of their whims. For Suetsumuhana to have "no speck of any such enthusiasm" (*nan no kokorogesau mo nakute*) toward the most earth-shatteringly handsome and talented man in the realm says everything. Her anomalous disinterest—which puzzles her women and Genji both—can be read as a kind of queer agnosticism that barely suits up for heterosexual courting.

In her physical and emotional distance from ideals of romance, Suetsumuhana sits askew of the heteronormative paradigm that captivates the people surrounding her: "'Please hurry out to him! Don't clam up: congeniality really counts!' they said, egging her on. Since she was of a mind not to refuse what people said, she spruced herself up more or less and scooched out. Genji faked as though he wasn't looking at her, gazing off outdoors, but he stole oddly numerous glances on the sly."[63] Her women long to have lives life enriched by some shining prince. Therefore, they haul her out from the house's inner recesses, proffering her as available for a suitor, even as that front earns "oddly numerous glances on the sly" (*shirime ha tadanarazu*) from Genji.

Yet unlike her enraptured gentlewomen, Suetsumuhana concerns her days with other, less fetching objects and objectives. As Genji visits the veranda, Suetsumuhana doesn't leap to his summons. Instead, she turns her back to him, reluctant to change her queer but comfy pace. That she tidies herself only "more or less" (*sasugani*, also "with reservations") marks her ambivalence in a bid to humor her ladies and take one for the team. And she doesn't stop there:

> "It would match my own sentiment much better if only you, the one lacking anyone to care for her, would forego your misgivings [*yurushiki onkeshiki nareba*] and grow fond of the man in the midst of courting you now. Your unyielding disposition is cold-hearted," Genji said, devising his exit excuse.
>
> *When the morning sun pierces ice hanging from eaves causing them to melt,*
> *why do these poor icicles hold out hope though frozen stiff?*
>
> Despite his poem, all she gave him was an "Mm," with a slight smile, and her wholly uncommunicative manner was so wretched that he up and left.[64]

Genji pleads with Suetsumuhana to admit him, but she freezes him out with her "unyielding disposition" (*yurushi naki onkeshiki*).[65] Unlike Utsusemi, she's not playing kittenish.[66] Not surprisingly, Genji perceives Suetsumuhana's unresponsive "Mm" (*mumu*) as an "abject failure" (*itohoshikereba*, also "wretched" or "pitiable"), denying him the entrance that he expects and—in his mind, at least—deserves.[67] The response is not unintelligible, just vexingly elliptical. Such a blasé attitude and cryptic refusal of Genji's alpha male antics confuses and disappoints him— and Suetsumuhana's ladies. Her comportment reads as queer here because of its orientation away from normative expectations for heterosexual romance. Like the warped proportions of her physical figure, her affective and rhetorical responses defy courtly common sense.

LAMENTING UNTIMELY TEMPERAMENT

This disinclination poses a problem that is as spatial as it is libidinal. For indeed, the frustration Genji, Tō no Chūjō, and Suetsumuhana's female intermediaries feel stems ultimately from her *reluctance to be moved*—physically or affectively. This reluctance simultaneously sparks and stifles suitors' desire. Moreover, such an indifferent posture—embodying its own brand of queer contentment—induces the go-between's sympathy for Genji: "Taifu mused, *I'd love to flaunt Genji to someone who would appreciate him, but alas, there's no fame to be found here. What a poor fellow!* But at least she could rest easy knowing that Suetsumuhana was conducting herself honorably and would likely not do anything reckless or too brazen for Genji to witness."[68]

"No fame/recognition to be found here" (*hae majiki watari wo*) reverberates in multiple registers. It speaks to the literal manner in which Suetsumuhana's dilapidated residence disallows infiltrations sought by men like Genji, along with prototypical romance. Suetsumuhana's asexual stance precludes the style of consummation that most hope will result in an heir. The ramshackle site hence symbolizes not just a bastion of waning customs but a vacant womb (*miya*) as well.

At another level, the "here" implies a place situated at some remove from expected vectors of felicitous heterosexual transmission and patrilineal succession. Remember that Suetsumuhana is the "last and best loved daughter born to his highness of Hitachi," who is "living in sad circumstances now that her father [is] gone."[69] This lack of any strong political paternal or maternal backing causes Suetsumuhana's "sad circumstances" (*kokorobosokute nokoriwitaru*). However, this lack also generates the spatiotemporal conditions under which a queer circumspection toward the motivating logic of compulsory heterosexual reproduction emerges.

Dowdy Suetsumuhana embodies a temporal lag and spatial displacement inhospitable to the fundamentalist bent of Heian marriage politics. "No fame to be found here" means there is no place for such a system of patriarchal inducements to settle now that the sponsoring father has left the building—physically, if not spiritually. With the symbolic figure's exit, Suetsumuhana's residence loses the guarantor of ascendancy suitors often seek. Yet this paternal loss also opens spaces that decenter. The Hitachi Prince's death disenfranchises his daughter, but it likewise displaces her from the cruel circuit of Heian courtship in which the unwed women of her retinue yearn to partake.

Unlike these restless ladies, Suetsumuhana is in no hurry to wed. This reluctance situates her beside a handful of female protagonists in *Genji* who refuse marriage.[70] Her lackadaisical disposition matches the regressiveness coating her clothes, customs, calligraphy, and capacity to respond to courtship "without a speck of such enthusiasm."[71] There are temporal repercussions to Suetsumuhana's disposition. Koike Seiji observes the deployment of three uncommon narrative devices in "Suetsumuhana," all of which, I would argue, characterize Suetsumuhana's queer relation to standard linear time. The first two are "redundant or duplicate time" (*chōfuku suru jikan*) and "flashback technique" (*kattobakku no gihō*).[72] These arise because her lack of commitment to participating in the prevailing temporal frame provokes protagonists to renarrate her predicament from alternate angles as they try to make her shape up. But she frustrates these attempts, stuttering time's passage. The third temporal device "Suetsumuhana" stresses is what Koike calls "blank time" (*kūhaku no jikan*).[73] This is represented most clearly in Suetsumuhana's comically blasé comportment toward Genji. Her "mms" and abject failure to reply drive Genji away. Suetsumuhana's lack of anticipation produces blank time, where the reader expects time to pass, but it doesn't, and narration of active events is scarce. Hence readers are placed in a position akin to that of her ladies-in-waiting. This untimely bearing syncopates courtship's narration and goads Suetsumuhana's gentlewomen to fill her empty hours with their anxious labor.

Fatherless, Suetsumuhana suffers (or enjoys?) a cushioned exile from the near-mandatory mores obeyed by ladies of her station. Whatever dispossession this brings registers as lamentable in the limited perspective of those so stuck within that matrix that they must view Suetsumuhana as pitiably alien, as "no footprint broke the vast, empty, and chillingly lonely expanse" of her grounds.[74] Genji explains that "this interminable distance your heart harbors toward me is so very wounding" (*tsukisenu ongokoro no hedate koso, warinakere*).[75] Suetsumuhana maintains emotional distance even on granting her suitor greater spatial access. Her discretion is an obsolete disposition that smacks of a lapsed style and era. Her propensity to reside so passively and passionlessly in such environs places Suetsumuhana outside the perimeter of their comprehension as anything but laughably pathetic.

Nevertheless, we would do well to understand her lapses as situating her beyond the manic presentism of heteronormative compulsions to be courted, wed, and impregnated (not necessarily in that order), and ideally to mother female children that would be serviceable to courtiers of Genji's trajectory. In being so irredeemably behind the times—inoculated against the flickers of anticipation felt by her attendants—Suetsumuhana unwittingly exempts herself from a lifestyle of jumping at callers and rushing to write replies designed to continually kindle the sexual interest or approval of men and women alike. As such, she is woefully heedless of courtship's conventions for correspondence:

> Prodded by the gaggle of voices around her, Suetsumuhana wrote out her poem on lavender paper from so many years past that age had drained its color to ash gray; her characters were predictably crisp and sturdy [*moji tsuyau*], following an archaic style, with the tops and tails of her columns evenly aligned [*kamishimo hitoshiku*]. It wasn't worth looking at, and Genji put it down. It was awful for him to wonder what she thought of him.[76]

Her glyphs' robustness reflects a bygone sensibility and a rectitude garnered from an enduring paternal influence. Similarly, the even alignment of her columns' heights means she eschews the variable placement of "strewn script" (*chirashigaki*), whose stylishly scattered lines convey a savvy she lacks. Here, the disquiet Genji feels (*omohiyaru mo yasukarazu*) could stem from his disgust for Suetsumuhana's dated calligraphic style with its unambiguous evenness and unnerving encapsulation of stubborn anachronism in handwritten form. Even as Genji deems her unfit, the indelible stoicism of her script makes him fretful of her ability to appraise him, too.

Those around her view Suetsumuhana as hopeless; she disabuses others of their aspirations. She garners such concern from her gentlewomen and is so demeaned by the narrator because she refuses to play the game to which everyone else has committed themselves. Yet the qualities that disgust Genji and mark her as hopeless—like the startling equipoise of her writing—suggest that the very rubric of appraisal according to which she is judged prizes harsh asymmetries. The even-handed lack of pretense Suetsumuhana's obsolete script exudes calls into question the crooked regime under which her legibility and value are appraised.

When we register the exasperation of Genji or these attending women, we encounter Suetsumuhana as a limit case for the coveted inequities of Heian courtship. For Genji, lightly refused on the balcony, Suetsumuhana's "indecision is tortuously harsh" (*tamadasuki kurushi*).[77] Her awkward silence proves so illegible and distressing to those around her that "a sprightly youngster named Jijū, a daughter of Suetsumuhana's wet nurse, felt so anxious and mortified [*ito kokoromotonau, katahara itashi*] that she drew close to Her Highness and answered."[78] In her fumbling nonchalance, Suetsumuhana lets other women remedy what they contend are her shortcomings. She lets young Jijū "draw close to her" (*sashi yorite*) to fill the void and rescue Genji's failing courtship. In doing so, she allows Jijū to sample slivers of the life the young woman yearns to taste, the same life Suetsumuhana turns her jutting back to.

For those anxious women encircling her, Suetsumuhana's backwardness takes a heavy toll. We see this when Genji's visit triggers an outpouring of shame and effort:

> Taifu felt so awful for Suetsumuhana that she feigned ignorance and fled to her own room. These young gentlewomen, as one might expect, given the wide renown of

his incomparable good looks, excused Genji's transgression and couldn't make some formidable protest bemoaning it, although it was quite unexpectedly sudden, and they worried that their mistress totally lacked the mindset needed for meeting men.

Suetsumuhana herself was wholly lost in a mortified daze, as though someone else, with nothing beyond her ashamed apprehension [*tada ware ni mo arazu, hadukashiku tsutsumashiki yori hoka no koto mata nakereba*]. Genji thus found this instance, unlike other moments, especially moving because she remained unversed in the world's ways and seemed to need someone to care for her. Even so, he found her clueless demeanor somehow quite pitiable. What about her could ever have captivated him?[79]

Genji's sudden entrance to the inner quarters shocks the women: "How awful of him! And he promised he wouldn't!"[80] Harsh phrasing in the original suggests that Genji's entrance wounds Suetsumuhana with a stunning shame; with his incursion, she contracts like a virus a strain of shame she didn't exhibit before, albeit one less intense than the jittery breed the women normally manifest. Yet Genji's brash encroachment seems to embarrass the women less than does their indelible association with Suetsumuhana. As Suetsumuhana's stock plummets, go-betweens like Taifu fear damage to their own reputations and spring to action like antibodies, lest the failings of their mistress ripple out to taint them, too.

The architectural contours of the women's quarters allow for the women's discomfiting identification with their mistress: their lack of physical distance from Suetsumuhana makes them susceptible to scathing embarrassment. For example, when Suetsumuhana ultimately sends Genji "an unforgivably sheenless and long outmoded light red [Chinese] dress cloak whose inner and outer colors were the same, making every inch of it strike one as utterly uninspiring, Taifu's face reddened [*omote akamite*] as she watched on."[81] Having been tasked with delivering the awful Chinese robe, Taifu must touch it, announce it, and present it, even as she aches to disown the horrid cloak: "I can't fathom how you could possibly view what's inside this without feeling pangs of awkwardness" (*kataharaitaku omohita-mahezaramu*).[82] That she is the servant means she is the one who must "[undo] its cloth wrapping" (*tsutsumi ni . . . oshiidetari*), opening the box to let her very pores be saturated by the shameful robe.[83]

Confidants like Jijū quell their mortification by answering in lieu of their fumbling lady: "Good heavens, [Genji] groaned to himself, what an awful poem! This must be the best she can do on her own—I suppose Jijū is the scholar who usually retouches her poems and guides her brush."[84] Suetsumuhana's spectacular incompetence lets female proxies take her enviable place as Genji's love interest. Her concealment behind shutters and folding screens lets her serve as the vehicle through which eager women enact romantic aspirations and express their lust.

This trope of gentlewomen interceding and questioning their lady's romantic competence or even sanity for not making herself more available to the high-ranking suitor appears elsewhere in *Genji*. For example, Ukifune's attendants worry that the young beauty is wasting her natural gifts by not capitalizing on the male attention being showered on her. Suffering reduced circumstances and removed from amorous intrigues, they seem to need another woman's romantic fate to latch onto and believe in. In their ostensibly compassionate concern, the nuns caring for Ukifune pressure her to answer her suitors. As Margaret Childs explains, they are "aghast at [her] refusal to reply"; they "argue that her rudeness reflects on them and resort to questioning her sanity to explain her silence."[85] Similarly, Suetsumuhana's women overidentify with her as participants invested in what Childs calls "coercive courtship."

The nature of this coercion, we should remember, entailed physical as well as psychological dimensions conditioned by the larger edifice of Heian patriarchal domination. As Childs notes, "Women of high birth, themselves badgered and bribed by the men pursuing their mistresses, often aided and abetted male suitors, most notoriously by secretly allowing them access to their mistress' bedrooms. They also echoed men's reproaches that it was cruel for a woman to reject a man."[86] The violence suffered by serving women at the hands of rapacious suitors (and those suitors' own anxious servants) metastasized into a mesh of microaggressions arrayed to sap their mistress' dissent. We should not interpret the way the serving women fall in line and "echo men's reproaches" as based in simple envy. Rather, we should acknowledge that the boundaries of self-interest can blur when your back's against the wall night in and night out. Operating within the Heian courtship apparatus, these women stand to gain both identificatory pleasure as intermediaries close to the romantic action and also some measure of relief from having momentarily sated the pack of suitors pawing at the shutters. Moreover, by selling out their mistress, the female attendants might moreover hope to earn some degree of socioeconomic reprieve from poverty for themselves.

As the residence's central occupant, who nonetheless maintains only a peripheral concern or wherewithal for the proper business of courtship's rituals, Suetsumuhana skirts social duty. Unwittingly, this clears room for other women to flirt on her behalf. Consequently, her obliviousness to the nuances of courtship greases the wheels of the Heian machine. Insofar as her uninterested ineptitude both stokes anxiety and makes way for more capable ladies to simulate her voice and take charge, Suetsumuhana's queer disposition obliquely fuels a regime of heterosexual relations she has neither the interest nor the skill to support.

That Genji finds Suetsumuhana's "comportment peculiar and somehow pathetic" attests to her insufferable queerness. She earns pity for not being as competently or energetically interested in men as her peers. Halfhearted at best, Suetsumuhana's dismal efforts at male-female courtship mark her as impenetrably queer in Genji's eyes: "He kept up a stream of pleasantries, bantering or serious, but nothing worked. In frustration before this evidence that she must be odd in some way [*samagahari*] or her feeling engaged elsewhere [*omohukata koto ni monoshitamahu hito ni ya*], he gently slid the panel open and entered."[87] Suetsumuhana's performance in courtship is so abysmal that Genji cannot help but understand her as being abnormal. Genji's narcissism opposes Suetsumuhana's composure, preventing him from recognizing her reluctance as legitimate.

Given the liability Suetsumuhana poses for her female attendants and the time Genji wastes in trying to court her, the question, "What about her could possibly have attracted him?" rings out. To venture an answer, we must look not just at Suetsumuhana's characterization but also at the way her failings, transpiring at behavioral and architectural levels, coax Genji closer to his bosom buddy, unlocking a space for attraction askew of routine courtship:

> Groaning, [Genji] took his leave late in the night. . . . He stole away very quietly indeed.
>
> He returned to Nijō and lay down to brood on and on over life's endless frustrations and to lament that anyone of this Princess's not inconsiderable standing should have so little to offer.
>
> These miseries were still whirling through his head when the Secretary Captain [Tō no Chūjō] arrived. "You are certainly sleeping late!" he said. "I am sure there must be a reason."
>
> Genji arose. "I was overindulging in the luxury of sleeping alone. You have come from the palace?"
>
> "Yes, I was there just now," his friend answered breathlessly. "Today is the day when the musicians and dancers are to be chosen for His Majesty's progress to the Suzaku Palace. I heard about it last night, and I am on my way now to inform His Excellency. I shall have to go straight back."
>
> "Well, then I shall go with you." Genji had them both served a morning meal, after which they got into the same carriage, though the other one followed it.
>
> "You still look rather sleepy," the Captain observed reprovingly, and he added with some rancor, "You have a good deal to hide."
>
> . . . Remembering with a pang of guilt that he owed [Suetsumuhana] at least a letter, he finally sent one that evening. What with the weather having turned wet and his not really being free to leave, he may well have wanted nothing to do with any "sweet shelter from the rain."
>
> At Her Highness's, Taifu felt very sorry indeed once the time to expect a letter had passed. She herself remained deeply ashamed.[88]

The "Suetsumuhana" chapter demonstrates the performative and often ludicrous character of Heian courtship. In their failure, Genji's and Tō no Chūjō's solicitations highlight a fallibility embedded in the larger Heian system within which courtship operates. In suspending these overtures, Suetsumuhana triggers a romantic disarray whose queerness stems more from the disruption of heterosexual romance than from any homoeroticism marking Genji's relationship with Tō no Chūjō.

Tō no Chūjō gains from his contrast with Suetsumuhana. Before, Genji was frustrated by his friend's nosy neediness. Now, unable to land the woman he wanted, Genji permits Tō no Chūjō's company again. As though magically granting Genji's wish, Tō no Chūjō rushes in right as his sulky friend "lay down to brood." Although the text makes no mention of intercourse, the sexual frustration Genji feels, his recumbent position, and Tō no Chūjō's panting, probing questions all sketch edges of its silhouette. After sharing their morning meal together, the men again share the same carriage, much as they did after bickering in the hedges, despite the plain availability of two vehicles. The empty carriage underscores the absence of the female lover originally sought, a reminder that neither man need ever fear the "luxury of sleeping alone."

That Tō no Chūjō has to go "straight back" implies undeviating haste; that he speaks to Genji "breathlessly" carries erotic implications even as Tō no Chūjō's exhaustion gives Genji something he might identify with as he broods. By his own admission, Genji wants no "shelter from the rain" because he would rather not have the chilly bed of Suetsumuhana's residence that goes with it. Genji's reluctance to send his awkward prey a letter stems from an ongoing frustration that Tō no Chūjō's welcome visit only galvanizes. His invitation to return to the palace seems preferable even despite the shade cast by the phrase "with some rancor" (to, togame idetsutsu), as Genji tries to hide his exploits from his stewing companion. Better to endure this intimate companion's barbs than another night stranded on some oddball's veranda. With Tō no Chūjō's breathless arrival in the middle of Genji's brooding defeat, Taifu's shameful worry that there is "no fame to be found here" (hae arumajiki watari wo) connotes homoerotic potential. Whatever heterosexual "something" might have blossomed between Suetsumuhana and Genji has been compromised. But Suetsumuhana has queered the playbook by baffling her suitors and leaving them lonely and exasperated. Consequently, the increased homoeroticism later in the chapter stems from the contingency her awkward actions forces them to confront. Thus Genji's interest in a rival with whom he has shared the bushes and a buoyant carriage signifies a bid for consolation. This homosocial bond outshines prospects with the dowdy misfit because its reliable eroticism reassures against her queerness.

HETEROSEXUAL PANIC AND SHAME'S SYSTEMIC FUNCTION

Rather than spotlight Suetsumuhana's failings, we might wonder why everyone becomes so mortified on her behalf. She becomes a locus for panic about the potential breakdown of optimal heterosexual romance. Her clueless celibacy undoes the natural order of things, even exposing its deficiency, like the "absurdly faded layer of licensed pink" (yurushiiro no warinau uhajiramitaru hitokasane) she wears.[89] For Suetsumuhana to engage her feelings elsewhere disappoints the protagonists (and narrator). Yet it also unlatches a space wherein those most captivated by heterosexual intrigue can redouble their investments in its social workings.

In response to this queer disengagement from heterosexual courtship, Genji and Suetsumuhana's gentlewomen venture to save her by prying her out of her

shell, bringing her to her senses, and making her over. The vicarious shame swirling around her adjoins Genji's suppression of shame, on the one hand, and the
investment in paradigmatic romance he shares with Suetsumuhana's anxious
ladies, on the other. However impracticable it proves, this farcical courtship
nonetheless remedies the violent humiliation Genji suffered in losing Yūgao. He
could compensate financially for his prior emasculation as potential patron of this
household, which would also hold incentives for its impoverished gentlewomen.

In discussing the mechanics of identification and group psychology, Freud
writes that features of the herd instinct include "the weakness of intellectual ability, the lack of emotional restraint, the incapacity for moderation and delay, the
inclination to exceed every limit in the expression of emotion and to work it off
completely in the form of action."[90] The gentlewomen's manic energy, outpouring of shame, and insistence on urgently rectifying Suetsumuhana's gaffes fit this
description. Freud goes on to explain that among the "primary" instincts "of self-
preservation, of nutrition, of sex, and of the herd . . . the last often comes into
opposition with the others."[91] Self-preservation, sex, and herd instinct actually go
together in this case, insofar as the Heian marriage system enforces an extensive
faith in officially recognized sexual reproduction with men of high rank as the
best bet for status and comfort, if not survival. Thus the shame Suetsumuhana's
compatriots feel and the guilt they force on her arises from a sense of duty to
their families, themselves, and to the system in which they have invested so much
of themselves, not to mention their dreams of a brighter future. Accordingly, from
their perspective, Suetsumuhana needs to get it together and pucker up.

We watch surrounding women grow envious of Suetsumuhana's (undeserved?)
capacity to garner Genji's interest. When we read that Suetsumuhana "was gaunt,
so acutely skinny as to seem skeletal" (*ito woshige ni sarabohite*), and that Genji
"could even notice her achingly jutting shoulders through her robe," it seems like
a literal symptom of her indigence, morbidity, and outworn sensibilities. However,
this corporeality also registers symptoms of the wounding system all these protagonists inhabit.[92] Like a nail that must be hammered flat, Suetsumuhana is goaded
back into the fold of normative courtship's hope-mongering. Shame disables the
majority's desire to self-examine so they can discipline the misfit instead.

Mixed with pity, Genji's experiences of losing his mother and Yūgao become
underlying factors in his projection of a pathological awkwardness onto
Suetsumuhana. The surrounding protagonists' and narrator's sprint to a paranoid reading of her disinterest as loathsome and unsound reflects deeper fears.
Specifically, their excitement and shame index the precarious nature of the sexual-
economic regime under which they subsist. Therefore, reluctance to participate
fully in that regime must be forcibly designated Suetsumuhana's own personal,
pathological shortcoming.

On this point, Judith Butler's notion of the law as "a prohibition that *generates* sexuality or, at least, compels its directionality" helps us understand the shape

and force of shame aimed at Suetsumuhana as issuing from a compulsion to normalize.[93] For Butler, "the 'performative' dimension of construction is precisely the forced reiteration of norms," and constraint represents "the very condition of performativity. . . . Constraint is not necessarily that which sets a limit to performativity; constraint is, rather, that which impels and sustains performativity."[94] This insight helps us understand courtship in *Genji* as being especially invested in an iterability and ritualized constraint. Suetsumuhana is ostracized so theatrically because her spatiotemporal and affective orientations threaten unspoken injunctions to maintain the directionality, speed, and temperature of Heian social intercourse. Her composure impugns that system's legitimacy. She manifests as grimy and misshapen to serve as the abject figure through which others ditch their misgivings and buttress their own frail faith in a cruel romantic regime. They fight to normalize her romantic interactions because the queer style of celibacy she practices undercuts their belief in the rumored virtues of Heian courtship.

Suetsumuhana's queerness activates a redoubling of investment in the most reductive narratives of romance available. So we shouldn't be surprised when the narrator self-consciously highlights the generic conventionality of the protagonist's ugliness: "It may seem mean-spirited to comment even on the various clothing she was wearing, but even in the ancient tales it appears they began by discussing the person's costume."[95] The ruthless depiction that accompanies this qualification trades on the pleasure accompanying the reading audience's disidentification with such a weirdo. The incident's narration helps us understand how desire circulates both within and around *Genji*. For instance, how should we interpret the desire of female Heian readers to witness Suetsumuhana's shaming unfold? And not just unfold, but surface through grotesque physicality that marks her as hopeless or unsympathetic?

Theorizing the relation between the rhetoric of embarrassment and the spatial structures within which Suetsumuhana's protagonists maneuver, we observe that Suetsumuhana's otherness strikes several characters as alienating and shame-inducing because it is too close for comfort. Its peculiarity infects their own prospects for social mobility. Here, we need to take into account the propensity of built-space to recruit from mid-ranking gentlewomen the hope and vicarious engrossment that fuels both sexual and readerly interest.

Suetsumuhana's house is a shameful place. Ragged fences and shabby gates notwithstanding, her residence *hosts* shame in all its vitalizing mayhem. For all their groaning, the protagonists need the shame Suetsumuhana anchors: their removal from the lustrous avenues of court life makes shame a welcome guest when no one else will visit. Blushing still counts as lowkey arousal. Wanting to help Suetsumuhana "succeed" in a pursuit she herself is ambivalent about helps inoculate oneself against the taint of her queer affect. It seems prudent to dispel doubts about the broader system by ridiculing her ineptitude in the realm of proper society. Suetsumuhana's incessant failures make room for intermediaries like Jijū and Taifu to take the stage intermittently and smooth out romantic relations their clueless mistress botches.

Drama builds as paradigmatic assumptions of heterosexual romance falter. Responding to Genji's incomparable appeal, these women spring into action as lubricating agents within the Heian matrimonial machine. These women's shame owes its intensity to the ideological dominance of Heian marriage politics as an institution beyond which little alternative can be imagined. Hence the primping and scooting to glimpse Genji's approach stems from an endemic inability to see past scented letters and would-be husbands. Granted, this activity might help the women's families economically, so we shouldn't malign them as insensible or self-serving. Nevertheless, consider how drastically a macro-level system induces micropolitical machinations.

Frantic group effort claws Suetsumuhana back into Heian patriarchy's grid. Indeed, her dingy clothes, tall back, bony shoulders, and stodgy writing all accent an angular disposition that warps accustomed styles of desiring and its outcomes. Unlike the flowing cursive executed by more stylish protagonists like Genji or Oborozukiyo, Suetsumuhana's staid, separated characters exhibit too much balance to entice Genji's eyes. That stiff regularity denotes a difficult seduction: despite her aberrance, her script implies that she sits resolutely, if vexingly, in line. Female surrogates must therefore enter the game to pinch-hit for their mistress, filling in the galling blanks left in her judicious, dispassionate columns.

The chapter elaborates a symbiotic relation between the dilapidated house, the disaffected queer mistress, and the regiment of anxious intermediaries primed to make this courtship system function at all costs. If the beams and lattice shutters, aisles and veranda railings supply the skeleton, then these serving women lend the marrow. Within this organistic institution, Suetsumuhana's queer withdrawal presses into action a teeming network of worry designed to metabolize shame for the benefit of Heian matrimony. They rally to reinscribe what Suetsumuhana lets crumble. Shame's fluctuation supplies a vital force of social cohesion among women of similar rank in the estate. At the same time, this microcosmic cohesion references a wider system of patriarchal organization dependent on the perpetuation of gendered class hierarchies in which women reproduce for the sake of gaining access to higher status and better lives.

ANTICIPATION, FASCINATION, AND CROOKED REDEMPTIONS

Genji's arrival glints with the promise of deliverance from suffocating boredom. The prospect of sex with Genji becomes the "thing" (*mono*) around which "stories are spoken" (*katari*). Hence *monogatari* names a paratactic discourse associated with sexual contact even as such talking only grazes the act. The primping gentlewomen's machinations attempt to yield a successful sexual, if not marital, union of Genji with Suetsumuhana, even as she herself occupies the sidelines, lukewarm.

Suetsumuhana's queerness—that erotic agnosticism marked by an absence of attraction toward the promise of heterosexual coupling—introduces a destabilizing risk into the Heian social system.[96] Indeed, this threat must be neutralized precisely because Suetsumuhana herself is so incorrigibly neutral. With her matted pelts, stiffly balanced script, and lack of even a "flicker of any such anticipation," Suetsumuhana threatens to infect the regime at large with the same corrosive neglect for prevailing social practices that pervades her lapsed estate.

The urgency displayed by residents of Suetsumuhana's house doing damage control derives from the dearth of visible alternatives to this patriarchal Heian framework. They fret so much because little else makes sense in so familiar and pleasurable a way. Ultimately, what this scenario underscores is the social utility of this woman's queerness, the valuable function it serves within a system focused most intently on reproducing itself. The giddy pomp of courtship highlights the need to reinforce the routines shaken by Suetsumuhana's inclination to comport herself otherwise. Her queer leaning thus becomes serviceable to this larger apparatus. To the extent that it spurs compensatory activities that pick up the slack, the system is able to incorporate Suetsumuhana's queer affect as a stimulus for maintaining homosocial bonds among mid-ranking women, on the one hand, and the institution of Heian marriage those bonds undergird, on the other.

To call the noncommittal Suetsumuhana's bearing a "refusal" ascribes it a deliberateness that doesn't fit. Her premodern Japanese example foregrounds limitations of queer theory steeped in a modern, Western, adamantly antinormative stance. Rajyashree Pandey's critique of modern conceptions of agency premised "on the assumption that behind every act there is the presence of an autonomous individual, who has the innate desire to strike out against the norms of her society," resonates here.[97] As she recommends, if we "were to let go of this anachronistic assumption, and were to decouple agency from liberal thought," that might "open up a space for imagining alternate readings of agency that do not presuppose the validity and universality of conceptions and norms based on modern notions of autonomy and freedom."[98] I read as queer the text's opening of such a space for imagining otherwise through Suetsumuhana.

Her posture entails a habit of hesitation befitting her medial position between the desires of Genji and those of her female retinue. While this puts her at odds with feminist or queer readings that prize erotic indulgence or denial as patent examples of agency and resistance, Suetsumuhana's half-hearted indeterminacy places her at a proximate remove from either gung-ho lust or wholehearted refusal. This interval poses a somewhat unfashionable question of celibacy, which Benjamin Kahan understands as "an organization of pleasure rather than a failure, renunciation, or even ascesis of pleasure."[99] Indeed, Kahan's discussion of celibacy's stepchild status within sex-positive ideals of feminist and queer activism and theory highlights blind spots in our capacity to recognize less active or less insistent dispositions. We might learn to discern and value figures who are stridently celibate or half-heartedly sexual.

Suetsumuhana flirts with such potential disregard. In contrast to behavior of female *Genji* protagonists like Onna San no Miya or Ukifune, whose hair-cutting flights to Buddhist monasticism or nonparticipation in written correspondence with suitors read more swiftly as oppositional, Suetsumuhana's attitude might be more accurately described as a lenient unwillingness to follow suit, and Suetsumuhana herself might be seen as someone whose illegible pleasures must be diagnosed as dysfunctional and promptly redressed. Although this ascription, to say nothing of the narrator's tone, paints Suetsumuhana pejoratively, a notion of dysfunction isn't entirely off mark.

For after all, the rhetoric of shame and the exasperated scurrying we hear tell of does in fact respond to a risk of societal malfunction raised by Suetsumuhana's dispassion. These affects and concerted actions surface to discipline or quarantine Suetsumuhana's queerness so that it doesn't impair operation of the larger apparatus to which Genji and the women bear allegiance. Hence the rally to smooth her edges, to make her more legible and more desirable within a network of courtly romance whose continual reinscription of generic ideals conditions intertextual and interpersonal affiliations alike. In this light, the narrator's self-conscious reference to such a scenario's fictionality—its "*monogatari*-ness"—accents links to a broader fictional lineage while Suetsumuhana's incapacity to assimilate underscores that genre's discontinuity. To keep her hidden and forge calligraphic couplets on her behalf is to disavow the simmering dysfunction stoking the Heian marriage machine.

An enigmatic figure, Suetsumuhana elicits paranoid fascination from both Genji and ladies of her own house. Flanked by these two contingents, Suetsumuhana becomes subject to their interlocked narcissisms. Their redemptive effort takes place as a disciplinary—if not persecutory—project to accelerate and straighten Suetsumuhana's slow, crooked ways. Suetsumuhana is perceived as epitomizing deficiency. Her ways are not timely enough, sensual enough, engrossing enough, fashionable enough, or serviceable enough to guarantee social reproduction in its most efficient guise. As such, the Heian system strains to draw her back into circulation as a properly functioning subject within its economy of enforcement—but fails to do so fully.

CONCLUSION: SUETSUMUHANA'S LAPSES
AND THE COMPULSION TO CURB QUEER TIME

Suetsumuhana's gentlewomen worry that she has no future. Her timeworn ways and lack of anticipation toward Genji's advances place her askew of a dominant vector of incessant forward movement. This entrenched trajectory proves merciless in its mandate for efficiency; it's embodied by the narrator's derision, Genji's sullen irritation, and the shame felt vicariously by Suetsumuhana's entourage. All the waiting Suetsumuhana performs—and, in her own retiring manner, *demands*—disturbs such a network of relations.

The arc of "Suetsumuhana" demonstrates how loss—of love or opportunity, actual or imagined—elicits intimacy between courtiers and women fearful of being continually or irrevocably dispossessed.[100] Suetsumuhana's loss of her father makes her both vulnerable and valuable as inklings of her own dispossession surface. Without paternal support, she lacks a considerable measure of protection, but she also controls an estate she might not were her father still alive. Moreover, as women's rights to property are curtailed over the course of the Heian period, courtiers encroach to inspect candidates for plunder. Therefore, Genji and Tō no Chūjō's rivalry for Suetsumuhana's affections cannot be divorced from her queer relationship to property and paternal inheritance.

Tō no Chūjō couldn't care less about her, ultimately; he's just courting her to keep Genji close and attentive. However, for Genji, barred from assuming full official privilege as an emperor's rightful heir, Suetsumuhana seems promising as a romantic conquest prone to grant him access to territory that might offset the maternal and material losses haunting him. Symbolically at least, the conquest of such an orphaned estate could help soothe his existential sense of dispossession.

But Suetsumuhana evades this conquest even as she fumbles through courtship's protocols. If, according to Judith Halberstam, a "queer way of life" is characterized in part by "alternative methods of alliance," then Suetsumuhana's queerness might extend from an unremarked on mode of familial attachment.[101] Namely, Suetsumuhana allies herself with the residual presence of her long-dead father: his written hand, his poetic diction, his moldering clothes. The awkward daughter is unwittingly yet indelibly steeped in paternal precedents that impede her capacity to court Genji successfully. Her attitude diverges from the "willfully eccentric modes of being" Halberstam advocates.[102] Suetsumuhana maintains an *unwillful*—indeed unconscious—yet formidable alliance to perished forms. This eccentric investment in obsolescence roots her belatedness, her much-bemoaned incompetence, and her negligible allegiance to the headlong rush of aristocratic romance.

We can understand Suetsumuhana's attachment to the past in nostalgic or melancholic terms. She wants to keep the material possessions and immaterial sensibilities bequeathed by her father. For a daughter like Suetsumuhana, the expectation is for her to find backing to replace that lost on her father's death—as soon as possible, preferably. Her unwillingness to hurry worries her women as her property rots and she threatens to die a spinster, dragging them with her. Ultimately, hostility so surrounds Suetsumuhana because her peculiar stance nudges those around her to question the naturalized sociality they love to take for granted. Her queer lag disrupts the widespread drive to outstrip extinction through rituals aimed at social reproduction. But property and pregnancy barely matter to such an outlier. And this is what spurs cravings to censure and reform her: the queer way her comportment questions how intimacy should transpire.

Genji's fictional portrayal of the affair with Suetsumuhana seems designed to earn laughs from Heian readers who knew all too well just how prone to malfunction and tampering the whole courtship enterprise was. For many of these heavy investors in the Heian court, Suetsumuhana's gaffes likely brought pleasure, since readers identified more agreeably with the scrambling gentlewomen or even Genji than the irredeemable basket case floundering in the dilapidated mansion. Her sheer abjection made it easy to disidentify through humor and scorn, much in the manner the chapter's protagonists themselves perform. And yet the recurrent trope of spatial porosity and the flood of infectious shame suggest that such humor, scorn, and schemes to solve or discipline Suetsumuhana's aberrance derive from an abiding unease about its capacity to transform the very nature of Heian sociality.

Despite the army mobilized to contain her energies, the dimensions of Suetsumuhana's personhood—like the distended proportions of her very body—momentarily evade delineation. Much paranoia is unleashed toward Suetsumuhana's grotesque obsolescence—akin to the "horror" of Merleau-Ponty's formulation. It is therefore not merely her failed courtship that marks Suetsumuhana as queer, in the sense that it demonstrates disinterest in ideals of heterosexual coupling. More significantly, it is her noncommittal posture toward the trajectory all her ladies and suitors covet. Her singular lack of even a "flicker of any such anticipation" denotes a queer commitment to the pleasure of pastimes that are as absorbing as they are unconcerned with the prospect of reproductive futurity. In her shabby belatedness, Suetsumuhana tarries along, incapable of appreciating the urgency—so often borne of fear and lust—that intermediaries like Taifu feel so keenly.

Suetsumuhana's clueless misalignment with the injunctions to court, conceive, and continually compete for public and private favor, proposes the possibility of other knowledges and other modes of being. The misogyny and homophobia unleashed at her behavior attest to how her mode of dwelling in the world roils deep fears not simply about sexuality but about the very process of yoking one's life to a logic in which hope doesn't dominate. *This* is the reparative sense in which we should comprehend and affirm Suetsumuhana as "hopeless."

We might say, then, that Suetsumuhana enacts queerness in being singularly half-hearted. Without being stubborn, she doesn't bend easily; nor does she fetishize divergence from the norm. There's no fearsome embrace of deviance here; she just happens to prefer the textures of outmoded, grimy pelts and of stiffer glyphs on thick, fusty paper. If we forgo the furor she inadvertently incites, we can recognize in her rapport with these unpopular inanimate objects a tendency that drifts away from the trendsetting fervor of her peers but without precluding their exuberance completely. She doesn't scream "anti" but rather reads as a figure quietly living a style of celibacy that is besieged.

To be sure, Suetsumuhana's eventual capitulation indicates how precarious this style and spatiotemporal interval can be. However, rather than interpret this in terms of failure or success, I'm inclined to read it as but another twist among a litany of reorientations that she browses without buying into. After all, to turn from passé objects of questionable worth toward courtship's promise is not necessarily to surrender one's soul. One can go through the motions without careening out of habit or desperation. While Genji and Tō no Chūjō struggle to make successful courting more efficient, Suetsumuhana's queer disposition outlines an alternate style of apprehending and inhabiting the world that bypasses such values for the sake of a life that others view as less optimal. But that life is for her, by the same token, *far more livable*.

In moving to the following chapter, which examines how Genji grapples with the dislocation and dispossession of exile, we should keep in mind the benefits of Suetsumuhana's queer orientation toward intimacy and loss.

4

Queer Affections in Exile

Textual Mediation and Exposure at Suma Shore

RESITUATING EXILE

Moving from "Suetsumuhana" to "Suma," the spatial and affective dimensions of queer intimacy gain new proportions. Exile emplaces Genji in a patently masculine space considerably farther away from the Capital's governing center than he was while at Yūgao's or Suetsumuhana's houses. While the asymmetry of homosocial power configurations—such as what we saw in the intense interactions between Suetsumuhana and her gentlewomen—persists, "Suma" shifts these dynamics by displacing such relations outside the circumscribed environment of the court.

Despite Oborozukiyo having been designated by the Kokiden faction as belonging to Emperor Suzaku, Genji is nonetheless caught cavorting with her—by her father, the powerful Minister of the Right, no less.[1] This treasonous affair results in Genji's exile, marked by disgrace, dispossession, and a disorienting dislocation from the locus of imperial authority. As Jonathan Stockdale notes, "Every narrative of exile imagines a certain constellation of power. . . . Yet the trope of exile was also harnessed by those more marginal, in narratives that sought to reimagine the hierarchies of inclusion and exclusion upon which Heian society rested."[2] I take up the "Suma" chapter as a textual venue in which these social hierarchies—and indeed the very concept of social relation itself—might be resituated and reimagined along queer lines.

Even for an aristocrat, exile can prove torturous, and as Charo D'Ectheverry notes, "That journey is far from linear, even at the level of exposition."[3] Against the sweeping oceanic backdrop of the landscape he enters, Genji must learn to orient himself differently than he did in the shadow-drenched residences we encountered him in before. He gains copious room to move but lacks physical access to the Capital's array of courtly women. This distance presses him to seek comfort among men as he tests methods of alleviating his despair. Forced to transfer possession of his belongings, Genji must establish a new home and learn to inhabit a space in which he lacks the authority he wielded back at his Nijō estate. Dispossessed and exposed to natural elements, Genji seeks refuge in practices of homosocial textual mediation as a way to mourn his loss of home and status. Deprivation and dislocation heighten his sensitivity to the new setting and to other men. Consequently, exile manifests a spatial and material dispossession that urges amplified affections that are less palpable in other settings.

According to Judith Butler and Athena Athanasiou, "Dispossession is a condition painfully imposed by the normative and normalizing violence that determines the terms of subjectivity, survival, and livability. . . . Dispossession involves the subject's relation to norms, its mode of becoming by means of assuming and resignifying injurious interpellations and impossible passions."[4] As punishment for sexual indiscretion, exile reads as a normalizing violence Genji suffers. However, to conduct a resignifying work as a mode of becoming aligns with Genji's creative textual practices and extemporized interactions as he tries to move past a designation as disgraceful. In this light we might ask, How does exile transform textuality, subjectivity, and sociality? How might we read these transformations as queer? And how might the resignifications performed in exile generate ways to imagine more livable alternatives?

Genji's banishment to Suma highlights the ways in which exile obliges alternative styles of mediation at textual and interpersonal levels.[5] I contend that these styles embody queer tendencies. These tendencies neighbor but are not delimited by male homosociality, and they are distinguished by visceral disorientation and receptivity. I analyze the portrayal of Genji's exile in "Suma" to argue three points. First, exile magnifies homosocial exposure and exchange. Second, exile compels practices of textual citation, production, and mediation that generate intimacies unachievable elsewhere. And third, exilic exposure intensifies affections that foster a queer critical reconsideration of dominant norms. I highlight exile's capacity to amplify queer tendencies, styles of attachment, and modes of becoming.

Haruo Shirane contends that Genji's exile makes him heroic: "Instead of portraying a defeated man plotting or preparing to return to power, Murasaki Shikibu presents a hero . . . who ultimately emerges, through a delicate weave of allusions and poetic language, as a victor even in defeat."[6] However, this emphasis on victory might presume embodiments and trajectories "Suma" in fact unravels, especially considering how broken Genji is by the experience. Rather than cast him as a hero, I prefer to theorize the Genji we encounter in "Suma" as a failed figure. This is to short-circuit certain anachronistic and culturalist assumptions about heroic masculinity unsuited to Heian fictional depictions. But it's also to cite a strain of queer theory invested in recuperating failure. Judith Halberstam writes that "under certain circumstances failing, losing, forgetting, unmaking, undoing, unbecoming, not knowing may in fact offer more creative, more cooperative, more surprising ways of being in the world" and allow "us to escape the punishing norms that discipline behavior and manage human development."[7] While Genji's exile is certainly a punishment, it might also be read as a space of escape where punishing norms don't reign. What would *not* succeeding at a heroic ideal of aristocratic manhood look like? What unanticipated possibilities for intimacy might emerge in the proximate remove from success? A queer reading of exile as a space of failed aristocratic masculinity helps us address these questions.

Terry Kawashima's analysis of how textual practices enact a gendered marginalization proves useful here. Rejecting the notions of "center" and "margin," Kawashima asserts that these static categories "do not exist as such. . . . Only the process, marginalization, exists. . . . In this paradigm, then, there is no single center surrounded by a single margin; instead, different and fleeting instances of marginalizer/marginalized relationships appear and reappear in a dynamic fashion."[8] I build on Kawashima's work to suggest that these "fleeting instances" of marginalization provide moments at which to perform queer readings. Although marginalization attempts to inscribe a putative center against a textually constructed periphery, the process cannot eradicate the contingency pervading such an aim. Therefore, Kawashima's arguments seem especially valuable for theorizing less rigid, more diffuse forms of relation where clear-cut desires to dominate are absent or insufficient for analyzing the multiple affects, social forces, and mediations of literal and metaphorical distance transpiring.

Jonathan Stockdale stresses the dual axis of distance/proximity upended by exile, arguing that "the particular sanction of exile thus represented a kind of double inversion, both of the distancing from the world and of the proximity to the emperor that the Heian court society normally strived to achieve."[9] This inversion evokes the figure of a proximate remove: a removal from the center that kindles unfixed potentials for proximity elsewhere. Newly imposed proximity to the periphery constitutes political punishment for heterosexual indiscretions. However, this banishment also spurs male homosocial intimacies in a singular fashion. Hence Genji's expulsion provides opportunities to reimagine one's habituated investments in hierarchy, protocols of social intercourse, and modes of interaction with the phenomenal world. In other words, exile catalyzes the narrative emergence of unaccustomed sensations, textual mediations, and relations ripe for queer reading.

The theme of exile resonates across premodern Chinese and Japanese literature, and "Suma" exploits this intertextual legacy to play up the trope's pathos and political undertones. However, we might also read such citational recourse as a bid for stability in historical and literary precedent, an effort that cannot fully resolve the destabilizing contingency faced in exile. Specifically, Genji supplements his invocation and evocation of famous exiles with a painted diary recording his personal affective experience—as tied to precedent but also singularly his own. Such a gesture highlights a desire and capacity to engage the nonhuman and elemental world through creative channels not totalized by courtly discourses of propriety, legitimacy, or community.

At a broader level, scholars such as Susan Mann and Gustav Heldt have discussed the theme of male fellowship in Chinese and Japanese culture, partly as a means of showing how homosocial practices sustain aristocratic privilege or male social dominance.[10] The theme of male aesthetic fellowship appears prominently in "Suma," but the experience of exile narrated there leads us away from those categories. As H. Richard Okada explains, "Far from being preoccupied with matters of aesthetic taste—'love'—or 'romance,' as the dominant *Genji* readings would have it, the narrative situates many of its most important scenes at intersections involving displacements produced by exile (or other forms of exclusion and transgression)."[11] And, as Jonathan Stockdale demonstrates, Heian prose fiction can register a "somewhat radical discontent" in casting "the world surrounding the Japanese court as a polluted place" or obliquely criticizing social realities such as "the Fujiwara use of exile to eliminate competing families and rival clan lines."[12] Similarly, Gustav Heldt's attention to "the essential ambiguity of Heian poetic expressions of desire" in court poetry helps us posit alternate readings of such expressions and alternative implications for forms of male homosociality occurring once Genji is displaced beyond the Heian capital.[13]

As my queer readings of exilic intimacy will demonstrate, "Suma" encourages us to reappraise political disgrace as productive for other modes of relation that courtly politics fail to encompass. This chapter examines two related arcs germane to my arguments about homosociality's place in literature: "The feminizing disgrace of exile intertwined with the masculinizing fraternity found once [one is] removed from court."[14] Although this removal magnifies Genji's homoerotic allure, I argue that such allure pales in comparison to the intensification of aesthetic production and embodied susceptibility to the natural environment he experiences. Transpiring outside the purview of courtship or competition, both of these experiences suggest alternate modes of dwelling in the phenomenal world that I interpret as queer. Hence my analysis considers the portrayal of a surge of homosocial desire in exile as significant not because it reveals some sexual secret but rather because it fuels the text's critical divestment from romantic and political ideals endorsed at court.

A PROTRACTED PASSAGE INTO EXILE

As the Suma chapter opens, the threat of exile hangs heavy, disorienting Genji:

> The world around him was so troublesome, filled with nothing save mounting enmity, that he determined that to just pay no heed and ride things out might only make them worse. As for that Suma, he had heard things like it had been someone's home in ages past and that now it was quite cutoff and lonely, with even a fisherman's hut making a rare sight, though it was no doubt still not his heart's desire to live jumbled up in some place bustling with people. That said, distancing himself from the Capital would surely make him restless for home. He ruminated in an unbecoming muddle.[15]

Suma represents an escape from hostility that also promises affiliation with another male exile, Ariwara no Yukihira, whose former presence there frames it as a resonant topos. The connection Genji might establish with this famous forebear is offset by disdain for the commoners he must encounter in leaving home. Even as Genji imagines redeeming ties to another aristocrat, exile confronts him with the risk of low-class contagion. These competing possibilities imply two types of sociality available to the exiled courtier: a singular empathy with a long-dead male peer, whose aura might anchor the newly dispossessed Genji; and proximity to the masses, whose very thought incites his "unbecoming muddle."

> Genji and Murasaki agonized that he could be away for years on end, as this was not some voyage whose span was fixed, and despite wanting their separation to end so they might meet again, it seemed that this fickle world had ultimately made this his last farewell. Hence there were times when he wondered, *What if the two of us secretly made off together?* But it would be too cruel of him to drag someone this tender to such a miserable coast, where she'd likely have no companions to join her save the waves and wind.[16]

By not taking his favorite wife into exile with him, Genji severs his fondest heterosexual connection and marks his exile as an exclusively male preserve.[17] As he departs Murasaki, the narrator comments that "the people who endured a hidden heartbreak despite his only having casually known them in his flittings here and there were many indeed."[18] This phrase delivers a swansong for Genji's romantic affairs with women, foreshadowing entrance into queerer environs. This aspect of Genji's self-imposed punishment fits the crime, which was his incestuous liaison with Fujitsubo. Being relegated to an exclusively male homosocial space thus symbolically counteracts the tumult his heterosexual transgression caused.

When Genji sets off, "He made no one aware of what hour he'd depart, setting out quite inconspicuously [*ito kasuka ni*] with merely seven or eight of the retainers who had grown closest to him."[19] "*Ito kasuka ni*" could refer to the unassuming way Genji departs, but it also means "shabbily," "feebly," or "in a lonely fashion," which all connote his shameful descent into powerlessness. The secrecy he practices helps avoid more public disgrace. Genji leaves his women while selecting a cohort of men to accompany and serve him, emphasizing the gendered nature of exile and the status hierarchy that persists despite his downfall. The secrecy continues when he "call[s] at His Excellency's under cover of darkness. His furtive entrance [*uchi yatsuretaru nite*] in a common basketwork carriage that looked like a woman's [*onnaguruma no yau nite*] was sad and might have been a dream."[20] Hidden and feminized, Genji's affection toward and reliance on male servants builds. This status and gender disguise anticipates the voyage to Suma's shore and reads like a closeting process.

Genji is "stripped . . . of rank and office" for his offense. Rather than be disgraced further by a forcible ousting by the Kokiden faction, Genji "resolved to remove [him]self from the world [*yo wo nogarenamu*] before [he] face[d] still greater dishonor [*kore yori ookinaru haji*]."²¹ Shame fuels Genji's desire to absent himself and becomes the affective force infusing Genji's growing bond to lower-status men. The romantic jaunts with higher-status women he enjoyed previously are now impossible, so through the trope of exile, lowlier men procure more space within the scope of Genji's affections.

This self-imposed exile deprives Genji of the prerogatives germane to his city existence, but it also creates distance between him and the factional enemies that fuel what the Emperor calls "the evil temper of the times."²² The Emperor cries about Genji's predicament even as his own "poor health . . . has obliged [him] to resign his office."²³ For his part, "Genji, too, could not carry himself with courage [*e kokoroduyoku motenashi tamahazu*]. Seeing his son the little lord toddling innocently back and forth, nestling close to this person and that [*korekare ni narekikoetamahu*], pained Genji's heart. . . . 'I am comforted knowing that the shortness of Aoi's life was a good thing, for her not to have seen such an inconceivable fate befall you,' said the Emperor."²⁴ The narrative juxtaposes the resignation of imperial office with the wavering motion of Genji's son, Yūgiri, to underscore the fraternal political stakes of exile. Both above and below Genji's station, the known order buckles. As the child flits between adults, without his father's anchoring presence, Genji feels paternal disquiet over his fate. The toddler's unsteadiness only magnifies Genji's concerns about the instability of patrilineal succession that exile causes.

For Genji, the boy's movements amplify affects of foreboding and shame. We interpret the following with these affects in mind: "Genji wept silently, and without really offering a reply murmured, *Now, I leave to see shores where sea folk broil brine raw, meanly mulling if yon smoke mirrors what charred clouds pyre black at Mount Toribe*. 'Can such heartache as this be anything save the parting at dawn?'"²⁵ Brine fires stain skies with Genji's guilt. Furthermore, the smoke's association with seafolk taints it with the low-status contagion introduced in the chapter's opening (e.g., "milling crowds"). Smoke also recalls a cremation pyre, suggesting the social death Genji suffers in banishment. The question of "parting at dawn" cites the motif of ending a night's erotic tryst; its emergence here implies that Genji approximates a feminine position on entering exile. The uncertainty implied by his question signals a queerness linking dispossession to refashioned gender roles. The trope is repurposed here to stress an ominous lack of eroticism in Genji's potentially leaving forever. As we'll see later, when Tō no Chūjō visits, Genji experiences another daybreak departure in exile that accentuates the trope's queer resonance.

ACQUIESCING TO A DWINDLED AURA

As Genji continues his incremental passage into exile, he attains an alluring vulnerability: "People peeped at him as he departed. In the keen brightness of the sinking moon, he struck a mournful figure of such immeasurably graceful beauty that even a tiger or wolf would have surely wept. All the more aghast, then, did those people who had observed from the start of his tender youth feel upon witnessing such an unprecedented shift in his air [*tatoshihenaki onarisama wo imiji to omohu*]."[26] Such observations suggest a loosening of the predominant male-to-female vector of *kaimami* seen earlier in the narrative and Heian prose fiction more broadly. While the shocking change mentioned refers to Genji's reduced station, it also evokes Genji's efforts to conceal himself by using a carriage that looked like a woman's. These details accent a feminization occurring as he enters exile, characterized by a slackening of normative patterns of viewing, feeling, and communing:

> At home again he found his own gentlewomen, who seemed not to have slept, clustered here and there in acute distress. There was no one in his household office, the men in his intimate service were no doubt busy with their own farewells, in preparation for accompanying him. It amounted to grave misconduct for anyone to visit him, and to do so more and more to risk reprisal, so that where once horses and carriages had crowded to him, a barren silence now reigned, and he felt the treachery of life. Dust had gathered here and there on the serving tables, some of the mats had been rolled up, and he was not even gone yet. He could imagine the coming desolation.[27]

The integrity of Genji's household starts to deteriorate. The loose cluster of distressed gentlewomen signals that exile has upset spatial relations in the Capital. This feminine assemblage heralds an implosion of an androcentric household structure. The women's presence only adds insult to injury as Genji surveys the gathering dust and absence of swooning crowds, the vacated space of his own residence expanding in "barren silence." As his residence empties, his body withers:

> The Viceroy Prince and the Captain came. Genji put on a dress cloak to receive them: an unpatterned one, since he had no rank, but which by its very plainness showed him off to still better advantage. Approaching the mirror stand to comb his sidelocks, he noted despite himself the noble beauty of the wasted face he saw. "I am so much thinner now!" he said. "Just look at my reflection! It really is too hard!"[28]

Exile reduces Genji outside and in. He trades his courtier's outfit for something base and remarks on his depleted appearance. Exile estranges Genji from his worldly possessions, his family, and even his own physical form, forcing him to redefine his place in the world. The mirror-stage of exile demands Genji relinquish formative identifications, habits, and markers of value. His reflection confirms his collapse while also opening space to fashion new connections and a revised persona. The arrival of two male intimates prompts his alienating trip to the mirror, framing the moment at which Genji's embodied awareness of exile's severity sinks in. The homosocial system of male rank and affiliation, an inescapable condition of courtly life, necessitates constant awareness of his relational identity. Where his physical location relative to the Capital defines exile's geographic character, the affective experience of Genji's exile materializes in wearing shame on his sleeves. In receiving his younger brother and his closest comrade in garments marking his demotion, Genji confronts a shocking disgrace.

Genji grows worried about the blow exile will deal to his legacy. For example, he says to Murasaki, "How lamentable it is that our time together has been so uneventful, these years having totally passed us by. My fate, thus far and going forward, will become a lesson for all."[29] The uneventfulness to which Genji alludes here is a child that Murasaki, his favorite wife, has yet to bear. Severing ties to the privileges of the Capital, Genji laments the fate of his progeny and property. His worry involves the loss of legal entitlements but also gossip that might overshadow whatever legacy he's built thus far. However, this is not to say he doesn't care about material possessions:

> He put his affairs in order. Among the close retainers who resisted the trend of the times, he established degrees of responsibility for looking after his residence. He also chose those who would follow him. The things for his house in the mountain village, items he could not do without, he kept purposely simple and plain, and he added to his baggage a box of suitable books, including the *Collected Poems* [of the poet Bai Juyi], as well as a *kin* [lute]. He took no imposing furnishings with him and no brilliant robes, for he would be living as a mountain rustic. To the mistress of his west wing, he entrusted his staff of gentlewomen and everything else as well, and he also gave her the deeds to all his significant properties—estates, pastures, and so forth. As for his storehouses and repositories, Shōnagon struck him as reliable, and he therefore instructed her on their care, assigning her for the purpose a staff of close retainers.[30]

Genji needs objects like Bai Juyi's poems and the lute to smooth his transition to Suma. These symbols compensate for the human contact—with women, especially—now foreclosed. Moreover, they help Genji mediate the experience of exile, forging an illustrious textual pedigree of male exiles to mitigate his contemptible exilic status.

Genji's transfer of property and certain administrative responsibilities to women stands out here as a corollary to the feminization he experienced earlier. As his claim to titles weakens, Genji must rely on trusted women like Murasaki, especially since he has no suitable male relative or heir to whom to entrust these duties. This massive transfer of wealth symbolically completes the gendered transformation prefigured by details like Genji's womanly carriage and exposure to peeping women "shocked to see him so changed."

Part of this change entails a diminished ardor when it comes to pursuing female lovers: "[Genji] renounced any heroic attempt to correspond with [Oborozukiyo] further."[31] Exile chastens Genji; this reluctance to push his romantic luck comes just lines after ceding control of his estate. This feminizing relinquishment seems to have diluted his earlier urges to court indiscriminately, as Genji learns his limitations and finds it hard to swagger like he used to.

FINDING FELLOW FEELING IN EXILE

The men recognize each other's comparable disgrace, building an empathy that we may see as part of the feminizing arc traced across the opening of "Suma":

> He left once the moon had risen, with a mere half dozen companions and only the closest servants. He rode. Needless to say, everything was so different from his excursions in happier days that those beside him were very downcast.
>
> One of them, a Chamberlain Aide of the Right Palace Guards, had been assigned to his escort that Purification Day; he had been denied due promotion, barred from the privy chamber, and stripped of his functions, and that was why he was with Genji now. The sight of the Lower Kamo Shrine in the distance brought that moment back to him. He dismounted, took the bridle of his lord's mount, and said,
>
> "I recall the days when we all in procession sported heart-to-heart, and the Kamo palisade calls forth a great bitterness."
>
> Genji could imagine the young man's feelings, and he grieved for him, since he had once shone brighter than the rest. He, too, dismounted and turned to salute the shrine. Then he said in valediction,
>
> "Now I bid farewell to the world and its sorrows, may that most wise god of Tadasu judge the truth in the name I leave behind."
>
> Watching him, these young men so enamored of beauty were filled with the wonder of his stirring grace.[32]

Bathed in moonlight, Genji rides exposed, unsheltered by his customary aristocratic carriage. These details accentuate the masculine vulnerability exile kindles. Demotion engenders emotion that brings these men together, having all been stripped of titles and rights they had enjoyed. Although residual hierarchy still deters the aide from reaching out to Genji directly, he nevertheless "took the bridle of his lord's mount," making physical contact with the carrier of Genji's physical burden before sharing his own tale of woe. That Genji "could imagine the young man's feelings" and "grieved for him" suggests an empathetic identification that becomes possible only at the Capital's outskirts and only now that both men must reckon with their respective dispossessions. Genji's mirroring gestures of dismounting, saluting the shrine, and reciting a doleful poem all speak to a conscious or unconscious willingness to develop new homosocial ties with lower-class comrades toward whom he was oblivious prior to exile. "Being young men so prone to affection, they watched his intoning figure, awestruck by a poignant wonder that pervaded their bodies" (*monomedesuru wakahito nite, mi ni shimite ahare ni medetashi to mitatematsuru*).[33]

The awe these young men feel toward Genji's "poignant wonder" pierces them as an attraction sparked by a mixture of shame and desire for consolatory recognition that he solicits by baring himself to the night air, dismounting to place himself literally on their level and confess a hardship akin to theirs. Paul Schalow stresses that "Suma is not a destination at all, but a yearlong journey through a year's worth of sexual and emotional deprivation, mitigated only by the companionship of sympathetic men."[34] These deprivations infuse the narration with erotic tension between Genji and his companions, though Genji seems too busy moping to notice their absorption with him.

Besides forming deeper ties with his retinue, Genji also seeks a renewed link to his recently perished father by visiting his imperial tomb:

> He reached the grave, whereupon rose to mind, as though before his very eyes, the figure of his father as he had been in life. Despite being of limitless imminence, even this Emperor had become someone now gone from the world, which produced unspeakable regret. Crying and crying, Genji told him all the myriad things that had happened to him, but his father's verdict was not clearly offered [*sonokotowari wo araha ni uketamahari tamahaneba*]. Hence, Genji felt hopeless thinking, *Wherever could all those various dying instructions father thought to bequeath have vanished to?*[35]

Genji is left emotionally adrift without a firm, clear judgment from his father. Genji lacks the paternal bastion that would center him in this alien landscape and quash the disorientation that gradually opens him to previously unfelt sensations.

While the tomb visit prompts Genji to ponder all he leaves behind in descending into exile, his concern about legacy becomes especially salient on reaching this site at which he must honor his father's memory. Visiting the tomb furnishes him with an occasion to solicit judgment from a patriarch "of limitless eminence." Although Genji sobs his story, seeking counsel, "his father's verdict was not clearly offered." Genji's desire to be judged in this dark hour—at a gravesite, no less—stands out. He has shirked judgment until now, worrying about being lambasted in the court of public opinion. Why does he crave it here and now?

Considering the intersection of homosocial desire and exile's dispossession lends answers. Genji's demotion literally lowers him—removing him from his high horse—to bring him closer to his new recruits. Part of what makes Genji so awe-inspiring (*ahare ni medetashi*) is the vulnerability caused by his dislocation. The anxiety Genji expresses regarding his imperiled legacy also heightens the male onlookers' sense of wonder, and Genji becomes more viscerally subject to exile's immediacy. This feeling of subjection manifests as a wish to be judged by "wise god[s]" but also as a newfound willingness to be potentially admired in reduced circumstances.

The tomb disorients less than the mansions of "Yūgao" and "Suetsumuhana" because it localizes foreboding at a single confined spot. Situated as a waypoint between the Capital and exile, the tomb marks a threshold Genji crosses from a space of rampant gossip to one of self-reflection. Hence even as he struggles to "find his way back again," he still escapes the omnipresent prying of the Heian court.[36] Genji's more focused scrutiny leads him to solicit the verdict he so avoided before.

Genji prays that his father's judgment might drop anchor as he drifts out to sea. Being acknowledged by the paternal ghost would grant some semblance of stability. Even if the spirit's judgment didn't expiate or vindicate, the mere force of such a gesture could amend Genji's fractured subjectivity. Even to be found guilty in his father's eyes would give Genji something to hold on to as his world crumbles.

Genji "shivered to behold a vision of his father as he had seen him in life. 'What is it his shade beholds when he looks on me—I, before whose eyes / the moon on high, his dear face, hides from sight behind the clouds?'"[37] Anguished and disoriented, Genji tries to imagine himself from his father's vantage. The gesture allows him to indulge momentarily the fantasy of residing on high, peering down at his fallen form from a celestial perch. This vision lets Genji sample the destiny his father wanted for him, even as the shrouded moon connotes the phantom patriarch's disappointment.

The tenor of shameful concealment carries over into Genji's final day at home:

> Genji also wrote a letter to Reizei, the heir apparent. It said, "to that gentlewoman" on it, since Genji had assigned her the task of managing affairs in his stead. "Today is the day I leave the Capital behind. What strikes me as foremost among my many woes is that it has become such that I won't be visiting His Highness again. Gauge all the issues at hand and relay my sentiments."
>
> *Whenever again in the Capital's ripe spring might I view blossoms, since now made a mountain dreg, all of whose time has run dry?*
>
> He attached the letter to a cherry branch whose blooms had all scattered off.[38]

The imperial ban placed on Genji bars his entrance to the palace. Therefore, he must have a trusted gentlewoman assume his responsibilities. That this woman is to visit Genji's secret son, the Crown Prince—guarantor of Genji's glorious legacy—sharpens the penalty's sting. Ōmyōbu's new status as executor for Genji also undercuts the integrity of a patrilineal ideal extending from Genji's deceased emperor father, through the commoner Genji, and on to his soon-to-be emperor son. The bare cherry branch reads as a phallic bequeathal, figuring the abortive fate of Genji's paternal line. The servant plays conduit for this transmission of homosocial sentimentality, her role as go-between fortified in direct proportion to Genji's withered authority.

The narrator further underscores the scene's pathos by describing the sadness of the lowest classes: "No one who had laid eyes on Genji could see his affliction without grieving for him, and of course those in his personal daily service, even maids and latrine cleaners he would never know but who had been touched by his kindness, particularly lamented every moment of his absence."[39] This sole mention in the narrative of latrine cleaners testifies to the far-ranging toll Genji's expulsion takes. These nameless figures surface now to stress Genji's appeal among even the dregs of court society. If their judgment suddenly matters, it proves how far he's plummeted. Moreover, their vocation indexes the depths of exile's affective repercussions.

Genji's expulsion draws reactions from both menials and aristocratic peers:

> Who could have remained indifferent to him, even in the world at large? [Genji] had waited day and night on His Majesty since he was seven, he had told him no wish that

remained unfulfilled, and all had therefore come under his protection and enjoyed his generosity. Many great senior nobles or court officials were among them, and lesser examples were beyond counting, and although they did not fail to acknowledge their debt, they did not call on him, for they were cowed by the evil temper of the times. People everywhere lamented his fate and privately deplored the court's ways, but apparently they saw no point in risking their own careers to express their sympathy, for many of them disappointed or angered him, and all things reminded him how cruel the world can be.[40]

The nobles' sense of risk stems from fears that proximity to Genji will contaminate them. Self-preservative instincts eclipse whatever affinity these courtiers held toward him. The space of the Capital stratifies subjects to the extent that it inhibits public display of sympathy toward the accused, highlighting the spatial constraints of affect's expression within Heian society. As we'll see, departure from the Capital's "cruel world" unlocks broader possibilities for tenderness to travel between subjects less hindered by expectations of reprisal.

THE TEXTURE OF EXILE'S LANDSCAPE

"Having never taken this route before, [Genji] felt unaccustomed to this kind of trip, experiencing a remarkable mix of dejection and joyful fascination [*kokoro-bosa mo wokashisa mo medurakanari*]."[41] Genji's mixed emotions attest to new leeway as he exits the Capital's confines. But the first site Genji's party encounters drains any delight: "The place called Ōe Hall was deplorably ruined, with only pine trees marking where it once stood."[42] To lay eyes on the decayed structure— the pine trees' position outlining the negative space the hall's absence has left—is to envision dispossession's concrete manifestation, hammering the stark reality of homelessness into Genji's skull. Importantly, this evacuated site initiates the chapter's inscription of exilic intertexts. The ruined building recalls a poem by the Chinese exiled poet Qu Yuan (340–278 BCE.), forming the first link in a lengthening chain of citations that helps Genji orient himself within an exilic topos.[43] Each allusion makes the landscape more legible—and livable. Acting as a stage for the gradual introduction of references to other exiles and foreign men, the ruins mark where a new home might be erected.

This poetry touches Genji's retinue: "Watching the waves wash the shore, then recede in turn, Genji murmured [*uchi zujitamaheru sama*], 'How I envy them'; although it was an old poem from a bygone age, he made it sound so fresh that seeing this the men accompanying him felt nothing but sadness."[44] "*Sama*" marks Genji's appearance as he murmurs, connoting visuality alongside the scene's emphasized aural qualities. By quoting the renowned lover Ariwara no Narihira's *Ise monogatari* poem, Genji aligns his forebear's homesickness with that of his new comrades. But by citing this poem, Genji also invokes its speaker's envy (*urayama-shiku mo*) toward the retiring waves. The subvocalized citation indicates an identification with those waves, suggesting a more fluid subjectivity brewing as Genji settles into exile, enabling male bonding at two levels. First, these spaces tie Genji to his exiled forefathers; citing their poems announces self-conscious participation in their lineage. Second, we witness the affecting confluence of the evocative shore and Genji's partial elision of the poem. Genji connects the residents of the landscape to poetic canon, uniting his all-male convoy in sorrow.

As Genji fortifies these affective ties to the men serving him, the allusions accrue. He "truly felt 'three thousand miles from home,'" referencing a Bai Juyi poem, and "the place he was supposed to live was said to be in close vicinity to the shabby 'draped seaweed dripping salt' dwelling where Counselor Yukihira had lived."[45] These tandem allusions intertextually scaffold Genji's residence. Yukihira's former presence, particularly, stamps Genji's exile with the imprimatur of poetic authority.[46] Nonetheless, we revise this exilic paramour's precedent as Genji refurbishes his quarters:

> The place stood a little back from the sea, among lonely hills. Everything about it, even the surrounding fence, aroused his wonder. . . . He summoned officials from his nearby estates, and it was sad to see Lord Yoshikiyo, now his closest retainer, issuing orders for all there was to be done. In no time the work was handsomely finished. The streambed had been deepened, trees had been planted, and Genji felt to his surprise that he could actually live there.[47]

Genji basks in the shadow of Yukihira's abode, feeling awe and chagrin as he realizes how far he has fallen. This explains his sadness at seeing Yoshikiyo talking to underlings; it reminds Genji that he must also interact more closely than ever with lesser vassals.

After Genji settles at Suma, he corresponds with his women in the Capital. However, maintaining ties over such distance makes for developments that undermine the communication's heterosexual character:

> The Rokujō Haven had successively joined four or five sheets of white Chinese paper into a scroll, on which she had written with fitful starts and pauses as she mournfully mulled things over; her brushstrokes bore a handsome mien. When he thought about how, despite her having been someone he cherished, his heart had veered callous upon pondering Aoi's death and his ardor had waned to make him quit the Rokujō Haven, Genji felt at this moment thoroughly grateful that something so desired had occurred. Because he found the perfectly timely letter so moving, Genji kept the messenger with him for two or three days, making him do things like recount stories of her life at Ise to him. This person in the Rokujō Haven's employ was young and of some sophistication. Since Genji now dwelled in such pitiable conditions, he did not keep even this kind of person at much distance from himself; catching glimpses of Genji's face and figure [onsamakatachi], the footman found him terribly wondrous and shed tears.[48]

By joining sheets of Chinese paper to form her sorrowful letter, the Haven attempts to extend a more substantive tether to the far-off Genji through the text's physical form. Exile alters the material composition of texts that mediate the gap between center and periphery. Furthermore, the lovely, fitfully written brushstrokes, Chinese papers designed in scroll format, and the sheer distance the missive must overcome to reach the exile all provoke Genji to indulge not just the female hand that wrote the text but also the male hands that ferried it to him.

Genji "welcomes even the servant" (*ontsukae sae mutsumashiute*), his reduced circumstances (*kaku aharenaru onsumahi nareba*) making him more solicitous of company. That Genji unexpectedly craves proximity to "this kind of person" (*kayau no hito mo onodukara mono tohokarade*), a menial, implies a paradigm shift whereby affections in exile nullify the status gulf that formerly prevailed. And we notice that this extraordinary closeness precipitates a weeping at male beauty we can safely assume to be unprecedented (*imijiu medetashi*), even taking the young man's relative sophistication (*keshiki aru*) into account.

The care Rokujō lavished on the text's construction moves Genji, but possibly not like she intended. For even as he peppers her messenger with questions about Rokujō's life, by detaining him Genji suggests that the experience of exile allows for affection to skirt its intended course. Distance from the Capital increases the value of a messenger who can move freely, where Genji cannot. Furthermore, the young man's sophisticated tinge sets him favorably apart from the Suma rubes surrounding Genji.

Collectively, these elements frame the queer potential of correspondence in exile—not in terms of male-male eroticism, but rather in terms of transcending status rifts to reshape affinity. Both mediums—scroll and messenger—resonate with motion easing Genji's rapport with the courier. Whatever the scroll conveys semantically or affectively, it also serves as a pretext for Genji's newfound interest in the youngster, who weeps on spying his beauty. Although the narrative doesn't say more about this character, that Genji replies to Rokujō's moving message only because he feels "bored and lonely" bodes better for the messenger than for Genji's lady pining at court.[49]

As Genji struggles through exile, he attempts to maintain connections with loved ones in the Capital. Elaborate letters like Rokujō's offer one mechanism to do so, even as the transmission introduces a queer potential into his Suma stay. These letters let Genji feel like a man. Insofar as "in this way, wherever they were, he still steadfastly exchanged missives with [his women]," he earns reassurance of their lasting attraction to him.[50] Unable to dress, move, or seduce like he used to, such letters become a privileged means of preserving a courtly masculine identity:

> *On and on I gaze at the ferns fringing the eaves of my dreary home / while the dew in ceaseless drops moistens my forsaken sleeves*, [Hanachirusato] had written, and Genji understood that in truth [the ladies of the village of fallen flowers] had no protection but their garden weeds. Upon learning that their earthen wall had collapsed in several places during the long rains [*nagaame ni tsuiji tokorodokoro kudurete namu*], he had his retainers in the city bring men from his nearby provincial estates to repair the damage.[51]

Given his limited mobility and shrunken sphere of influence, Genji longs to extend his reach. To be sure, the poem's references to the "fringing ferns" growing in the thatch of a woman's neglected roof and the water moistening her sleeves signal sadness. However, these images also highlight an architectural disrepair caused by Genji's absence as caretaker. Genji realizes that the women lack protection from the elements and springs to action, marshaling the troops to plug the holes and rebuild the fallen wall. This gesture of organizing men from two locales—the city and the provinces—to fix the structure from afar lets Genji assert what little authority he retains to consolidate manpower across vast distances. Consequently, he can feel like a man despite his dispossession, snug in his role as Mr. Fix-it.[52]

The nature of the repairs also matters. The long rains, connoting endless weeping, have made the residence problematically porous. Redressing this porousness becomes symbolically important to Genji to counter his emasculating withdrawal from the Capital. This porosity signifies masculine neglect on Genji's part, and the potential encroachment of more able-bodied men while he languishes elsewhere. The "ferns" (*shinobu*) echo homophonically as "remember fondly" but also denote "sneaking in." Genji's masculinity is tied to his ability to reinscribe the boundaries of his outpost in the city, thus ensuring his women and property stay secure.

AESTHETIC MEDIATION AND CONSOLATORY TEXTS

Genji's issuance of work orders lightens his worries, but it is ultimately a poor substitute for inhabiting the Capital and an insufficient remedy for his eroding personal and residential ties to it. As these ties wane, Genji's link to Suma deepens:

> At Suma the sea was some way off under the increasingly mournful autumn wind, but night after night the waves on the shore, sung by Counselor Yukihira in his poem about the wind blowing over the pass, sounded very close indeed, until autumn in such a place yielded the sum of melancholy. Everyone was asleep now, and Genji had hardly anybody with him; he lay awake all alone, listening with raised pillow to the wind that raged abroad, and the waves seemed to be washing right up to him [*nami tada koko moto ni tachikuru kokochi shite*]. Hardly even knowing that he did so [*warenagara ito sugou kikoyureba*], he wept until his pillow might well have floated away. The brief music he plucked from his *kin* dampened his spirits until he gave up playing and sang, *Waves break on the shore, and their voices rise to join my sighs of yearning* [*kohiwabite naku ne ni magahu uranami ha*]: *can the wind be blowing then from all those who long for me?*
>
> His voice awoke his companions, who sat up unthinkingly here and there, overcome by its beauty, and quietly blew their noses. What indeed could their feelings be, now that for his sake alone they had left the parents, the brothers and sisters, the families that they cherished and surely often missed, to lose themselves this way in the wilderness [*ge ni ika ni omohuramu, wagami hitotu ni yori, oyahara kara katatachi hanaregataku, hodo ni tsuketsutsu omohuramu ie wo wakarete, kaku madohiaheru*]? The thought pained him, and once he had seen how dispiriting they must find his

own gloom, he purposely diverted them with banter during the day and enlivened the hours by joining pieces of colored paper to write poems on, or immersed himself in painting on fine Chinese silk, which yielded very handsome panels for screens. He had once heard a description of this sea and these mountains and had imagined them from afar; and now that they were before him, he painted a set of incomparable views of an exceptionally lovely shore.

"How nice it would be to call in Chieda and Tsunenori, who they say are the best artists of our time, and have them make these up into finished paintings!" his impatient companions remarked. He was so kind and such a delight to the eye that the four or five of them forgot their cares and found his intimate service a pleasure.[53]

As autumn arrives, the exilic topos emanates melancholy. The winds of Suma shore and Yukihira's poetry weave against waves' rhythm to produce a synesthetic tether to the landscape. Genji's raised pillow makes him more susceptible to the hypnotic sounds of winds and waves that "seemed to be washing right up to him."[54] The waves approaching the sleepless exile speak to his inability to maintain a boundary between interior and exterior. The sea's water saturates his subjectivity, surging past the threshold of Genji's residence and skin to pour from his eyes inadvertently.

Moving from instrumental to vocal music in his quest for consolation, Genji sings as "waves break on the shore, and their voices rise to join [his] sighs of yearning."[55] Genji becomes one with the Suma shore as music dissolves the boundaries between him and his environment, and between Genji and his all-male retinue. Just as the sea sounds enter Genji's song, so too does this plaintive strain of melody permeate his comrades' hearts. Genji's switch to other media soothes their pain, and the paintings ultimately reproduce "incomparable views" of the very shore whose rhythms prompted Genji's crooning.[56]

The poems on joined paper and the paintings on silk enable Genji to sublimate the anguish Suma's exilic topos evokes. Remarks by Genji's "impatient companions" about having his ink paintings finished up in color might reflect a desire to create distance between themselves and the pervading landscape. Inscribing paper or silk with ink transposes an overwhelming terrain into a more manageable, tangible medium.[57] These texts let Genji and his men feel less subject to the setting through artistic skill, rescaling and externalizing the sense of loss they feel.

Genji's texts reformat and displace the immediacy of exilic experience, allowing for a homosocial rapport to develop. By deferring exile's pain and interposing layers of silk and cellulose between alienated subjects and their all-too-invasive environment, these media deflect longing for home toward longing for Genji. In his role as artist, Genji consequently becomes a mediating presence whose ability to both produce and exude beauty within misery attracts gratitude shaded by admiration. Through Genji's lens, the men are able to regard their poor fortune as finite. Furthermore, the text's appearance right after the description of the losses suffered by the Chamberlain Aide accompanying Genji, who "had been denied due promotion, barred from the privy chamber, and stripped of his functions," suggests the textual mediation also aids in building an altered family to offset the ones these men left behind. In other words, these poems and paintings bind the men after an ethos of loyal servitude wears thin.

These companions in exile feel lost, having left behind parents and siblings "they found difficult to be apart from even momentarily" (*wagami hitotsu ni yori, oya harakara katatoki hanaregataku, hodo ni tsuketsutsu omohuramu ie wo wakarete*). To be lost like this (*kaku madohi aheru*) connotes a spatial dislocation, but it simultaneously signifies a removal from conventional familial structures that extends the customary range of affections of the men. Removal from a realm of ingrained relations, along with its concomitant expectations and responsibilities, reconfigures their responsiveness to Genji, producing a newly unmoored inclination swaying between loyalty and longing.

As the textual mediation tightens ties between the men and eases them into a state of relative comfort in exile, the distance of formality dissolves:

> One lovely twilight, with the near garden in riotous bloom, Genji stepped onto a gallery that gave him a view of the sea, and such was the supernal grace of his motionless figure that he seemed in that setting not to be of this world at all. Over soft white silk twill and aster he wore a dress cloak of deep blue, its sash only very casually tied; and his voice slowly chanting "I, a disciple of the Buddha Shakyamuni . . ." was more beautiful than any they had ever heard before. From boats rowing by at sea came a chorus of singing voices. With a pang he watched them, dim in the offing, like little birds borne on the waters, and sank into a reverie as cries from lines of geese on high mingled with the creaking of oars, until tears welled forth, and he brushed them away with a hand so gracefully pale against the black of his rosary that the young gentlemen pining for their sweethearts at home were all consoled [*furusato no onna kohishiki hitobito, kokoro mina nagusami ni keri*].[58]

That the "admiring men forget the matters of the world" (*natsukashiu medetaki onsama ni, yo no mono omohiwasurete*) augments their closeness with Genji, manifesting here as cheerful service to him (*chikau nare tsukaumatsuru wo ureshiki koto nite*).[59] Such intimacy intensifies in these environs, even gaining spiritual magnitude as the displaced Genji assumes the mantle of a makeshift Buddha. His superficial resemblance to Shakyamuni overlays the men's devoted servitude with a capacity for spiritual succor. We can read their abandoned concern for the world as aroused by the ministrations of an exiled prince-cum-bodhisattva.

Having reconciled his connection to Suma's landscape, Genji has become comfortable enough to lower his guard. Whereas he formerly lay awake listening to the unnerving sound of waves edging his pillow, Genji now greets the beckoning sea. Twilight blossoms contribute color to a drab tableau. Genji saunters to a porch to peer at the ocean as night sets in, and he lets his robe's sash wilt. The composition of texts has relaxed Genji—toward his men and his environs—such that he is now willing to unfasten himself before them.

To produce the texts, Genji crossed a threshold of dispossession that exposes him to environmental phenomena in a more generative fashion. Exposed in this way, bathed in evening light at the veranda, with his sash loose, Genji surrenders to the state of exile and solicits men's attentions. In this charged environment where sights, sounds, and the scent of ocean air intensify sensitivity, Genji's sonorous prayer triggers a disproportionate response from singing seamen.

The topographic shift grounding this homosocial affinity revises the gendered schema of *Genji*'s nearest literary forebear, *The Tales of Ise*. That Genji did not travel alone to Suma challenges the *Ise* archetype straightaway, since it plainly disables the trope of heterosexual erotic adventure (*irogonomi*). Yet this doesn't necessarily foreclose the possibility of erotic relationships; it merely transfers that option from a heterosexual vector toward affections shared between men. Gotō Yasufumi notes that aristocratic men's geographic consciousness determines how love or lust play out, allowing for *Ise*'s literary depiction of these men's foul treatment of provincial women.[60] By invoking this topos, *Genji* encourages Heian readers intimately familiar with the *Ise* paramours' heterosexual exploits to judge them against Genji's newfound homosocial sensitivities in exile—likely to his benefit.

Genji's prayer sets off a chain reaction: its call provokes a choral response from the sailors, which precipitates cries from flying geese, that in turn "mingled with the creaking of oars" (*kaji no oto ni magaheru wo*) to provoke sobs.[61] The geese seem gendered male, and their seasonal decampment symbolizes exile. The sonically rich scene also shines visually. The sudden multimodal effusion of timbre, color, and texture springs from the recent portrayal of artistic production. Not unlike the ink absorbed by paper and silk, these artistic pursuits by Genji soak into the adjoining scene to form a layered, transmedia portrait of male affection.

Oars creak with the boatmen's effort against the rolling tide; meanwhile, Genji's pale, graceful hand brushes teardrops from his face and black rosary beads. The contrast in sound, sight, and degree of physical exertion between the male subjects on land and those on water establishes a desirous asymmetry.[62] Stuck at sea in their rowboats, these rougher men can't help but be seduced by Genji's charms. Genji's disarming lassitude encourages the fishermen, "pining for their sweethearts at home," to view him as a substitute for their absent female lovers. "Consoled" (*nagusami* [*ni keri*]) in fact has a wide semantic berth; the relief that comes from masturbation or sexual intercourse with a partner can fall within its scope.

The description of swelling voices, sinking reverie, spilling tears, and rough or smooth hands clutching wooden oars or caressing rosary beads builds an extraordinary erotic momentum. Although a more explicit account of the action will always remain "dim in the offing," tender moments like this pour forward with singular potency in exile. Genji's wind-pierced home and loose sash index a degree of exposure inconceivable in the city. To the extent that exile undoes the standard hierarchies operative in the Capital, status distinctions that might ordinarily separate an oarsman from a weeping noble melt at Suma.

Similarly, Suma's openness incites an overflow of affect that outstrips the boundaries of sexual orientation. Displacement from the Capital's aristocratic circuits of heterosexual courtship allows freer flow between classed and gendered subjects. As a result, sailors can harmonize with fallen courtiers, Rokujō's lowly messenger can be treated like a prince, and men separated from the confines of courtship and its social climate can unwind along the beach to savor Genji's image. Hence the dislocating dispossession suffered in exile also imbues a mobility along queer lines. In exile, freed from strict notions of propriety and pressed together into a porous space of reduced duty and incessant leisure, the men find each other's "intimate service a pleasure."[63]

This pleasure echoes in sights and songs that rise as the chapter nears its end. Among these, a string of poems from men joining Genji at Suma rings out. Just after the mention of consoled sweethearts at home, Genji and three of his exiled associates solidify their ties to one another through poetry. The chain of responses carries an orgiastic tenor as each man piles his verse atop his comrade's. The motif of wild geese recurs to link the poems while phrases like "wild geese fellows" (*kari ha kohishiki hito*), "all in one line, one memory on the next streams" (*kakitsurane mukashi no koto zo omohoyuru*), "abandoning of their own will their eternal home" (*kokoro kara tokoyo wo sutete*), and "we find it comforting at least not to lag behind" (*tsura ni okurenu hodo zo nagusamu*) amass to underscore intimate fellowship's urgency.[64] I'm convinced the ink's seep into silk and the loosened sash are what set desire reeling. The all-male sequence spotlights exile's propensity to intensify homosocial ties. This exchange culminates in music, which becomes a privileged venue for mediating the exilic experience and for male bonding, as Genji's plaintive lute draws tears from his ensemble mates.

Owing to its porous roof, Genji's residence is coated in icy moonlight, exposing him even further and making him feel more vulnerable to scrutiny from on high. The spatial dimension heightens an oppressive feeling of subjection framed by the physical access lower-status men now have to Genji and by his fallen social position. Genji's interiority dovetails the space of his "poor refuge" as swarming with the disabling indignity that overexposure inflicts. In contrast to Genji's first steps into exile, when he visited his father's tomb to seek solace and judgment, here Genji meets a naked moon whose radically penetrating sight singles him out as irredeemably depleted. Unlike the shame that simmered throughout Suetsumuhana's residence, this shame strikes brutally. It pinpoints Genji, hitting right as he confronts the fact that "everything about Suma's look and feel was bizarre, and even the baffling impression of low rustics, who he was unused to seeing, struck his own sensibilities as glaringly offensive. Time and again smoke came drifting quite close by. . . . What they did on a ridge behind where he lived was something called 'burning brushwood.'"[65] Genji feels shame at his proximity to the mountain folk, a status bigotry that stems from backwoods poverty and clings like the soot of rustic fires.

For all the intimacy exile fosters between men, status barriers persist. Genji's annoyance displays a prejudice underpinning camaraderie, as fondness for formally titled servants does not necessarily extend to his new Suma neighbors. (Singing boatmen get a pass by being far enough removed to look and sound poetic.) Meanwhile, the mountain folk engaged in "what people called 'brush' burning on the slope behind his home" come too close for comfort, offending Genji with char's sight and smell.[66] Thus status conditions intimacy's spatial logic. Although Genji's initial desolation seems to disable his awareness of social distinction, his bias rebounds as he tries to resign himself to life in exile while holding out hope to reclaim his stature.

This reversion occurs as winter comes, along with bitterness at having to play music while rustics burn bushes behind his humble house. Genji's attempts to weather exile with his makeshift ensemble read not just as consolatory measures but also as small reassertions of courtly protocol outside the Capital. Genji's companions see him as "something so wondrous that they felt solely in awe of him and hence could not abandon his sight, being unable to allow themselves even brief trips home."[67] Such loyalty heartens Genji but clashes with the behavior of rustics, "who were a mystery to him" (*mitate shiranu . . . mitamahinarahanu onkokochi ni*) and who lack the manners to defer as swiftly as his fawning expatriates.[68]

INTIMATES IN EXILE: TŌ NO CHŪJŌ'S SECRET VISIT

This gulf between the proximity Genji can comfortably tolerate with natives of Suma versus those loyal comrades who have accompanied him from court widens as time in exile passes. Fresh contempt enters the picture as "at Suma, the new year came, with longer, humdrum days, and the sapling cherry trees Genji had planted started to bloom faintly."[69] This malaise sets the stage for Tō no Chūjō to materialize:

> While the awful tedium of Suma wore on and on for Genji, Tō no Chūjō made Consultant, laden with the society's formidable acclaim due to his excellent character. But without Genji, the world felt woefully lifeless, and [Tō no Chūjō] missed him every moment, until he made up his mind—*What does it matter if word gets out and they charge me with crimes?*—and sped to Suma without warning. Upon laying eyes on Genji, tears of both delight and sorrow spilled forth. Genji's residence had an unspeakably Chinese air. Besides its surroundings being of the sort one would wish to paint, the crudeness of the woven bamboo fence encircling the house, its stone stairs, and the pine pillars was enchantingly exotic. Resembling a mountain peasant, Genji wore gathered trousers, with a charcoal-green hunting cloak atop a robe not of forbidden crimson but licensed rose with yellow overtones; his unassuming fashion was deliberately rustic, and looking at him, one couldn't help but smile at Genji's stunning beauty. The furnishings he used were also bare-bones, and his exposed room let anyone peer right in.[70]

The suddenness with which Tō no Chūjō appears at Genji's door after "miss[ing] him constantly" is striking given the excruciating slowness with which Genji made the same trip. Koike Seiji designates the chapter's opening slog as participating in a "reverse time" (*modoru jikan*).[71] I see this as queer time: a temporal protraction laden with negative affect induced by abandoning the Capital's standard tempo. Similarly, with this brisk reunion, yearning's sheer intensity vaporizes spatiotemporal distance along with the gap between thought and action. As Tō no Chūjō throws caution to the wind, overwhelmed by a desire to see his exiled friend, the narrator syncopates his passionate impatience by relating the men's encounter with lingering detail.

For instance, the modesty of the "indescribably Chinese" house ratchets up exoticism and highlights a disparity in rank between the former peers that fuels their arousal on reuniting. For Schalow, this overwhelming Chineseness (*sumai tamaheru sama, iwamukatanaku kara mekitari*) serves to "emphasize the utter masculinity of the environment."[72] But at another level, this Chineseness inscribes a desirable foreignness, amplifying possibilities for men's relationships to morph. The lavishness of the Chinese façade, with all its studied authenticity, overloads the very notion of masculine conventions. The poetic surplus marshaled to erect this guise betrays the crevices inescapable in citing precedents—masculine, Chinese, or otherwise. Thus, much like the exile himself, "utter masculinity" longs to be rescripted less strictly.

We note the overlapping textures—woven bamboo, stone, and pine—not to mention the delicate bleed of colors. It's as though the narrator forgoes charting distance only to transfer that descriptive energy to the meshed haptic and optic sensations in this erotic elaboration. The men's forlorn affection yields tears of joy and sorrow. As the narratorial gaze implicitly tracks Tō no Chūjō's passage from the outer fence, up the stairs, and to the pillar, it insinuates intercourse between men with its rising movement across the house's bamboo threshold, upward to the erect pillars, and then into the pleasure of melding hues.

And yet some boundaries persist, some even enhancing the men's rapport by inscribing disproportions that augment desire. For example, comporting himself "in the simple manner of a mountain peasant," Genji elicits sympathy from his friend "of great esteem."[73] The status rift invigorates this scene of desire by providing a top-to-bottom frame that obviates quarrels like those fought when the two men's ranks nearly matched. Simultaneously, Genji's low-class masquerade implies its own enticements: "purposely rustic" clothes and the unshielded room invite longer, closer perusal of Genji than usual.

Genji's porous house and rustic costume also recall the well-worn trope epitomized by his exilic forebears, Ariwara no Narihira and Yukihira. These famous paramours' exploits with callow seashore girls—at Suma, no less—are the stuff of *Tales of Ise* legend.[74] Their visits from the Capital established a spatial vector of desire that Genji's exile inverts. Rather than acting as the studly city courtier come down to pluck women from the provinces, Genji assumes a feminine position on the occasion of Tō no Chūjō's sudden visit. In his tidy unscreened home, he occupies a domestic space of waiting, akin to the ladies of romantic tales who, similarly exposed to view and unable to travel freely, sit pining for suitors to select them. Genji's lowered status, unhampered visibility, and exotic costume all contribute to an inviting occasion:

> Tō no Chūjō sang a bit of "Asuka Well," and between laughing and crying, the men shared tales of the past months. Since they talked on without end, I couldn't possibly recount everything they discussed, or even fragments of it. They didn't sleep, and instead traded Chinese poems through the night until dawn came. Although he'd said he cared nothing of the scandal that might erupt should he visit Genji, Tō no Chūjō nevertheless grew anxious at the thought of rumors of his exploits spreading, and thus cut his trip short to hurry home, only heightening Genji's heartache. . . . Both the men shed tears. Each of them seemed to regret having to part so soon. In the dim glimmer of sunrise, a line of geese crossed the sky. . . . Saying, "Take this to remember me by," [Tō no Chūjō] gave Genji among other things an exceptional flute of some fame, though they made no keepsakes of anything that might elicit people's censure. Slowly but surely the sun rose, and with a restive heart beating, Tō no Chūjō glanced back again and again as he hastily set off [*hi yauyau sashiagarite, kokoro ahatatashireba, kaherimi nomi shi tsutsu idetamahu wo*]; watching him leave, Genji looked all the more bereft.[75]

As these old friends converse, the initial topic is how the Emperor pities Genji's son, a concern reminiscent of what Sedgwick calls "men promoting the interests of other men."[76] In mentioning this homosocial compassion straightaway, Tō no Chūjō cites an imperial, intergenerational sympathy that validates Genji's own self-pity. This disclosure and the singing that precedes it soften Genji up for more tender exchange. The narrator herself conspires, preserving shreds of privacy by concealing everything they shared in lieu of sleeping.

Stimulated by Suma's ocean air and the unchecked view (and the narrator's collusion), Chinese poetry keeps Genji and Tō no Chūjō trading verses through the night. This transaction euphemizes intercourse, operating in a register reserved for learned men. Indeed, the text's admission right afterwards that Tō no Chūjō "grew anxious at the thought of rumors of his exploits spreading" suggests that even as his poetic exchange with Genji surrogates sexual contact, something about the length, depth, or force of his pleasure triggers self-censorship. Given the relative prevalence of male-male sex among courtiers of the time, one wonders what rumor's risk might be, if not sexual intimacy itself.

The trepidation might stem from Tō no Chūjō's cognizance of the duration of his visit and a fear that, if careless, he might ditch his courtly life for pure indulgence at Suma. Unlike Genji, whose exile exempts him from the temporal and political constraints of the Capital, Tō no Chūjō has a stature that demands this visit stay secret. Whereas the lower-ranking lackeys Genji conscripted to Suma have little choice but to stick close, Tō no Chūjō's lofty rank means that prolonged exposure to the tainted exile would cost too much. Thus the fear of rumors that might stain his reputation should he linger at Genji's side makes him abridge his stay. Tō no Chūjō draws intimately toward Genji until dread reminds him that the threats of proximity demand a tactical remove.

Abruptly, the exchange's pleasure stops as stigma invades. Awareness of social prohibition can wane temporarily, but it does not disappear from aristocratic consciousness. Stealing to the periphery mutes imminent risk, but the conviction to overcome enduring misgivings can't be sustained. Consequently, we're left to wonder what more Genji and his caller could have shared had shame not encroached on their makeshift harbor.[77]

The men indulge during their transient reunion in conversation, wine, songs, poems, and flutes. As they fraternize, each medium layers associations to assuage the pining that plagues them both. The cups of wine accompanying manly gifts of a black horse and a flute speak to a love the narrator claims "would be impossible" to relate (*tsukisubeku mo araneba, nakanaka katahashi mo e manebazu*).[78] The surfeit of exchanges, which culminate with the "fine flute of considerable renown" (*imijiki fue no na ari keru*), stoke and sublimate desire between the men.[79] Recalling how they piped away merrily on flutes in the shared carriage ride following their tiff in Suetsumuhana's yard, this recurrence of the motif appends a vestige of that bliss to this sad bestowal of keepsakes.

Dawn dissolves their night together; the men part as geese in flight remind them of the arrows leading home. Such strict lines chafe as this exilic interval lends reprieve from courtly protocol, allowing them to savor one another's presence beyond the Capital's purview. The efficient formation of flight paths countermands the unrushed, circuitous luxury Genji and Tō no Chūjō reveled in all night. We see the poetic motif of geese flying wing to wing revised in this environment—past its heterosexual provenance. Tō no Chūjō's reply, "*A lone crane, adrift, forsaken amidst the clouds, now echoes my cries: still yearning for that old friend I soared beside, our wings linked [tsubasa narabeshi tomo wo kohitsutsu]*," substitutes a male companion for the female lover usually eulogized with such an image.[80] Normally, the "aligned geese" motif resonates as the ultimate symbol of a lifelong partnership between a man and a woman. However, this tweaked notion of flying wing to wing deploys the image of the timelessly pure crane to evoke the agonizing duration of the men's separation, made more painful by Tō no Chūjō's lofty location "amidst the clouds" (*kumoi ni*; i.e., in the Capital), far from Genji's Suma dwelling. That Genji and Tō no Chūjō invoke these associations here, as they prepare to part ways, emphasizes their lasting affection for one another: "[Tō no Chūjō] answered, 'I now so often regret, after all, having enjoyed the undeserved privilege of your friendship!'"[81] We soon learn that "Tō no Chūjō's departure did not go at all smoothly, and the lingering grief of his returning home left Genji gazing off more and more sorrowfully until the day finished."[82]

Whereas Genji's earlier interactions with Tō no Chūjō in the Capital displayed a rivalrous edge, that subsides here in exile. The men neglect games like *go* and backgammon to spend the night not competing but affectionately talking, drinking, and sharing poetry. This altered temperament intersects with Tsukahara Tetsuo's assertion regarding *The Tales of Ise* that "the Heian nobility, bound by a bureaucratic system and forced to forfeit its humanity, was able to realize its humanity outside the bounds of the logic of a political system. If erotic adventure represented the recuperation of humanity between the sexes, then friendship represented the recuperation of humanity between members of the same sex."[83] Tsukahara's observation highlights the desirability an exilic space like Suma might possess, despite its being tied to dispossession, that is, the prospect of indulging "humanity" to an extent inaccessible in the Capital. But while we should avoid a paranoid anticipation that all same-sex friendships harbor erotic aspirations, we should also not unduly partition homosocial desire's ample continuum of possibilities—platonic, erotic, and otherwise. Displaced from his seat of masculine privilege within the Capital, Genji has been reoriented so that his gendered habits slacken to allow for other styles of contact, as his strength and rapport with his men attests. But Tō no Chūjō's visit marks a turning point. We can read Genji's incremental openness with and physical exposure to his lesser, nearer-to-hand comrades as having paved the way for this most intimate encounter of his exile.

The reverberations of this metaphorical turning point physically reorient male bodies. Specifically, we see "Genji's friend set out in haste, with many a backward glance." The repeated act of twisting to look back at the beloved object—throughout the process of its abandonment—stands out. At one level, this turning signifies an ambivalence about staying with Genji or leaving him, even as Tō no Chūjō's sensitivity to rumor ultimately wins out. However, at another level, the iterative intermittency of the turns discloses an instability in the normative mores that call him home. To return straight and steady, like the regimented geese, would signal a certain faith in the validity of these conventions. But desire interrupts that route. Transpiring in the interval between home and exile, the turns highlight suppressed contingencies. The turns are insistent and, importantly, seem to emerge spontaneously. Along Suma's shoreline, they accrue like granules to raise doubts about the spatial and sexual configurations installed by the legislating center. Consequently, Tō no Chūjō's tentative gesture foregrounds the contrapuntal impulse homosocial yearning emits against mandates to quarantine deviance and enforce cruel distances.

A heart-rending visit from his favorite male companion leaves Genji "gazing off more and more sorrowfully." Yet it is the reunion with this loving man that makes Genji ponder all he has lost and, as the chapter ends, stiffens his resolve to escape exile:

> Seated there in the brilliance of the day, he displayed a beauty beyond words. The
> ocean stretched unruffled into the distance [*umi no omote uraura to nagiwatarite*],

and his thoughts wandered over what had been and what might be. . . . When Genji, too, briefly dropped off to sleep, a being he did not recognize came to him, saying, "You have been summoned to the palace. Why do you not come?" He woke up and understood that the Dragon King of the sea, a great lover of beauty, must have his eye on him [*miiretaru*]. So eerie a menace made the place where he was now living intolerable.[84]

Genji's sorrow at losing Tō no Chūjō leads his mind to wander, his ruminations conferred a wide berth by "the ocean stretch[ing] unruffled into the distance." The expanse of such a placid space summons contrary thoughts of livelier, tighter quarters, such as the Chinese house in which they traded verses or the rollicking carriage they shared leaving Suetsumuhana's estate. While the textural juxtaposition of the Suma residence's architecture and elements of Genji's outfit suggests an escalating desire, this fresh calm implies desire's abatement. In its capacious smoothness, the sea invites thoughts to unfurl across its surface while reminding Genji of unceasing absence.

Still dumbstruck by Tō no Chūjō's departure, Genji confronts a moment of unfettered possibility, an interval lacking any clear or imposed telos. The charged, ephemeral intimacy shared during his reunion with Tō no Chūjō has left Genji a blank slate of sorts, stripped of routine aspirations, unable or unwilling to move forward, and stranded "at a crossroads of unknowing" (*yukuhe mo shiranu ni*). The ambiguity narrated here lets us wonder about the erotic potential of "what might be" (*yukusaki*, literally "[future] destination") as a fierce storm hits and "the sea gleamed like a silken quilt beneath the play of lightning. . . . [Genji and his men] barely managed to struggle back, feeling as though a bolt might strike them at any moment, . . . and the rain drove down hard enough to pierce what it struck [*harameki otsu*]."[85] This explosion of violent weather manifests an eruption of sexual tension that had been building since Genji first reached Suma. With the texture of crashing waves, electric fear of being pierced at any moment, and the undulation of the sea's silken quilt, the landscape itself seems to convulse vicariously to simulate the liberating rupture anticipated as Genji's thoughts wander.

The storm underscores homosocial bonds and homoerotic subtext with unprecedented potency. It unites the men—regardless of status—in shared purpose to redirect their energies toward home. Genji's dream extends the storm's erotic outpouring by introducing the penetrating gaze (*miiretaru*) of the Dragon King's desirous eye. This final convergence of Tō no Chūjō's visit, the storm, and the dream consummates the multifaceted homosociality that has infused Suma since day one. While the Dragon King's lustful scrutiny of the overexposed Genji precipitates his decision to leave Suma, we can't ignore the languorous interval savored between Genji and Tō no Chūjō just prior to this upheaval. Genji's reluctance to see his companion leave is what triggers his own epiphany to quit Suma. In this regard, male-male intimacy both thrives in exile and amplifies the desire to exit exile and foster such relations in less precarious settings. Hence the stormy climax reads as queer not for its homoerotic tenor but rather for how it literalizes embodied contingency: the brutal layering of dislocations protagonists suffer as intimacies are broken and rebuilt.

CONCLUSION: EXTENDING THE QUEER
TURN IN EXILE'S EXPANSE

Genji's exile at Suma demonstrates how homosocial intimacy plays out at two levels. First, this intimacy emerges as a practice of intertextual homosociality in which exile induces a desire for closeness that requires the citation of masculine textual precedents. As Genji attempts to come to terms with being cast out of the Capital and abandoned at Suma, he looks desperately to the infamous men who have preceded him in exile. The exilic topos of Suma evokes an archive of poetic references that help orient Genji in this foreign place. Through a poetic tissue of citations, Genji is able to soften the edges of his alienation and establish a textual connection to the natural landscape to which he is subjected. Exile heightens Genji's sensitivity to the imbricated materiality of text and place. By composing poetry akin to that of his literary forebears and painting his heart out along the gorgeous shore, Genji tries both to root himself in these new environs and to assert mastery over them with his artistic prowess. These attempts at mediation offer a means of recuperating something of the privilege lost on banishment from the Capital.

Genji's exile at Suma also shows how dispossession and exposure within a marginal space reorient social relations. Thus the second way homosocial intimacy plays out involves an unprecedented degree of physical exposure to the natural elements, other men's gazes, and their desire for closeness. The disorientation of exile brings Genji physically and emotionally closer to lower-status men particularly. Stripped of rank and the formal costumes that go with it, Genji is tossed into a liminal space in which dear companions and passing seamen may lay eyes on him more or less unhindered. This exposure stirs homoerotic desire and lays the ground for Genji's heart-rending paintings. When his exile is over, these exceptional images convey every ounce of his suffering to politically vindicate him within the context of a life-altering competition on his tortuous return to the Capital:

> The Left [Genji's daughter's team] had one more turn [in the picture contest's final round], and when the Suma scrolls appeared, [Tō no Chūjō's] heart beat fast [*on-gokoro sawagi ni keri*]. His side, too, had saved something special for last, but this, done at undisturbed leisure by a genius at the art, was beyond anything. Everyone wept, His Highness the first among them. Genji's paintings revealed with perfect immediacy, far more vividly than anything they had imagined during those years when they pitied and grieved for him, all that had passed through his mind, all that he had witnessed, and every detail of those shores that they themselves had never seen. He had added here and there lines in running script, in Chinese or Japanese,

and although these did not yet make it a true diary, there were such moving poems among them that one wanted very much to see more. No one thought of anything else. Emotion and delight prevailed, now that all interest in the other paintings had shifted to these . . . the Left had won.[86]

In Jonathan Stockdale's reading of this scene, the audience's tears signify sympathy for Genji's plight: "He has heightened the affinity of those present for Genji and his faction" and, through his artistic command, perhaps made the audience feel "sentiments of affinity toward other paradigmatic figures of exile."[87] However, while the diary certainly transmits something of Genji's personal exilic experience, we also notice the trace of paranoia emerging in this venue where private, peripheral expressions are revealed publicly. For before delight prevails, we perceive the quickening pulse of the man who stole away from the Capital to visit Genji in exile. Tō no Chūjō's quiver of alarm at what will be divulged in this public space vibrates as a vestige of the anxiety aroused by his sleepless night at Genji's side when, despite his pleasure, "the Captain was sensitive to rumor after all, and he made haste to leave."[88] Even within a context in which male-male sexual relations weren't uncommon, this climbing pulse suggests fears of some secret excess being outed—not the content of the men's closeness in exile per se but rather the crime of breaching courtly protocols by visiting Genji.

This scene displays the potency of affective forces that circulate along homosocial routes. Long after Genji's exile has ended, the "perfect immediacy" of his artwork attests to how well the residual yearnings of that period have been preserved through aesthetic mediation. We should therefore read the audience's "want[ing] to see more" of the intensely personal record as symptomatic of the record's capacity to give vent to the desires vitalizing its sheets. As Genji prepares to unsheathe his Suma journal, his "looks were such that one would have gladly seen him as a woman."[89] The return of this desirous phrasing in the "Eawase" chapter refreshes tinges of the eroticism of "Suma."[90]

The experience of exile impelled Genji to assemble his overpowering archive of pure feeling. Queer exposure he experienced in banishment redoubles the affective intensity of his compositions such that, when he is transported back into the heart of courtly life, they land with indisputable political impact even though "these did not yet make it a true diary." Qualities like the object's formal definition or veracity matter little when the content so overflows generic conventions. The off-line bearing of the efforts at aesthetic sublimation testifies to the profuse sensations experienced in exile. The Suma archive's unmatched value stems from an oblique style of aesthetic mediation that exudes powerfully moving queer traces while strategically withholding full disclosure of them. Thus the paintings, which exhibit "here and there lines in running script, in Chinese or Japanese," embed inscriptive traces whose variation and discontinuity register the ebb and flow of a mutable queerness elicited along Suma's fraught shore.[91]

It is here that Tō no Chūjō's backward glances toward Genji come to matter most. How should we dwell with those parting glimpses? As daybreak quickens pulses, those bittersweet pivots dilate our perception. They alert us not only to the gravitational pull of shame but also to shame's inability to fully circumscribe the movements of queer longing. This is a longing not for sexual intercourse between men but rather for a space and time not delimited by norms devoted to sustaining shame as a means of social reproduction and political control. The secrecy and urgency with which Genji and Tō no Chūjō rendezvous at Suma seems almost to imply that the political shame of exile is a pretext for a degree of male-male intimacy impossible to indulge otherwise and elsewhere. But this might allow us to reclaim shame for its generative, if not unequivocally positive, repercussions. For what blossoms outside the Capital are affections, yearnings, and a latent receptivity only made possible as a product of shame's propulsive, vitalizing energy.

Indeed, we might read the intermittent pivots as manifesting a queer impulse that worries the superficial stability of straight, unidirectional routines at moments in which the diminished subject transitions across a spatial boundary. We saw this happen at Suetsumuhana's house, in the suitors' friction at her frayed fence, and similar twists surfaced in the "Yūgao" chapter, when "Genji could only look back time and again, his breast brimming with anguish as he rode off. Along the dew-drenched route, he felt like he hadn't a clue where he was, set adrift within an abnormally dense morning fog. *Yūgao looks as she did when alive, lying there in that crimson robe of mine from when we traded ours*."[92] The matching phrasing in both instances of looking backward (*kaherimi nomi*) likens bereavement to the loss of having one's beloved companion return to the Capital, just as the exchange of robes before Genji's lover died recalls the gift giving he and Tō no Chūjō performed before parting at Suma.

This confluence shows how homosocial separation mimics mourning's gestures. The reappearance of backward turns at Suma begs comparison with death's aftermath. The turns accent continuity along a spectrum spanning heterosexual and male-male desires and connote congruence between homosocial and heterosocial losses. Moreover, this parallel movement suggests that when one experiences the metaphorical social death of exile, the added deprivation of a beloved's presence can send the subject reeling as though wracked by an actual demise.

And perhaps something does truly perish at Suma. The intense, noncompetitive interaction savored among men there suggests styles of homosociality far less hostile than at court. Here, my interpretation recalls Ellis Hanson's claim that "faced with the depressing realization that people are fragile and the world hostile, a reparative reading focuses not on the exposure of political outrages that we already know about but rather on the process of reconstructing a sustainable life in their wake."[93] When Tō no Chūjō looks back, we should apprehend this gesture as him unsuccessfully mourning the loss of a homosocial intimacy not wed to the preservation of dominative paradigms or crippling asymmetries. For all its drawbacks, exile also hosts development of a reparative atmosphere. While in no way devoid of inequalities that trail the men outside the Capital, Suma's permissive expanse nevertheless obviates much of the violence germane to court life, making a fuller range of relations possible.[94] Returning to the notion of exile as a space of failed aristocratic masculinity, we watch vicious courtly habits wane. Alas, the patriarchal territorialism that awaits Genji back home will revive them. But the night shared with Tō no Chūjō marks a momentary lapse in those strictures that is unique to the exile of "Suma."

Looking toward the next chapter, I want to stress the backward turns as a hinge that connects queer mediation and melancholic mourning. I examine how the sons of Genji and Tō no Chūjo extend the trajectory of homosocial intimacies pioneered by their fathers. The pivot backward returns in this context of grieving, as aural and haptic mediations of loss sculpt mourning's queer contour.

From Harsh Stare to Reverberant Caress

Queer Timbres of Mourning in "The Flute"

What styles of attachment does mourning solidify or dissolve? In this chapter, I explore the link between queer gestures and the portrayal of mourning in the *Genji* narrative and its twelfth-century illustrated handscroll version. Examining the rhetorical and artistic techniques through which male bonds and dead bodies are rendered in the "Kashiwagi" (The Oak) and "Yokobue" (The Flute) chapters, I argue that *Genji*'s spectacular depictions of deathly encounters foreground mourning's queer contour. I take up texture as a useful concept through which to theorize the aesthetic, spatial, and affective dimensions of this melancholic terrain, suggesting that mourning in *Genji* hinges on queer intimacies that surface most palpably in death's wake. Furthermore, I argue that a queer reading of mourning foregrounds how these dimensions destabilize patriarchal aspirations for clear-cut legacies, suggesting richer forms of affection and affiliation.

Why focus on Kashiwagi—the eldest son of Genji's rival, Tō no Chūjō—along with mourning, and the multisensory negotiations portrayed? Kaoru Hayashi explains Kashiwagi's genealogical significance:

> As first son of the household, Kashiwagi is supposed to be heir to the family name, if not property and family enterprise. However, I argue that he oscillates and transgresses boundaries between several families. It is only through his experiences of being possessed, dying, and then possessing others that he is finally able to establish a kinship that is closely related to that of the Fujiwara ancestry and that he will pass down to his descendants. Kashiwagi's episodes embody the hybridity of kinship that refuses to be sorted out in merely one line of genealogy.[1]

Extending Hayashi's argument, we might ask what shape that hybrid kinship takes, especially when exceeding straightforward lineage. This tendency, with the multimodal mourning accompanying it, leads me to read Kashiwagi's episodes as queer. "Yokobue" demonstrates how musical mementos come to embody the hybrid kinship often overshadowed by monolithic lines. More than sight, sound, and touch offer sensory means of apprehending the nature of latent traces surrounding Kashiwagi's life and haunting legacy. In this vein, attunement to the phenomenological dimensions of homosocial intimacy, mourning, and inheritance helps us gather a fuller sense of these veiled ancestries and apparitional attachments.

Specifically, I delineate a movement from visual toward aural sensation to demonstrate how sonic texture, or timbre, indexes degrees of posthumous intimacy and pleasure inaccessible in life. A poignant act of observation plays out in the deathbed encounter between two courtiers: the dying Kashiwagi and Yūgiri, the companion who mourns him. Analysis of this primal scene sets the stage for a discussion of "Yokobue," in which hearing displaces vision as the dominant sense through which queer contact persists beyond death. Here, the illustrated handscroll rendition of the scene provides an illuminating counterpoint as one especially spectacular response to the original *Genji* text. By considering the portrayals of "Yokobue" beside those of "Kashiwagi," I perform a transmedia reading that supports art historical analysis with textual evidence to demonstrate how melancholic attachments pose questions through their queer timbre. Finally, I develop this engagement with timbre to theorize the queer reverberations of touch as a disorganizing yet generative sense.

THE ENTICEMENTS OF A DYING BODY

Genji is tainted by his mother's problematic status and her father's death, inheriting her insufficient political backing at court. This precarious position represents a form of contingency that propels the narrative. Genji's pursuit of imperial dominance—in deed if not in name—consumes him, with consequences for those in his way. Enter Kashiwagi, who seals his fate by conceiving a child with one of Genji's wives, Onna San no Miya. To cuckold Genji like this is a fatal affront. I want to theorize the homosocial intimacy that accompanies Kashiwagi's demise and the fraught longing that ensues.

How might the stylized spectacle of death queer the confluence of intimacy and loss that emerges in mourning? In this final chapter, I incorporate visual art into my examination of queer textuality by reading between the narrative text and the illustrated handscroll that reenvisions it. *Genji* has inspired countless commentaries, translations, imitations, and visual reproductions over the centuries. The most famous is the *Genji monogatari emaki*, or the *Illustrated Handscrolls of The Tale of Genji* (ca. 1160). Constructed roughly 150 years after *Genji* was composed, these handscrolls represent the oldest extant text of the narrative.[2] Orchestration of the *Genji Scrolls* represented a nostalgic enterprise, as they reproduced an impression of *Genji*'s world that commemorated a lustrous bygone era both intimately

FIGURE 1. *Genji monogatari emaki*, "Kashiwagi 2 Original Painting." Tokugawa Art Museum. © Tokugawa Art Museum Image Archives / DNPartcom.

familiar to the cloistered Heian nobility and increasingly illusory as their court collapsed during the late twelfth century.

Although most are now lost, sections corresponding to each of *The Tale of Genji*'s fifty-four chapters probably existed at one point. Each scroll section consists of a painting of at least one scene from a *Genji* chapter. Each painting was originally preceded by a calligraphically rendered narrative excerpt (*kotobagaki*) that primed readers for the painted scene.[3] The alternating format of lavish tracts of calligraphic text followed by multilayered paintings illustrating the text formed, in Melissa McCormick's words, "a pictoliterary object of unusual sophistication that provided customized viewing experiences for its audiences."[4]

I consider the "Kashiwagi 2" painting to be the most compelling of all those in the *Genji Scrolls*. It captures an intimate deathbed encounter between male aristocrats while provoking a host of questions about the nature of spectacle, intimacy, and the repercussions of desires to approach a body visibly more vulnerable than one's own. The painting beckons the beholder in a fashion that parallels Yūgiri's lingering gaze at his beloved companion (see figure 1).

The handscroll painting capitalizes on Yūgiri and Kashiwagi's tender deathbed moment to make the extent of the men's closeness unmistakably clear. I have argued elsewhere that at key moments like this, the *Genji Scrolls* highlight the spectacular aesthetic possibilities available in rendering bodily decomposition and performing the work of mourning through virtuosic calligraphic or painterly techniques.[5] The cultural plotting of grief includes beliefs about seclusion to combat death's polluting force; a metaphorical and material emphasis on darkness in poetry and clothing; the experience of emotional distress and physical enervation; and feminization, such as when the Kiritsubo emperor mourns Genji's mother.[6] Importantly, I demonstrate that "*The Tale of Genji* represents mourning as a spatiotemporal interval of concentrated textual investment."[7] Here, I expand on that notion to emphasize the queer potential of that interval, primarily as a space wherein melancholic attachments are wrought and rewritten.

Although the verbal exchanges quoted below indicate the emotional turmoil Yūgiri feels, what recedes in the narrative when compared to the image is the striking physical proximity between male bodies foregrounded by the painters; Yūgiri's domineering posture toward Kashiwagi; and the impression of an urgent if not oppressive masculine voyeuristic desire to scrutinize a dying male body.

The scene depicted in the "Kashiwagi 2" painting derives from the moment Yūgiri visits Kashiwagi, cries about not knowing why his friend is so ill, and tells Kashiwagi, "You're looking so much more handsome than you usually do!"[8] Yūgiri adds to this flattery a rueful accusation: "We promised ourselves that neither of us would go before the other."[9] Beyond wanting Kashiwagi to stay by his side, Yūgiri also wishes to know why his companion is dying: "I can't even make sense of what's made this affliction of yours so severe. We share such an intimacy, and yet I have only the vaguest idea what's wrong!"[10] By framing his ignorance of the cause of Kashiwagi's illness in terms of "closeness" or "intimacy" (kaku shitashiki hodo), Yūgiri implies that increasing proximity to the enigmatic object would resolve this mystery.[11]

Residing momentarily in this space with Kashiwagi and getting so close to him highlights a thinly veiled desire to make his dying body produce responses Yūgiri craves. Ostensibly, Yūgiri's frustration stems from secrets kept about an illicit liaison Kashiwagi has shared with Genji's wife. And yet the desire to know more exceeds a wish for mere verbal confession; it spreads into a desired exposure whose physical vibrations generate resonances irreducible to gossip or pillow talk. As we will see in the subsequent analysis of the "Yokobue" chapter and painting, the implications of this desire for proximity emerge as Kashiwagi dies and Yūgiri begins the volatile work of mourning him.

Consumed by illness, Kashiwagi's disintegrating body captivates Yūgiri. The text recounts the details of Kashiwagi's appearance partly from Yūgiri's point of view: "Kashiwagi wore more or less a court cap, his head pushed into it, and although he tried to sit up a little, this proved too fatiguing. He lay with the covers pulled over him, wearing numerous layers of pleasingly supple white gowns. In and around the room was pristine, with sweet hints of incense, and he lived in an elegant fashion, seeming to have kept his wits despite his wilted condition."[12]

The mention of incense and soft gowns lends an erotic tinge to the men's encounter, as Kashiwagi's inability to right himself emphasizes his physical vulnerability relative to the inquisitive Yūgiri: "They had long been so close that nothing could come between them, and no parent, brother, or sister could have felt greater pain at the prospect of parting [wakaremu koto no kanashiu kohishikarubeki nageki]. . . . 'Why is your health failing this way? I thought that the congratulations due you today would make you feel a little better.' [Yūgiri] lifted a corner of the standing curtain. 'Unfortunately, I am no longer the man I was.'"[13]

FIGURE 2. *Genji monogatari emaki*, "Kashiwagi 2 Original Painting" (detail). Yūgiri at Kashiwagi's deathbed. Tokugawa Art Museum. © Tokugawa Art Museum Image Archives / DNPartcom.

These companions share an intimacy that transcends blood ties. In this vein, one man's concern for another man's suffering and the hidden reasons behind it presses customary notions of familial closeness into queer relief. Endō Kōtarō notes how elegiac homosocial exchanges can eclipse the logic of gender itself.[14] As a later response to the *Genji* narrative, the handscroll painting capitalizes on Yūgiri and Kashiwagi's tender moment to make the extent of the men's closeness unmistakable. The bamboo blinds to the deathbed dais are raised, and the curtain past it has been pulled to the right to allow both Yūgiri and the scroll viewer unimpeded looks at the prostrate Kashiwagi. By contrast, we see that five women line the leftmost third of the painting; they are clearly cordoned off from the bed and not privy to the degree of access Yūgiri enjoys (see figure 2). A standing curtain separates the women from the tender scene (visually, at least, but not aurally), partitioning the bedchamber to give the men at least the impression of some privacy.[15]

This juxtaposition of gendered spaces reveals how furnishings like standing screens or curtains focus sensory attention or filter stimuli. Exposed visually and to some degree aurally, Kashiwagi dies in this scene. The subsequent transition from "Kashiwagi" to "Yokobue" portrays Yūgiri's multimodal negotiation of unaccustomed sensations as mourning intensifies his sensorial experience.

READING MOURNING'S SENSATIONS

How might we apprehend affect in *Genji*? The following scene, which recounts Yūgiri's visit to Kashiwagi's widow following his funeral, helps solidify the link between mourning and the sensations attending it:

> The funerary observances were unusually impressive. Naturally, the Commander's wife, but especially the Commander [Yūgiri] himself, added to the scripture readings deeply fond touches of their own. The Commander called often at the Princess's Ichijō residence. The skies of the fourth month somehow lifted the heart, and the color of the budding trees was lovely everywhere, but for that house, plunged in mourning, all things fed a life of quiet woe, and he therefore set off there as he did so often. The grounds were filling with new green, and here and there in shadowed places, where the sand was thin, wormwood had made itself at home. The near garden, once so carefully tended, now grew as it pleased. A spreading clump of pampas grass grew bravely there, and he made his way through it moist with dew, mindful of the insect cries that autumn would bring. The outside of the house was hung with Iyo blinds, through which he caught cooling glimpses of the new season's gray standing curtains and of pretty page girls' hair and dark gray skirts—all of which was very pleasant were it not that the color was so sad. . . . He looked out sorrowfully on the trees that grew in the grounds, indifferent to human cares. There stood an oak and a maple, fresher in color than the rest and with their branches intertwined. "I wonder what bond they share, that their mingling branches should promise them both so happy a future?" he said, and he quietly went to them.[16]

Genji's portrayals of affect help us reconsider poetic motifs and scenic descriptions we've come to take for granted as stock emotional metaphors. We should energize its botanical motifs with a phenomenological awareness—not just a sensitivity to the four seasons. Doing so lets us rethink simplistic notions of feeling that bypass the sensate body to praise the yearning heart. The absence of scattered cherry blossoms notwithstanding, this passage could seem like a stereotypically rhapsodic Heian literary depiction of nature: Kashiwagi has died; people are sad; the landscape reflects this sadness. However, we might notice sorrow while responding further to the physicality of perception portrayed.

Mourning alters sensation: it accentuates the panoply of stimuli surrounding the bereaved, amplifying perception of otherwise unremarkable details. Yūgiri had "called often" at the residence he now visits after the funeral. Yet this routine's character has changed "somehow," slipping past conscious deliberation to lend this familiar place uncanny tinges. Echoing Sedgwick's contention that touch undermines "any dualistic understanding of agency and passivity," Yūgiri moves voluntarily but out of habit, seeming to relent to an unaccustomed susceptibility to his immediate surroundings' stimuli.[17] This reorientation—which is also behind Yūgiri's impulse to add "deeply fond touches" to the funerary observances' scripture readings—magnifies how he perceives the surface of familiar environs. The color of freshly budded branches prickles against the downcast household's austere blinds and gray curtains. As he moves, the "quiet woe" of his paces arises from the mélange of textures flickering unevenly across the residence grounds: flora draped in patches of shadow, wormwood surfacing where the garden's sand has thinned.

Though still charming on this mild summer day, the garden, "once so carefully tended," approaches disarray as it "[grows] as it please[s]," literally "following its heart" (kokoro ni makasete), disregarding customary strictures.[18] The image also highlights the mourning subject's porosity as he walks, proprioceptive sensation heightened by his trousers passing through unkempt tracts of moist grass. That Yūgiri is "mindful of the insect cries that autumn would bring" as he makes his way through the damp grass suggests a temporal overlap of season—this melancholic scene shares more of a traditional poetic affinity with autumn than summer—but it also implies a synesthetic experience not dominated wholly by the visual: the dewdrops transferred from static grass to moving fabric exceed the sense of touch to stimulate an aural imagination, "transform[ing] the effects of one sensory mode into those of another," in Brian Massumi's words.[19] Like the braided branches of the oak and maple trees, Yūgiri treads forward silently as the passage closes, with sound interlacing touch as he drifts through a landscape refashioned in death's aftermath.

Finally, Yūgiri's walk over to those trees culminates an apprehensive sensibility Kashiwagi's death has nurtured. This sensibility involves a tentative willingness to acquiesce in unaccustomed ways to surrounding phenomena. The passage chronicles an unhurried wondering about newly perceived textures of once-familiar surroundings. Details like trousers weighed down by dew-thickened grass pinpoint elements of the materiality conferring this ambience. In approaching the trees to get a better sense of what has brought their branches so close, Yūgiri's question about the bond they seem to share is transformed from a rhetorical gesture of supposition to an embodied physical action performed to resolve it. The way the branches of different tree species entwine compels the mourning subject to "quietly approach them" (shinobiyaka ni sashi-yorite), with the prefix sashi- adding soft emphasis. The branches beckon toward something other than "their mingling edges promising a future," something Yūgiri can't quite place and feels drawn to pursue as he contemplates their bond. The feel of the tree's mesh intrigues him, coaxing him into reciprocating contact.

FROM VISION AND TOUCH
TO A QUEER EROTICS OF TIMBRE

Even as we unpack the visual politics of Kashiwagi's exposure, the garden scene reminds us that other sensations activate Yūgiri's function as an intermediary for viewers. Sound (accompanied by scent and touch) is a pivotal medium through which bereavement transpires. Yūgiri joins the majority of court in mourning Kashiwagi on the one-year anniversary of his death. Yūgiri's sense of duty to his beloved friend outweighs even that of Kashiwagi's siblings, to the extent that Kashiwagi's parents "had never expected to find [Yūgiri] more devoted than their son's own brothers."[20]

Following Kashiwagi's request, Yūgiri visits the family of Kashiwagi's widow, Ochiba no Miya, and reminisces: "The residence felt quite silent and forlorn, with a slightly ramshackle air about it."[21] Amid insect cries that remind him of the absence of human noise, Yūgiri tries to lighten the mood by adding sound of his own making to the desolate scene:

> Yūgiri pulled the *wagon* [Japanese zither] close. It had been tuned to the *richi* mode, and having resonated with copious playings, was suffused with a human aroma that stirred fond reminiscence [*hitoga ni shimite natsukashiu oboyu*]. *In a place like this, a man boasting a lustful heart prone to heed its own whims might well discard restraint, exposing uglier qualities, and end up making an abysmally tarnished name for himself.* He continued musing about such things as he strummed. This was the *wagon* his dead friend had usually played. Playing a little of a charming piece, Yūgiri said, "Alas, what a truly sublime tone he used to pluck forth! I gather some of that must be stowed within that instrument of Ochiba no Miya's, too. How I'd love for her to grant me a thorough listen!"[22]

Yūgiri accesses scents and sounds evocative of Kashiwagi by touching the stringed instrument. "Suffused with a human aroma" (*hitoga ni shimite*), Kashiwagi's favored instrument sparks "fond reminiscence" (*natsukashiu oboyu*) that coaxes Yūgiri's thoughts toward his dead friend.[23] In plucking the strings himself, Yūgiri fastens those thoughts to something tangible, even as their vibration calls to mind a fuller resonance that Kashiwagi's passing has deprived him of.

Yūgiri enjoys inklings of arousal as he strums the cherished instrument, toying with the notion of unleashed longing. His perished companion's instrument resounds with an insistence that drowns out the distinction between bereavement and libido, prurience and prudence. Although chastened by mourning's prescribed decorum, Yūgiri nonetheless has his passions piqued by the bleak tenor of the residence, not to mention its untended, downbeat women. Inexpert and apprehensive as it is, what reverberates as most queer in this sounding gesture is how the musical object's multisensory breadth can transpose and sustain otherwise partitioned or dissonant desires. Echoing in the wake of losing Kashiwagi, intimate contact with the resonant memento thus bestows a fuller frequency range: a bandwidth brimming with potentialities barely discernable until loss took its toll. Alone, neither intimacy nor loss could imbue such a transformative vibration. Rather, they work in concert; their proximate remove from one another is what activates the disorienting refusal of finitude I consider queer.

Touching this memento, Yūgiri accents the way this "truly sublime tone" (*ito medurakanaru ne*) seems to have waned—unlike the surviving scent.[24] Recognizing the insufficiency of what remains, Yūgiri scours for a supplement: some remnant of Kashiwagi's idiosyncratic contact with the strings that lingers hidden in the echoing wood (*komorite*).[25] "It is the middle string that would convey his touch and yield a truly remarkable tone," Yūgiri says. "That is what I myself was hoping to hear."[26] Importantly, he touches Kashiwagi's instrument in search of some reciprocal caress, and not for its sound per se. Yūgiri hopes to hear Her Highness's rendition only insofar as her playing might bring him closer to the touch he longs for. In this sense, she's just a conduit—like the musical instrument itself—for the two men to sustain their posthumous affinity.

When the Second Princess finally plays something, Yūgiri is moved to stroke strings again: "Hoping to hear more from her, Yūgiri took up a *biwa* [lute] and, with quite a tender tone [*ito natsukashiki ne ni*], played 'So Adored Is He.'"[27] The Princess's performance prompts Yūgiri to continue his timbral pursuit, this time with a lute, expressing his heartache in an idiom that outstrips verbal communication.[28] The lute boasts a sound chamber held against the torso; as Yūgiri's ardor burgeons, he thus transitions from a floor-based instrument to one that is more resonant against his body. As if transposing his sonically manifested desire to a visual canvas, "the moon shone in a cloudless sky while lines of geese passed aloft, wing to wing."[29] We saw this motif at Suma as Tō no Chūjō prepared to part with Genji at dawn. Here, geese highlight the scene's devotional tenor, their patterned movement symbolizing transmission of a message across untold distance.

Yūgiri's melancholic progression through instruments culminates with receipt of Kashiwagi's beloved flute:

[The Haven, Ochiba no Miya's mother,] gave him a flute as a parting gift. . . . The Commander examined it. "I am unworthy of such an attendant," he replied. Yes, this instrument, too, was one that [Kashiwagi] had always had with him; he remembered him often saying that he did not get from it the very finest sound it could give and that he wanted it to go to someone able to appreciate it. He put it to his lips, feeling if anything sadder than ever. "I could be forgiven for playing the *wagon* as I did in his memory," he said, stopping halfway through the *banshiki* modal prelude, "but this is beyond me" [*kore ha mabayuku namu*]. The Haven sent out to him as he was leaving, "Here beside a home sadly overgrown with weeds a cricket now sings in that voice I knew so well in those autumns long ago." He replied, "Nothing much has changed in the music of the flute, but that perfect tone missing ever since he died will live on forevermore."[30]

Putting lips to his friend's flute need not carry homoerotic connotations. And yet, the flute's shape and status as token of patriarchal inheritance mark it as a phallic symbol, a fetish for sublimating desire for intimacy. To blow through it, placing his mouth near its tip, Yūgiri must make more intimate contact than with the previous instruments. Making deeper physical contact with Kashiwagi's most prized instrument ends up being "beyond" Yūgiri (*mabayuku namu*).[31] Whereas plucking the strings of a *wagon* or *biwa* takes dexterity, the flute demands more of the player's body. Mouth as well as fingers must be used, and he must impart breath, literally conveying energy from his body's cavity into the wooden rod's. It is not just the intimacy of physical contact that taxes Yūgiri, then, but the fuller somatic commitment made in investing one's life force.

Breath defines the flute's tone. The texture of mourning shifts with the timbre of each particular instrument. Yūgiri moves through devotion, affection, curiosity, hope, and fond remembrance with the *wagon* and *biwa* to feelings of inadequacy when he realizes his inability to do his friend's flute justice. It is arguably this extra respiratory effort that proves too much for Yūgiri; besides any question of musical skill, the very shape and modality of the instrument foregrounds a hollowness that hurts. Compared to the once warm bedchamber, the perforated hollow object, which Kashiwagi "always had with him," evokes his absence more cruelly than taut strings. The flute drills home Yūgiri's inability to fill the hole that opened since Kashiwagi expired. As such, Kashiwagi's admission that he "did not get from it the very finest sound it could give" only amplifies Yūgiri's recognition of his own insufficiency, signified by the admission, "I am unworthy."

Yūgiri's confession reveals a classic symptom of melancholic mourning: "The melancholic displays something else besides which is lacking in mourning—an extraordinary diminution in his self-regard, an impoverishment of his ego on a grand scale."[32] Here, Yūgiri experiences a masochistic pleasure in disparaging his own skill while underscoring the merits of the deceased as he tries to recapture some trace of his companion through touching abandoned instruments.

THE SOURED DREAM

Having been conjured incrementally by Yūgiri's instrumental remembrances, Kashiwagi rematerializes:

> [Yūgiri] dozed off a little and dreamed that the late [Kashiwagi,] Intendant of the Gate Watch, dressed exactly as he had been then, sat beside him and that he picked up the flute and examined it. He wished even in his dream that the departed had not come to its sound. "I would have the wind, if I may indulge that hope, blow upon this flute a music for generations to pass on down in my own line. I had someone else in mind," the figure said. The Commander was about to ask a question when he woke up to the crying of a baby boy.[33]

Yūgiri mourns not just Kashiwagi's absence but, moreover, Kashiwagi's unwillingness to reciprocate affection in the style Yūgiri prefers. While this could be tolerated immediately following Kashiwagi's death, it galls Yūgiri now that even his own fantasies betray him a year later. The restless spirit of Kashiwagi returns, but only to ensure his line survives, not to grant Yūgiri the pleasure of his presence. This haunting moment displays how the sheer amplification of affective resonances can conjure queer alternatives.

Yūgiri's vision of Kashiwagi revives the ailing courtier in perfect form, "dressed exactly as he had been then," with "then" denoting a point prior to his atrophy: "Yūgiri found it hard to forget the lingering image of Kashiwagi [on his death-bed] and felt intensely saddened—more so than Kashiwagi's own brothers."[34] Not mentioning illness suggests a fantasy of wish fulfillment on Yūgiri's part, wherein Kashiwagi's appearance is restored along with clear, audible communication—not the faltering script or hoarse whispers offered as he died.[35]

Confronting the dead even in a dream's diaphanous space brings discomfort despite all the desire Yūgiri has poured into summoning his friend. This might explain his wish "that the departed had not come to [the flute's] sound." Here, the apparition's statement, "I had someone else in mind," intersects the feeling of melancholic deficiency Yūgiri felt in trying to do justice to the displaced flute he knew to be "beyond" him. Kashiwagi's reemergence to deny Yūgiri ownership of the prized flute manifests a melancholic self-reproach that lodges the conscious sentiment of his earlier "I am unworthy" comment into the unconscious.

Yūgiri's rejection fantasy is a melancholic symptom: "The self-tormenting in melancholia, which is without doubt enjoyable, signifies . . . a satisfaction of trends of sadism and hate which relate to an object, and which have been turned round upon the subject's own self."[36] In putting Kashiwagi's flute to his mouth, Yūgiri tries to incorporate the lost love-object, attempting to fuse the external physical object that exudes Kashiwagi's presence to Yūgiri's cherished internal image of him. Music replaces the words he longs to share with Kashiwagi but can't, anticipating the dream in which Kashiwagi returns to tongue-lash Yūgiri.

But before Yūgiri can respond to Kashiwagi's voice or move from trepidation to savoring his friend's apparition, an infant's scream snatches it away. Yūgiri thinks back on his dream after the baby drama subsides: "Recalling his dream, Yūgiri thought, 'My, but this flute has such a troublesome aspect to worry over [*wadura-hashiku mo aru ka na*]! It's an object that commanded his ardent concern, and I am not the one it should go to [*yuku beki kata ni mo arazu*]. A woman's passing it down is worthless [*onna no ontsutahe ha kahinaki wo ya*]! What could Kashiwagi have been thinking?'"[37] Yūgiri's vexation about what to do with the flute suggests meanings and functions outside conventional use. As a symbol of paternal connection, the instrument should have been passed down to Kashiwagi's son, though Yūgiri isn't yet sure Kaoru is the rightful heir.[38] However, the abundance of feeling aroused by the redolence of precious instruments and Yūgiri's longing for his dead friend marks the flute as an erotic symbol of nonsexual masculine love.

We hear hints of baffled complaint in Yūgiri's question. This slight speaks to the melancholic ambivalence Yūgiri feels toward Kashiwagi. As Freud notes,

"The loss of a love-object is an excellent opportunity for the ambivalence in love-relationships to make itself effective and come into the open."[39] Yūgiri is angry with Kashiwagi for leaving him, but the death's anniversary and his affinity toward his companion don't permit him to chide the dead man outright. The question, like the dream, signals conflicting feelings regarding lost love that simmer without being articulated fully.

At the same time, Yūgiri's question also carries a more jealously misogynistic edge, implying that business between men should have been delegated to him, free from female interference. The direction of this precious inheritance matters; Yūgiri balks at the idea of a female custodian for this bestowal. For him, its value can be preserved only through patrilineal—and, failing that, male homosocial—transmission. This prejudice has deep intertextual roots. Susan Mann explains that sonic understanding is a symbol for male friendship and emotional accord, but also that all-male exclusivity has a long history in Chinese letters ranging from the third century BCE through the Qing dynasty. Invoked obliquely through the Chinese tenor of Genji's Suma rendezvous with Tō no Chūjō, this trope is encapsulated by the phrase someone who "knows my sounds" (zhi yin).[40]

Sound's ephemeral performative nature makes it less stable in transmission than calligraphy or concrete objects that leave a visible, tangible trace. Tone amplifies contingency outside more circumscribed, linear, and knowable markers of succession. This indeterminacy underpins the notion of success or failure to produce the same sound—despite using the same instrument. Such transience underscores how ineffable Kashiwagi's perished sound becomes. The multimodal poignancy of that lost tonality consequently drives Yūgiri to vicariously restore—in part, at least—Kashiwagi's material legacy to his true son, Kaoru. By entrusting Kashiwagi's flute, a resonant symbol of paternal inheritance, to Genji, Yūgiri facilitates multiple overlapping intimacies through a single gesture. He solidifies a fragile trust with his own father, Genji, in not acknowledging Kashiwagi's cuckoldry; he fulfills his duty to his friend; and he symbolically plays surrogate father to Kaoru—for the span of a few sour notes.

As Kaoru Hayashi notes, "Similar to skill in kemari [kickball], musical skills and instruments tended to be inherited within members of family. Only by dying and becoming mononoke [a possessing spirit] is Kashiwagi able to ensure a continuation in his descendants."[41] Notably, this desired legacy is sought through a male homosocial sonority. Kashiwagi's ghost asserts its wishes in poetic form: "Would that I could have the wind blow through this flute bamboo, bestowing lengthy tones/roots for generations to come" (fuetake ni / fukiyoru kaze no / kotonaraba / sue no yo nagaki / ne ni tsutahenamu).[42] The emphatic -namu underscores the seriousness of Kashiwagi bequeathing the flute to his male heir. The dual valence of ne links Kashiwagi's sound to his son, Kaoru, who earlier in the chapter "clutched a bamboo shoot and mouthed it, drooling," while playing with Genji.[43] Moreover, as Melissa McCormick notes, "Phallic connotations are also implied, with the word

FIGURE 3. *Genji monogatari emaki*, "Yokobue Original Painting." Tokugawa Art Museum. © Tokugawa Art Museum Image Archives / DNPartcom.

for 'root' (*ne*), a term for genitalia, reflecting the paternity anxiety inherent in the Kashiwagi storyline."[44]

Given this preponderance of paternal anxiety for preserving long "roots" through the ages, Yūgiri's own shifting melancholic desires and nebulous fears about inadequacy add some spite to his appraisal of women's unfitness. This resembles a classic case of projection. Were he himself more worthy, he wouldn't view a woman's transmission of this object as repellent. For the melancholic Yūgiri, the flute's value evaporates outside an exclusively male relationship, and "a woman's passing it down is worthless." It must be shared between men—passed from father to son, customarily—and symbolizes an inheritance intended for the deceased's son that veers astray because of Kashiwagi's tragic tryst with Genji's wife.

But the intimacy Yūgiri shared with Kashiwagi suggests the flute's possession of sentimental value beyond hereditary logics. The flute continues to bring poignant pleasure despite its genealogical misplacement, which speaks to its capacity to exceed any heterosexual reproductive legacy. Reunited through the flute, Yūgiri and the spectral Kashiwagi momentarily indulge melody in lieu of adhering to ancestral lines. Though their encounter lasts only a dream's length and pressure to entrust the flute to the proper recipient mounts for Yūgiri, this brief interval lets Yūgiri consummate a hunger for fuller contact with his dead companion, which he previously sought through song.

Sensual reminiscences on sound precipitate a dream of Kashiwagi. But Yūgiri is wrenched awake by the screams of a retching baby. In this way, the human product of heterosexual reproduction fractures the sweet fantasy Yūgiri entertains for another man through the phallic wooden object. The handscroll painting elaborates and magnifies the physicality of Yūgiri's mournful homosocial attachment—the subtle gestures of which are imperceptible in the original text. When he appears in the "Yokobue" painting, sound recedes as sight and touch burst forward: Yūgiri clutches a pillar as he locks eyes on a baby suckling at Kumoinokari's bare breast (see figure 3).[45] This painting portrays a scene rife with queer vitality, despite—or indeed, *because of*—the transfixed gesture embodied by the melancholic voyeur.

THE VALUE OF PILLAR CLINGING

At Kashiwagi's deathbed, Yūgiri's actions highlighted the men's intimacy and Yūgiri's dominant vitality. The "Yokobue" chapter immediately follows "Kashiwagi," and its scroll painting—like "Kashiwagi 2"—features Yūgiri as a voyeur. The scene in which Yūgiri views the nursing of his infant son runs as follows:

> [Yūgiri] was about to ask a question [*tohan wo omohu hodo ni*] when he woke up to the crying of a baby boy, frightened in his sleep. The boy was crying very loudly and retching up milk [*tsudami nado shitamaheba*]. His nurse arose in haste while the lady of the house had the lamp brought near, tucked her hair behind her ears, wiped and tidied the baby, and held him in her arms. She bared a beautifully full, rounded breast for him to suck. He was a very sweet baby, ever so white and pretty, and she enjoyed comforting him this way even though she had no milk. "What is the matter?" [Yūgiri] asked, going to her. The commotion of the women scattering rice must have completely dispelled the mood of his dream. . . . The way he looked at her made her shy, and she fell silent after all. "Now, stop that. I am not fit to be seen," she said. Her bashful figure in the bright lamplight made quite a nice picture.[46]

The *Genji* narrative makes numerous references to sights—like Genji's fashionable figure, or blossoms at their peak—being "like a picture" (*e no gotoshi*) and thus well worth seeing, or striking enough to compel the viewer to illustrate it: "It is often not simply that something *resembles* a picture, but that the speaker would actually like to *make a picture of it*. This implies a degree of fashioning and of control."[47] This desire to shape the scene to the viewer's whim arguably matters more when the act of picturing potentially involves not just the objectification of observed phenomena but the exploitation of vulnerable bodies.[48]

While he doesn't bring the lamp, Yūgiri nonetheless frames and focuses the scene by vicariously guiding the viewer's attention. He is the first character encountered by the viewer in moving leftward along the scroll's horizontal axis in "Kashiwagi" and the character in the "Yokobue" scroll painting who is situated most stably, at a perpendicular angle to the painting's grounding plane. Perched at the edge of the frame within this domestic tableau, Yūgiri stares, engrossed, standing as though fused to the pillar. This central structure anchors the interior pictorial scene, serving as a rectilinear boundary between it and the larger frame that embeds it. Yūgiri's figure presses the inner spectacle's border into relief by buttressing the scene from the left-hand side, his right hand palmed parallel against the vertical edge of this stage-like dais. The contact of the male courtier's hand against the architectural scaffold activates the frame of viewing through touch. Vision inspires a craving for direct physical contact that is gratified at least partially by the hard pillar.

But what does Yūgiri reach for? His adherence to the structure can be read in at least two ways. First, it marks his reliance on the larger architectonic systems within which it sits; second, it suggests his susceptibility to the sway of spectacular bodies. The nursing woman seems his most obvious focus in "Yokobue," but we mustn't forget the rapport Yūgiri shared with Kashiwagi just a chapter ago. There, both the painting and the calligraphic preface betrayed a suffocating desire to touch Kashiwagi's spectacular dying body.

That desire resurfaces in this "Yokobue" painting, in Yūgiri's hand touching the pillar. Touch registers a proximate remove by embodying a simultaneous inclination and restraint. Yūgiri's contact with the pillar as he stands transfixed highlights both desire's expression and its limit, troubling a boundary between activity and passivity. The pillar stands as a phallic symbol against which Yūgiri might steady his balance, maintain a fantasy of control, or imagine suppler textures. This touch is ostensibly oriented toward Yūgiri's full-bosomed, seminude wife. However, as Yūgiri has just woken from a dream of Kashiwagi, it might instead by proxy betray a lingering desire for the gaunt companion at whose deathbed Yūgiri wept. Rajyashree Pandey resists an erotic reading of the scene, noting that "what is noteworthy . . . is not the breast as a sexual object. . . . It is the image of [Kumoinokari] as an ordinary wife, comforting her own baby rather than relying on the wet nurse, that the text draws our attention to."[49] Hence what looks like a spectacle of heterosexual lust in fact evokes homosocial longing and a notable exception to the standard aristocratic system of child-nurturing labor.

Yūgiri's scrutiny aims to remedy the grief he feels for Kashiwagi—or at least distract him from it—as he rejects morbid portents for the baby embodying life. By staring hard, Yūgiri can deflect the unresolved attachment he harbors for his beloved companion. That Yūgiri's dream of Kashiwagi fractures to lead him here, only after he's waxed poetic about yearning to hear his dead friend's tender tone again, accents the utility of different sensory modes. Where instrumental mementos allow a sensuous aural engagement with Kashiwagi in the form of posthumous echoes of the past, vision concretizes a connection to the living present, a space in which old ties must be reined in or severed for the surviving witness to move forward. For Yūgiri, vision would thus appear to operate as a compensatory sense through which he attempts to save himself from sinking further into reverie: sight tries to eclipse the call to mourn and curb the prospect of further loss. So Yūgiri swoops in after hearing the baby's scream, straightens himself against a pillar, and turns to stare at the woman to both renounce sorrow and bolster his commitment to a less precarious style of manhood.

Yet in its phenomenological richness, the gesture of touching proves ambiguous at best. For instance, the pillar seems extreme as a support. Why rely on this enormous object to confront the eerie scene? What's more, Yūgiri's eyes consume the baby and the breast it suckles in vain. On spying a lamp-lit bosom lent to soothe the crying child, the scene of breastfeeding promises a surface impression of comfort. And yet whatever consolatory function is served by the sight of an infant suckling at an empty breast is undercut by an ominous unnamed presence infiltrating the scene.[50]

Whereas the infant seeks simple comfort, Yūgiri wants to expel his discomfort to rid himself of grief, attraction, and doubt—like so much puke. But as an adult, his relief must assume other forms. This occurs first musically and now visually. The transition from stringed to wind instruments matters, not just in terms of timbre but also symbolically. We move from plucking to blowing, charting a progression in Yūgiri's yearning imagination from Kashiwagi's fingers to his mouth, only to end—once Yūgiri's dream breaks—at the mouth of a baby suckling in vain from an empty breast.

The baby's futile suckling thus concretizes an unfulfilled desire to be sated by intimate contact with another human body. The infant symbolizes Yūgiri's melancholic predicament of being unable to derive a full pleasure from the desired object he's lost. Handling the flute allows the melancholic Yūgiri to express his longing in a sublimated though ultimately unsatisfying form. The stare at the baby's own frustrated mouth-work only literalizes Yūgiri's own yearning for succor.

Yūgiri chokes back his desire for Kashiwagi. His effort to manage this emotion aligns with his desire to stand straight—at a calibrated distance from the scene's locus—and stabilize himself more than when faced with Kashiwagi's dying, tempting form. Compared to his solicitous lean in the preceding "Kashiwagi 2" painting, here Yūgiri looks like a new man. He is standing, not sitting, and thus his vantage is now less vulnerable. This gesture seemingly allows him to recover whatever he may have surrendered during Kashiwagi's deathbed vigil.

Yūgiri's standing with his hand against the pillar and his stare thus become gestures through which to recuperate a compromised masculinity and to approximate a closure of the wound opened by Kashiwagi's death. Together, the two gestures signal a desire to retrospectively redress these losses indirectly. This exertion of pressure rightward also pushes against the leftward temporal unfurling of the scroll. "Tangled-script" passages in the Genji Scrolls' calligraphic prefaces make this counter-movement most visible, but this specific instance shows that the gesture can materialize within painted images as well.[51] Yūgiri's push backwards, against a movement forward stresses the difficulty of severing ties; clinging to the pillar thus parallels the folding calligraphic columns as a melancholic gesture designed to defer the work of mourning.[52]

QUEER ATTACHMENTS AND THE REFUSAL
TO MOVE FORWARD

Yūgiri's clinging enacts a melancholic gesture of refusing to release Kashiwagi. Since he cannot keep Kashiwagi with him or draw him close enough to know him

FIGURE 4. *Genji monogatari emaki*, "Yokobue Original Painting" (detail). Yūgiri transfixed at pillar, staring at nursing baby. Tokugawa Art Museum. © Tokugawa Art Museum Image Archives / DNPartcom.

fully, Yūgiri must settle for surrogates, clinging to the surface of concrete proxies, frustrated that his dream of deeper contact vanished too soon. By staring at his own son, Yūgiri keeps knowledge of Kaoru's true paternity at bay. Revising Edelman's view, Yūgiri looks past painful memories of loss to focus on the child not as an emblem of the future but as a distraction from the past.

Several elements complicate this picture. For example, the shift in Yūgiri's posture from the "Kashiwagi 2" painting to the "Yokobue" painting signals a reorientation toward time and space. Before, Yūgiri leaned unstably leftward, overlooking his dying friend and literally facing, if not confronting, the grim future that awaited. But now, braced rightward against the sturdiest vertical boundary in the frame, Yūgiri installs himself against the forward horizontal vector of the handscroll, his palm extending in a gesture toward the past, not the future (see figure 4).

This orientation indicates Yūgiri's reluctance to release his attachment to Kashiwagi, expressed at the deathbed when Yūgiri laments, "We promised ourselves that neither of us would go before the other [*wokure sakidatsu hedatenaku to koso chigiri kikoeshika*]. This is a terrible thing!"[53] What sounded like compassion there rattles here as what Lee Edelman calls compassion's "morbid obverse, paranoia."[54] Now that Kashiwagi has preceded him in death, Yūgiri reaches backward in an anxious yet futile gesture to mend that broken vow to stay together.

Yūgiri's posture therefore expresses, if not a death wish, then at least a disinterest in moving forward, insofar as it would mean leaving his beloved Kashiwagi behind. To promise "that neither of us would go before the other" is to pledge to die in sync.[55] According to this vow's logic, the simultaneity of the men's demise attests to the sincerity of their devotion. This does not constitute a suicidal willingness or even fatalism but rather refuses any future apart. By having vowed to share the same instant of their deaths, the men reciprocally affirmed their unconditional commitment, insisting moreover on a mutual denial of futurity itself. Without reading it as necessarily homoerotic, this refusal can be read as an act of affirmative queerness precisely to the extent that it negates the promise of reproductive futurism.

If we recall Lee Edelman's formulation, the figure of the child represents the linchpin of a compulsory heteronormative regime bent on optimistic, reproductive injunctions. By contrast, "queerness names the side of those *not* 'fighting for the children.'"[56] For Edelman, queerness aligns itself with the death drive and is directed against the "presupposition that the body politic must survive."[57] This notion of queerness reframes our impression of Yūgiri's postures and gestures. He is preoccupied with Kashiwagi's survival, which overshadows any concern for the long term.

Expanding his theory to argue against a ubiquitous narrative of procreative heterosexuality, Edelman states that "far from perpetuating the fantasy of meaning's eventual realization, the queer comes to figure the bar to every realization of futurity."[58] This description of an obstructed futurity aligns queerness with an orientation against procreation and epistemological reassurance. Recall Yūgiri's lament: "I can't even make sense of what's made this affliction of yours so severe. We share such an intimacy [*kaku shitashiki hodo*], and yet I have only the vaguest idea what's wrong!"[59] The same intimacy stoking his need to understand his companion's fate demands the secret be buried. If Yūgiri's search for rationales when Kashiwagi dies situated him in pursuit of meaning, his later position against forward temporal progression—and against the "fantasy of meaning's eventual realization"—halts this course.

Lodged against the pillar, Yūgiri stares at the bare but empty breast, itself a symbol of a tempting expectation of fulfillment that in fact grants no sustenance, no true comfort, no realized meaning. In this light, Yūgiri's ostensibly licentious stare might in fact bypass heterosexual lust to instead relish an icon of reproductive futurity's interruption. And Yūgiri's rightward push against temporal progress gestures even further. Inasmuch as it follows his leftward lean toward Kashiwagi in the earlier "Kashiwagi 2" painting, it presses beyond an interruption of futurity to figure the retrospective consummation of a desire to touch left unfulfilled by Kashiwagi's premature death.

Although we can read this motion as a gesture of refusal insofar as it thirsts for the past and symbolically staves off untimely death, such a backward inclination simultaneously manifests queer feelings. In theorizing the possibility of queer history in relation to the politics of loss, Heather Love outlines the concept of "feeling backward," reading "figures of backwardness as allegories of queer historical experience."[60] Yūgiri's pose, situated in opposition to the handscroll's forward vector, embodies a style of feeling backward. Opposing the future, the disconsolate survivor opens his palm to touch the most reliably tangible object available: a pillar that in its sturdy materiality vows not to abandon the grieving man riveted to its side. With the pillar now situated behind Yūgiri in the scroll's spatiotemporal configuration, we watch the mourner literally feeling backward. Yūgiri performs a push rightward—against the handscroll's leftward temporal advancement—attempting to apprehend some more substantial trace of his dead friend than dreams or echoes offer. Yūgiri's pillar touching signifies as doubly queer: it both flouts normative time to disavow the future and sublimates the disorienting pain of melancholic attachment through the stabilizing sensation of nonhuman contact.

CARESSING THE INCALCULABLE

One way to understand the utility of a queer orientation toward the world would be as a means of undoing one's habitual subjecthood and reshaping it in relation to other objects and organisms. For Yūgiri, debts to his family and the crying baby in particular represent the constraints of everyday life. But the dream, instruments, and touching of the pillar introduce new relations toward nonhuman others and objects. These are not just mementos—mere indices of enduring past attachments—which is why the pillar matters so much: it demarcates an interval of tangibly queer instability amid quotidian limits. This gesture of touching the pillar is infused with melancholic desires; these desires trigger an irruptive moment in which the visual vectors of both heterosexual lust and homoerotic longing are pressed into question. Yūgiri's turn to touch embodies a queer gesture consonant with José Esteban Muñoz's notion that the promissory nature of queer politics and queer politics of life "is most graspable to us as a *sense* rather than as a politic."[61] This formulation leads us toward "an understanding of queerness as a sense of the incalculable and simultaneously, the incalculable sense of queerness."[62]

We fathom slivers of this "sense of the incalculable" as Yūgiri samples instruments, indulges dreams, and caresses a pillar. For indeed, while all of these phenomena convey something of Kashiwagi, his irreparable absence means that

Yūgiri's melancholic pursuit must continually confront mortal loss. The very inability of such depletion to reside firmly within a single perceptual realm makes its impact felt across multiple sensory registers. More of Kashiwagi than what was cremated persists in perceptible, if incorporeal, form. Yūgiri's search for solace reads as an attempt to comb an archive of past sensations, tangible and imagined, to locate some more livable future.

Yūgiri's gesture recalls Lauren Berlant's notion of world-making as a reimagining of the political in terms of a "lateral exploration of an elsewhere."[63] It can be hard to distinguish between melancholy and hope here, because both would appear to inspirit the same gesture of lateral exploration: an outstretched palm inclined toward something that doesn't wholly exist—like Kashiwagi's desired presence. To call the gesture utopic would overlook the lingering caution that surrounds heartache. Rather, Yūgiri's persistent, desirous tentativeness—the earnest explorative disposition accompanying his melancholic plight—qualifies as queer.

Mourning enjoins a process of hypothesizing one's way through varied sensations to ask: Where do I belong now, and where should I turn? This unmoored, querying stance recalls Sara Ahmed's attention to disorientation's inescapable banality and its queerness. Her phenomenological emphasis becomes especially pertinent in this context of melancholic mourning. What does melancholic male desire for male bodily presence produce? For one, it excites a heightened affection toward substitute objects and a search for the proper surface along which to impart one's hopes and dreams.

In Yūgiri's case, he tries to make contact with Kashiwagi through musical instruments. These arouse poignant memories of the deceased, incurring unsavory sensations by accident. Instrumental music is meant to fill the vacant spaces death leaves. Whether as an atmospheric resonance as strings ring out or as nervous notes on a flute to which one lacks proper claim, the desire to sublimate the loss makes sense. But what stands out in these scenes are the ways in which those sensible grasps for solace largely fail. Something's always off: the breast milk is spent, or the timbre is unbecoming. Despite these frustrations, residues persist that blunt grief's pangs. A plucked string punctures the numbness of autumn nights. Its frequency can't shatter mourning, but the act of laying hands on reverberating wood can grant seconds of reprieve. Similarly, the breast comforts not with its contents but with the fleshy cushion it provides a gaping mouth.

These male mouths go searching as loss echoes. They make a contact with objects that only intimates the true tenor of abandonment. And still, this insufficient touching has its place. It doesn't resolve the feelings of loss but does allay its pain. The survivors are allowed to introduce a bit of distance between themselves and grief's leaden everyday.

This gap can spur fantasy, and Yūgiri's dream gushes from the rift caused by straining to caress what's absent. He touches the pillar and mouths the flute and plucks the lute, all because he cannot touch his dead companion. We see Yūgiri crave closeness with Kashiwagi; when that doesn't pan out, scrutiny from his phantom suffices. Yūgiri's desire surfaces as self-reproach for his poor playing and deficient tonality. Yūgiri translates the unobtainable ideal touching for which he yearns into self-flagellation, which still counts as contact despite its sting.

While Yūgiri's dream may materialize out of mourning, it conveys pleasure at having the lost love return and reprimand him. This pleasure comes partially from Yūgiri being designated as insufficient. After all, whatever hurt comes from having one's failings noted nevertheless allows for the possibility of further contact. Having the chance to improve his tone and be of use as a mediator between Kashiwagi and Kashiwagi's son, Kaoru, allows Yūgiri to fulfill commitments to his dead companion.

As Yūgiri stares at the baby, its pliant white skin becomes a screen that reflects some partial semblance of Kashiwagi. The suppleness of the infant's willowy skin beckons to Yūgiri as a surrogate body for the one he so misses. The child's suckling shows Yūgiri an image of a closeness whose transposed terms allow him to see himself as part of that intimate equation that Kashiwagi's death had otherwise foreclosed. Like the bawling baby, Yūgiri produces sounds, trying to externalize the bitter remnants of his grief. Whereas the baby's purer bile materializes literally as vomit, Yūgiri is mature enough to encase his hurt in melody. Taking up the flute, Yūgiri is able to sublimate loss through musical abstraction. Like the instrument itself, though, Yūgiri's consolatory abstraction proves porous: the strings' vibration is found lacking; the flute's new tone doesn't measure up. Akin to the son attached to the milkless teat, Yūgiri seeks succor from a hollow vessel.

And yet there's something earned, something intuited—not total satisfaction, but some sliver of relief. This is where Yūgiri's posture at the pillar and the baby's cradling at the barren teat mirror one another as queer questions. Why cling to an object that doesn't yield what you yearn for? Both males here do so because some shred of intimacy survives, enveloped in that contact's lack. While far from perfect, contact with stolid wood or sagging skin nonetheless grants a whisper of solace. Given the stony finitude of death, the textures of hollow flutes, empty breasts, or sturdy columns all offer incalculable comfort despite what they withhold.

Lag is central to these efforts at impracticable closeness. For as much as timbres matter, the temporality of waiting in vain hope pervades them all. Call it cruel optimism's queer spell. Even ambivalent contact with objects relinquished by the dead unlatches tiny optimistic intervals. Little anticipatory possibilities percolate as Yūgiri positions his fingertips along the bamboo apertures, fills his lungs, and readies his embouchure before blowing. On instinct, the anxious infant tries to draw sustenance from a breast that is not his wet nurse's. No milk dribbles out, but even so, he stops crying because the nipple can still occupy his vacant mouth. Empty breast in empty mouth—two intervals of absence overlap.

Whether with breast or flute or pillar, the fit is off—askew of an ideal. However, these objects deposit impressions of density for now, and that counts for much when so much has already been taken. All this suggests that when maneuvering through mourning's proximate removes—its vibrant vacant spaces—taxonomies of timbre, texture, or flavor matter infinitely less than the question of how unassimilable presence brushes skin.

CONCLUSION: IMPLICATIONS OF THE REVERBERANT CARESS

In the wake of Kashiwagi's death, Yūgiri's circuitous quest for consolation queers mourning. The ways in which Yūgiri struggles to make sense of his attachment to his dying companion or to resolve the pain of loss pulse along a continuum of homosocial and homoerotic tendencies.[64] From staring to leaning, to listening, to plucking, to strumming, to blowing, to dreaming, to clutching, to staring again, Yūgiri's behavior accentuates a range of tactics fumbled through to recoup some facet of what's absent—and no single sense proves sufficient to the task. Yūgiri's actions suggest that to mourn is at some level to apprehend the texture of the lost object through a host of interrogative gestures. Touching proxies reanimates what has perished—partially. To the extent that the object itself can't be regained, the next best thing is to caress remnants whose tactile impressions suppress the object's absence. Encountering these textures prompts a host of unsettling desires to lean in, stand upright, or turn one's back to the future. Such contact queers with the questions it poses.

Given all this, what might an attention to queer timbres, textures, and gestures lend our critical work? For one thing, they sketch a frame for apprehending stimuli and spatial practices that fall outside a strictly heteronormative telos. These queer moments intensify synesthetic leakage, such as when touch, sound, scent, and taste meld once Yūgiri samples his dead companion's instruments. We notice the text's granular sensitivity to sensorial perception materializing at such junctures of posthumous intimacy, homosocial or otherwise. To read these touches reparatively is to delineate the affective fringe along which queer movements meet mourning. Such a practice suggests the outline of a method cognizant of the intimate interdependence of sensory experience— especially in death's aftermath.

During Yūgiri's exercise in managing attachment to the absent object of affection, the work of mourning emerges as a queer process of mediation and reorientation. This iterative labor escalates as it recurs, with Yūgiri drawing surrogate matter into mouth or grasp to produce for himself a richer sense of presence in the wake of Kashiwagi's demise. The "Yokobue" chapter underscores the extent to which mourning's labor can be beset by failure to achieve resolution or complete detachment. Even so, Yūgiri's movement from flute to pillar suggests that the failures accrued in the midst of handling mortal loss compel the mourner to seek a steadied position within a space of loss rather than to escape it—to brace oneself alongside the most resonant or rigid objects available in the hope that one might reside in perennial contact with something vibrant and sound. Yūgiri's gesture reads as queer insofar as he reaches back to embrace the ambivalence animating his rapport with humans, ghosts, and material and immaterial objects. He stares at his sexualized wife, but he also looks past her; he identifies and disidentifies with his own son in the same glance; he longs to touch the flute but accepts that he can't rightly possess it. In this sense, his melancholic labor takes embodied shape in a queer gesture "that signals a refusal of a certain kind of finitude."[65]

In reading this account of Yūgiri's negotiation of the anguish that follows Kashiwagi's death, I have tried to depict the work of mourning as a practice of reorienting attachments that reverberate—against skin, strings, air, hollowed cylindrical wood or its dense rectangular counterpart. I have stressed a queer erotics of mediating loss orally, aurally, and haptically. Kashiwagi's death produces a queer texture of loss that should be felt within the context of the homosocial intimacy he shares with Yūgiri. What this episode suggests, then, is that the work of mourning involves not just severing enduring interpersonal attachments but also reorienting perception to remediate loss. This remediation alters the materiality and position of both the mourning subject and the mourned object, transposing them to make loss more palatable, more sonorous, and more smooth, as the lost object is simultaneously coveted and disavowed.

These pivots gesture toward queer attachments that push longing subjects askew of futurity's telos, orienting them in the here and now to magnify what Merleau-Ponty called "the vital experience of giddiness and nausea, which is the awareness of our contingency."[66] Such contingency suffuses Yūgiri's melancholic scenario as a constitutive element whose "vital experience" is played out aurally and haptically as a queer practice of turning to reckon with loss and feel one's way past it.

The sense of contingency that resonates throughout both scenes of Yūgiri's voyeurism draws Yūgiri toward the bedridden Kashiwagi and makes him reach for support as he stands and tries to reside stably within the space left vacant by Kashiwagi's death. Allure couples with repulsion in that mournful space of visceral contingency. However, we nevertheless observe here how death enables a posthumous queer intimacy to take hold.

Through the remnants of Kashiwagi's life, Yūgiri satisfies desires for a closeness that was unattainable when his companion lived. Specifically, the sensuous contact Yūgiri indulges in with Kashiwagi's cherished instruments was formerly withheld. But now, within extended intervals of reminiscence, their timbre can be savored at will, and amply, albeit with the risk of phantasmic reprimand lurking. Even as the dream of Kashiwagi seems to spoil Yūgiri's reverie, the aural, oral, and tactile stimuli he absorbs exceed the scopic fixity enforced at his companion's deathbed. These sensations contribute to a more disorienting—and indeed more *vital*—impression of Kashiwagi's postmortem resonance.

An awareness of this type of phenomenological contingency should make us rethink how we oversee our scenes of analysis. Our goal should not be to unify readings but rather to find ways of letting them unspool in less foreseeable ways. Hence a heightened sensitivity to Heian cultural production's queer texture might allow us to perceive gestures that surface only to flee our grasp—like restless apparitions—leaving traces whose refusals of finitude encourage us to pursue a vibrant contact without capture.

Conclusion

Learning from Loss

We've visited a range of settings to address questions posed by *Genji*'s queer gestures only to arrive at a provisional endpoint. These readings only scratch the surface of a vast area of inquiry into the relation between intimacy and loss, to say nothing of larger concerns regarding discipline and method. That said, several insights bear revisiting as this exploration ends. I'd therefore like to consider what we can learn from *Genji*'s queering of intimacy and loss. Let's work backward.

Chapter 5 demonstrated how touch reverberates, discharging sensual repercussions irreducible to rational or intentional delimiting. Tactile engagement with the texture of objects undoes dominative styles of regarding the world. Melancholic fixations aside, touch grounds an altered self-regard that, unlike Yūgiri's experience, needn't require self-abasement. If we forego his loathing, we might discover a beneficial humility through praxis. Musical instruments amplify Yūgiri's grief, but transposed to a different register, they might allow a generous reconsideration of his skill unburdened by regret. What might've happened had he not stopped playing? So let's play the music through and see if it doesn't lend some more viable perspective on the value of our lives and efforts. Not playing to recapture what has been irrevocably lost but rather playing to retrieve from the present less remorseful resources for thriving.

Chapter 4 examined how privation in exile can connect men physically, emotionally, and textually. Exile's punitive displacement from the Capital seeds a reparative potential for intersubjective and intertextual intimacies to take root—beyond the domain of sexuality or textuality per se. Nourished by an oceanic expanse, the microaggressions germane to the paranoia of courtier life evaporate. One lesson here is that spatial and social constraints can foreclose capacities for creative modes of affiliation and artistry. Yet the energies generated through creative work reach leagues beyond the site of dislocation. Home, for all its comforts, swarms with quotidian restrictions. So when Tō no Chūjō heads home, he keeps turning to wonder what might bloom outside its confines. The recursive quality of this questioning compels me. Eroticism and longing fuel the gesture but can't delimit its momentum. This apprehensive gesture shows that Tō no Chūjō is no longer preoccupied with childish gotcha games and chiding that shroud loneliness and envy. Instructively, in Tō no Chūjō's departure from exile, we witness a will to power fade.

Suetsumuhana is my favorite character. Chapter 3 celebrates her beleaguered queer sensibility. Maybe it's my penchant for oddball underdogs, but I empathize with her and like her offbeat style. I appreciate the cadence of her living, which looks late only because haters loathe someone dwelling in the world in a manner heedless of the breakneck tempo of their own insecurities. Hence Chapter 3 is dedicated to the Suetsumuhanas of the world: all the folks out there trying to do their own thing and who aren't actually lost—despite the din that tries to drown out their contentment and convince them otherwise. Vernacular translation: "Haters gonna hate." So let them hate. Put their hatred to work; metabolize it. Let them do their jobs, then redirect that energy. If they whine, just remember: troll tears are *delicious*.

I was a Suetsumuhana once. I think of the bullies and bully wannabes who called me "faggot" growing up—not for being gay but for being smart. Intelligence was offensive because of White supremacist legacies we didn't comprehended because they so saturated the banality of Chicago life for us. That homophobia was normalized, sutured to racial and class-based formations we lacked conceptual and material tools to theorize or evade as children. I'm forty-one now, and some of those grade school classmates are dead. In this light, Suetsumuhana's lesson echoes as "Do you."

Chapter 2 recounts how Genji's machismo gets splintered, along with his ability to orient himself without admitting a debilitating awareness of his own contingency. Genji's aspirations for dominion are nipped in the bud as he gets lost and is rescued by his manservant. Genji learns the hard way not to let his reach exceed his grasp—especially when jealous spirits are involved. Although he ignores this lesson, "Yūgao" tells a cautionary tale, recommending against haughty incursions. Here, *queer* names a reoriented perspective and priorities, and a humbled acceptance of help in surviving the darkness.

Chapter 1 outlined contemporary queer theoretical interpretations alongside premodern accounts that both parallel and challenge modern assumptions regarding the politics of subjectivity, textuality, and disciplinarity. Here, *queer* and *Genji* become provocations to rethink our sense of both notions through a genealogical examination of their cultural assumptions, blind spots, and geopolitical baggage.

LARGER LESSONS

These little lessons kindle larger questions. How does *Genji* queer? And where might queer readings of this text push the field of premodern Japanese literary studies? In the spirit of Ruthie Gilmore's definition of racism as "the state-sanctioned or extralegal production and exploitation of group-differentiated vulnerability to premature death," we might say that Murasaki Shikibu's text highlights the calibrated, disproportionate exposure of vulnerable bodies to privation and premature death.[1] Whether it be Genji's mother, Kashiwagi, Yūgao, Aoi, Murasaki, or Genji himself, several protagonists suffer forfeitures of stature and vitality from micropolitical violences indebted to patriarchal domination. In response, *Genji* delineates necropolitical sinews striating the Heian body politic. The narrative queers by casting into radical doubt the logics perpetuating this system and by charting the depleting, often fatal violence through which it secures optimal function.

Genji queers to the extent that its fictional portrayals undermine the validity and trajectory of imperial authority. These depictions present Genji as a charismatic, deeply *problematic* product and perpetrator of violence shaped by imperial ambitions. The text queers by foregrounding the fictive, aspirational nature of normative and normalizing claims, giving the lie to systems that subsidize normalcy's enforcement. It deploys figures like Genji to interrupt facile notions of order, prompting readers to question dominant logics of family, romance, reproduction, power, movement, virtue, affection, striving, and feeling. To echo José Esteban Muñoz's gesture, *Genji* queers by refusing the finitude of the systemic inequalities that underpinned its circulation within Heian society.

The field of premodern Japanese literary studies could learn from such a refusal. For a queer impulse toward questioning pressures to conform applies not just to *Genji*'s fictional realm but also to the actual world in which we undertake our intellectual work. We should therefore preserve a wary stance toward structures, tendencies, and rubrics whose investments in normativity (tacit or otherwise) dictate what questions get asked or don't—and by whom—to say nothing of how that questioning takes place. What then might be lost or gained by queering Heian literary studies? One risk would involve estranging familiar conceptual routines. Another would entail revising the perimeter of queer theory's comfort zone past a modern, Anglophone purview. Both risks deserve exploration through critical gestures that oppose the respective hermeticism of each territory.

This book can only pursue that project piecemeal. Granted, I'm more concerned about the fate of premodern Japanese literary studies than I am about the future of queer theory. But by the same token, those of us interested in attempting interventions in either field should locate ways to continue queering queer theory, by reminding it of other archives and experiences that fail—in conceptually generative ways—to align with activism, discrimination, legal discourse, or concerns with sexual identity, orientation, or preference that feel most familiar to us today.

The goal would be to vitalize questioning, fostering a spectrum of perspectives rather than policing such views under the aegis of academic discipline—or, for that matter, rather than adopting a self-congratulatory progressivism whose conception of *queer*'s utility has proved myopic in its presentist agenda. We'd lose the coziest claims to expertise but could gain insights whose value is not preordained.

To queer is to question the conditions by which—and price at which—affiliation, productivity, and evaluation occur. Queer inquiry remains dubious of protocols for producing instrumental knowledge, having no time for concerns tied to discipline for discipline's sake. To queer the discipline would be to avoid conventions trained on insular expertise to the impoverishment of more worldly discernment. Masao Miyoshi explains that "we are now experts rather than authorities. This difference is hardly trivial: an authority knows not only her/his specialty but also understands its place in the scheme of learning. An expert, on the other hand, is trained only in the field of specialization, and refuses to take even a step beyond it."[2] A queer critical practice would sidestep this refusal to trespass in ways that ensured a less parochial sense of knowledge work's broader stakes.

If *queer* signifies an impulse to question systems of oppression enforcing explicit and unspoken injunctions to conform, then to queer Heian literary studies would be to interrogate not just the Heian texts themselves but also the parameters according to which the domain "Heian literary studies" directs textual analysis. The field could benefit from infusions of queer critical energy that proved generative precisely to the extent that it lacked aspirations to be productive; it had no craving to reproduce disciplinary routines that strove for closure. To queer would be to resist desires for conceptual fixity—or legacy.

It's because I'm cautiously optimistic for the future that it feels important to look back, like the protagonists Genji, Suetsumuhana, Tō no Chūjō, and Yūgiri do in their own queer ways. I think for instance about the serviceable role Japanese literature and Heian exemplars like *The Tale of Genji* played within a larger modern geopolitical context. Beyond the orientalist fantasies that flourished from the nineteenth century onward, the postwar context reprised this repertoire of tropes toward a different imperialist project. Namely, a focus on milquetoast texts distant from the nitty-gritty of an anticommunist battle for hearts and minds abetted a program of censorship whose legacy far outlasted the official departure of U.S. Occupation forces. Thus Kawabata's rhapsodies to Old Kyoto and *Genji*'s portrayals of seasonal sensitivities and tapestries of romantic melancholy overshadowed more strident political works to help stem the tide of Soviet realism. To assure capitulation to American-style ideals, a more manageably benign brand of cultural production was advanced in service of liberal democracy and its capitalist patron.

As containment strategies aimed to suppress threats of resistance or revolution, this cultural agenda discovered fond fellows in Heian literature and other canons like it. Subsidized by government funding and deployed within the U.S. academy, these containment strategies entailed their own styles of supervision and neglect marked by Japanese studies' own penchant for certain brands of positivism and, historically at least, an allergy to theory. In contrast to the Marxist critical tradition that informed so much of European and other non-U.S. criticism, emphasis on close reading in the style of the New Critics attempted to sever texts' ties to their broader political contexts. Hence notions of passionate, pathos-filled Heian aestheticism upstaged other interpretive inclinations for decades. Whatever basis in reality such characterizations may have had, they nonetheless reflected Cold War desires for docile partnership that domesticated potentially subversive Japanese resonances. This "friendship" enforced a client-state hierarchy whose bliss remains as queer as the 1945 photograph of MacArthur beside Hirohito makes it look.

I wonder about the future of the field as the scholars central to its formative Cold War flourishing retire or die off. I also wonder about those students who gravitate away from premodern Japanese literature. Maybe it's because we haven't convinced them that the discipline is queer enough to merit their investment? And I don't mean in a cheap sensationalist way that barks "Sex! Samurai! Boy's Love manga!" Alternately, there are students who retreat to studying premodern Japan precisely because it promises sanctuary from the scarier world outside, with gauntlets of Japanese language bestowing bonus XP.

Regarding scary real-world matters, I also think about the students terrified to have "queer" show up on their transcript for fear of what questions it might raise. Whatever discursive damage the scholarly version of a paranoid hermeneutic might cause, its parental counterpart could prove far more damning for students. Parents' homophobia and sense of moral and economic value can make it difficult if not impossible for them to view such courses as worth spending tuition on. I'm not sure whether a queer studies course beats out a Heian literature course for Most Questionable Offering. However, it seems safe to say that within the context of burgeoning concerns within the contemporary university and society more broadly for securing a return on educational investment, both courses raise the question of value and prospective utility in threatening ways. Such courses not only precipitate potentially uncomfortable confrontations regarding students' sexual identity, they also out the students as frivolous, guilty of wasting time and money on ventures deemed unproductive according to a narrow, profit-based logic of productivity.

In the U.S. academy, at least, *queer* underscores a luxury already endemic in a less legibly utile field like premodern Japanese literary studies. Maybe *Genji*'s masterpiece reputation helps, but within this economy the text signifies as queer in its ostensible failure to produce a recognizable impression of future payoff. It is under the banner of caring and responsible counsel that parents might dissuade students from entertaining such queer pursuits. More than any latent homophobia, the performativity of logics of futurity resurface to protect an imagined projection of children's employment prospects; for example, "But Angela, what about your *future*?!" The question of value underwrites a suppression of endeavors askew of seemingly sure bets. Come registration week, the Potential Employer looms like a boogeyman.

Not for everyone, though. For indeed, the perceived threat, distaste, or skepticism—or lack thereof—intersects gendered, regional, racial, and class constraints that shape course selection long before syllabi enter the picture. The choice of queerer topics predisposes itself to students whose backgrounds tend to allow for more risk. Class entitlement, in particular, would seem to grant students the most leeway, especially when graduating in efficient fashion feels crucial and course credits don't come cheap. Hence wealthier, Whiter students tend to enjoy a wider berth—a longer span to remain "undeclared"—and potentially suffer less fallout from making less economically rational choices.

One lesson here might be to deflect stigma by incorporating queer approaches into courses on premodern Japanese culture whose official titles needn't trigger paranoia. One could even take up the opportunity in such a course to discuss with students the nature of curricular, political, and affective constraints within the academy—particularly as it relates to disproportionate distributions of vulnerability for folks marked as queer, colored, poor, and otherwise. Although no cakewalk, this kind of conversation could capitalize on latent paranoia to reparative effect. The result could be a critical sensibility grounded in more worldly awareness of how prejudice inflects what we study, how we learn, and how we perceive intellectual rigor and its risks.

PARTING LESSONS: QUEERING THE CLOSURE
OF EXPERTISE

For all its investment in charting a kinship between intimacy and loss, *A Proximate Remove* tries not to forfeit disorientation's generative (and even pleasurable) potential. In this regard, I intend the book to be an intervention that queers an encounter with *The Tale of Genji*, to the benefit of our methods of critical intuition. My hope is that these readings arouse an awareness of our contingency—and of the limitations of our modern disciplinary expectations and investments—that does not instill horror but instead vitalizes our sensitivity to the fissures *Genji's* passages enfold. This seems worthwhile, if tough. Indeed, this very process of queering our apprehension of *Genji* might mean slowing down to rethink the disciplined stances we tend to take.

Considering the question of queerness within the context of medieval European texts, Carolyn Dinshaw stresses asynchrony as a temporal theme: "I explore forms of desirous, embodied being that are out of sync with the ordinary linear measurements of everyday life, that engage heterogeneous temporalities or that precipitate out of time altogether—forms of being that I shall argue are queer by virtue of their particular engagements with time."[3] For her, certain textual engagements demonstrate the collision of multiple temporalities within the now, attesting to the heterogeneity of the present. This occurs especially when "amateurs—fans and lovers laboring in the off-hours—take their own sweet time and operate outside of regimes of detachment governed by uniform, measured temporality; these uses of time are queer. In this sense, the act of taking one's own sweet time asserts a queer force. *Queer, amateur:* these are mutually reinforcing terms."[4]

Dinshaw's approach challenges reductive—and from a late-capitalist standpoint, cruelly *productive*—notions of time, also opening a space for altered relations to time that animate other modes of being. In theorizing proximate removes as queer gestures, my own readings of *Genji* here also highlight protagonists' desirous, embodied, out-of-sync-ness with surrounding regimes: Genji's horror at losing his bearings and feeling as though his male servant has taken a millennium to rescue him (chapter 2); the syncopation Suetsumuhana inserts into the standard love triangle's evolution (chapter 3); Genji's long span in exile, punctuated by Tō no Chūjō's fleeting visit (chapter 4); and Yūgiri's loitering with musical instruments his dead friend has abandoned (chapter 5).

What I also appreciate about Dinshaw's account is how, through praising amateur engagement, it questions rubrics of competency routinely taken for granted. This relates to larger disciplinary issues at stake when trying to study gender and sexuality in Heian cultural products. We should consider two contiguous interventions that accentuate Dinshaw's points: one in English literature and one in Heian literature; both literary and queer—explicitly or otherwise; and, serendipitously enough, both published in 1990. The first is Eve Sedgwick's *Epistemology of the Closet,* in which she endorses "the unrationalized coexistence of different models."[5] Sedgwick had contemporary models of sex and gender in mind, but her stress of "unrationalized" attracts me. Models inhabiting yet not adhering to modern categories vexes knowledge workers much as it does the categories themselves. Opposing the prohibitive epistemologies designed to make queerness make sense, Sedgwick emphasizes plurality as part of a nonconformity to a modern, often oppressive heterosexist logic.

Sedgwick's recognition of the dangers of enforcing conformity to modern categories and desires for unifying clarity recalls the second intervention: Hideki Richard Okada's caution against domesticating *The Tale of Genji.* Taking issue with scholarly approaches to make sense of *Genji* either through a feminist project that highlights the tale's novelistic portrayal of "heroines" (Norma Field) or through insistence on its "poetic" unity (Haruo Shirane), Okada criticizes such moves as exclusionary and narcissistic:

> Despite my remarks, naturalizing and domesticating representations of the *Genji* text based on expert referrals to secondary scholarship as demonstrated in [Field's] *Splendor* and [Shirane's] *Bridge* will seem to many the proper (if not the only) way of reading *Genji monogatari.* What I hope to have pointed out, however, is that without bearing in mind the exclusionary consequences of any attempt to preserve such traditional categories or disciplinary boundaries as the "literary" (with its requisite

privilegings of the lyrical, the novelistic, or the heroic), your representation of the Other faces the prospect of turning into a variant of your own image.[6]

In Okada's reading, Field's and Shirane's frameworks, while expertly productive, nevertheless resort to comfortable categories that efface the text's queerest traces. His own preferred concept, "resistance," might commit a similar sin, though it likely curtails those traces less.[7] Importantly, Okada's remarks bridge Dinshaw's interest in the queer forces discharged through amateurs' textual engagements with Sedgwick's preference for the "unrationalized coexistence of different models." Although Sedgwick was unfamiliar with Heian literature and Okada was unfamiliar with queer theory, both scholars oppose the naturalizing, exclusionary, and unduly unifying tendencies of a modern will to disciplinary knowledge.[8] Although not explicitly focused on questions of gender or sexuality, Okada's skepticism toward "proper" ways of reading *Genji* nonetheless parallels Sedgwick's skepticism regarding unitary meanings and her advocacy for a queer "politics that values the ways in which meanings and institutions can be at loose ends with each other."[9] Moreover, Okada's critical posture evokes the queer force Dinshaw mentions, particularly as it touches the question of estrangement. As he notes, "In my experience, I have found that students are perfectly capable of re-situating themselves to handle what may at first seem alien; not only that, they are often quite willing to allow themselves and their received notions of 'literature' to be subjected to transformation in the process."[10]

Note the turn to "students" here (cf. "scholars"). This turn matters as a critique of regimes invested in limiting styles of knowledge. Such investment can overpower an amateur's willingness to think and feel in more malleable ways than authorities tasked with edifying them would prefer. Okada invokes the figure of the student to question dominant models of academic authority, disciplinary rigor, and scholarly value—models that can, at their worst, twist the study of premodern Japanese culture into a suffocating enterprise for students and scholars alike. In this regard, Stefano Harney and Fred Moten's strong preference in *The Undercommons: Fugitive Planning and Black Study* for "study" over "knowledge production" resonates with Okada's suggestion.[11] Okada's critique shuns the specious disciplinary assumptions governing how knowledge about premodern texts is normally produced and evaluated. If assailing these assumptions makes them "dissolve to reveal the shape of other, earlier categories, discourses, logics, coherences," then "the challenge facing *Genji* scholarship now would seem to be to find ways . . . to make *Genji* strange, to read the non-excluded Other, rather than yet another version (no matter how well intended or documented) of ourselves."[12]

This notion of estrangement underscores the queer potential of reading *Genji*. Let's therefore append to *queer*'s expanding resonances a notion of generative estrangement. The concept also returns us to *queer*'s etymological roots as "strange," "not quite right," or "off-center." This is not to subsume or dismiss *Genji*'s historical particularities under the veil of an untheorized strangeness. Rather, it is to reorient our sense of the text, our position toward it, and our presumptions about what it ought to reflect of its time—or our own.

Okada anticipates that *Genji*'s "unconcern with closure may lead to conceptions of openness that complement contemporary notions of fragmentation or juxtaposition."[13] Indeed, it is this "unconcern with closure" that continually returns me to the pleasures of thinking through *Genji* and that confers the transformative potential that students embrace in their "amateur," as yet only partially disciplined, engagement with it. *Genji*'s unconcern with closure has most certainly induced centuries of expert inquiry aimed at disclosing its secrets. Yet that same unconcern could well authorize an inexpert method that allowed us to take our own sweet time to apprehend more amply the queer forces pulsing through it. To queer *Genji* would thus be to approach it from a proximate remove, estranging it in a generative fashion by incrementally posing questions toward the text that refuse finitude.

Regardless of one's feelings toward the term or its long-term analytic utility, *queer*, for the time being at least, helps me estrange *The Tale of Genji* in what I hope will be pedagogically affirmative, yet not definitive, ways. I embrace both the term and the text provisionally and intently. Despite the tale's distance, I continue to approach *Genji* as an inexhaustibly fascinating realm whose gravity proves too strong to release me from its orbit. So here's to the joys of long hauls and loose ends, to the incalculable cadence of study, unbeholden to any demand to produce knowledge. In the end, my hope is that these readings encourage students to imagine otherwise and pursue a reparative rapport with the text that, in a certain way, kindles light and heat for thriving. For to dwell with this Heian text's proximate remove from our own hostile world might teach us lessons lost within our present, lending us sustenance drawn from *Genji*'s luminous unclosure.

Teaching Removal

How might queer reading dislodge restrictive notions of evidence, empiricism, or expertise—the epistemological assumptions anchoring disciplinary identities and investments? What should rigor look, sound, and feel like if it were attuned to a queer frequency? While I'm not sure, my intuition says things would likely feel different than they tend to now. I wonder, for instance, about how a dispersive textual energy I mark as queer—*Genji's* irrevocable unclosure—might encourage the curiosity of students. For all the formidable research done on premodern Japanese literature, passages remain whose conceptual resources rest untapped because the proficiencies we've inherited prove too coarse to make other futures tangible—especially for folks who've been offered little reason to invest their precious time and energy in this queer little corner of the map called premodern Japanese studies. The most authorized notions of competency can obscure the value of transformative insights. But this value may prove more legible to learners still unimprisoned by discipline.

This book has tried to oppose a deadening tendency within the field to break students down rather than build them up. This tendency seems to stem from a particular machismo underpinning the discipline, one I've hoped to queer—to question and rework—through interpretive gestures explored herein. In this sense, the book embodies an effort to make my current disciplinary home more livable, both for myself and for those learners who might aspire toward something other than what "expert" customarily delimits.

A Proximate Remove revisits loose ends, theorizing relations that exceeded the readings of mortality and calligraphy *Textures of Mourning* (2018) performed.

Additionally, this book has also held space to recommend less circumscribed ways of apprehending premodern Japan. Its approach has refused the finitude of a strain of positivist inquiry untrained to welcome creative, questioning students who "are perfectly capable of re-situating themselves to handle what may at first seem alien," students who "are often quite willing to allow themselves and their received notions of 'literature' to be subjected to transformation in the process."[1]

This quotation from Hideki Richard Okada foregrounds a queer potentiality activated through pedagogical encounters with literature. This capacity for students—and teachers, too—to resituate themselves toward initially alien phenomena and this willingness to allow themselves and their received knowledge to be transformed both raise the specter of violent disorientation or a paranoid hunt but convey it toward a more reparative interpretive pose. Okada tried to locate a viable balance between disciplinary norms and a kind of intellectual work more valuable than mere profession. For him, to stress *Genji*'s unclosure was to resist efforts to diminish its meanings and transformative potential. Those domesticating efforts would truncate or straighten *Genji*'s constitutive queer arcs. Therefore, *A Proximate Remove*'s readings have sought not to deaden those textual energies but to reconjure them. Hopefully I've been able to destabilize certain normalizing notions and chart Genji's queer gestures without inducing the nauseating horror Merleau-Ponty notes.

Concluding this book, I'm reminded that my first graduate school essays were written for Okada. The first was on "Nietzsche, Genealogy, History"; the second examined intertextuality in "Suma." "Good start," he commented, but there was much more happening that deserved consideration. Indeed. As it happens, those essays' ideas inspired this book's fourth chapter. Time flies. These two essays were the only ones I ever got written comments on. This could seem—as it did to me then—negligent and undisciplined. But in retrospect, it has also proven instructive. For whatever frustration I felt then gave way to a renewed sense of what truly mattered in the grander scheme of things: the worth of my own ideas, irrespective of what professorial or institutional appraisals dictated, and the incalculable value of sharing wonderful conversations. Written comments paled against the push and pull of debates that filled seminars and spilled out into countless impromptu chats over the years. At the end of the day, those invaluable exchanges still resonate with lessons—positive and negative, conscious and unconscious—that I carry close in the wake of his departure.

This book lingers with that ellipsis, in what I hope is a palpably reparative spirit, continuing a conversation we can no longer enjoy in person. Hideki is removed yet still proximate in readings that continue to draw vitality from his thoughtful presence. With this, my mourning work is ended. Taking my leave, I turn to look back, and wish my teacher and friend farewell.

NOTES

PREFACE

1. See Jagose, "The Trouble with Antinormativity"; and Chen, *Animacies*.
2. Crenshaw, "Demarginalizing the Intersection."
3. See Kimura, "Love and Sexuality in the Heian Text."
4. Field, *Splendor*, 15–16.
5. Field, *Splendor*, 16.
6. Field, *Splendor*, 16.
7. I thank Grace Ting for this point.
8. See Shimizu, Tarumi, and Nakagawa, "Kuia riidingu," 4, 22.
9. Shimizu, Tarumi, and Nakagawa, "Kuia riidingu," 22.
10. Berlant and Warner, "What Does Queer," 347.
11. Berlant and Warner, "What Does Queer," 343.
12. Berlant and Warner, "What Does Queer," 344–45.
13. Berlant and Warner, "What Does Queer," 345.

INTRODUCTION

1. The "novel" designation stems from aspirations to cast *Genji* as a national exemplar, imbued with cachet bound to a European genre consolidated in the eighteenth century. However, the cultural hierarchy underlying the terms of comparison and the exclusions concomitant with such an ascription are problematic. For a disagreement with the designation on formal grounds, see Miyoshi, "Translation as Interpretation," 79.
2. On *Genji*'s reception since the Edo period, see Emmerich, *The Tale of Genji*.
3. See Mitamura, *Genji monogatari: tennō ni narenakatta ōji no monogatari*.
4. For an overview of cultural practices, see Reddy, *Romantic Love*, chapter 5.
5. Okada, *Figures*, 69.

6. Selden, "Discourses of Desire," 8.

7. See Pandey, *Perfumed Sleeves*, 26–30.

8. Heldt, "Followers," 1.

9. I am grateful to Edith Sarra for raising this valuable point.

10. Stockdale, *Imagining Exile*, 44.

11. Vincent, "Queer Reading," 71.

12. Pandey, *Perfumed Sleeves*, 2.

13. I thank an anonymous reviewer for this characterization.

14. *GM* 1:126; *Genji*, 69. All translations are mine unless otherwise noted. "*GM*" refers to Yanai et al., *Genji monogatari* (five volumes) in the *Shin nihon koten bungaku taikei* (*SNKBT*), with the format "volume:page." Citations marked "T: page" refer to quotations from Shikibu, *The Tale of Genji*, trans. Royall Tyler. I include "*Genji*, page" for readers to refer to Tyler's translation; however, any translations from *Genji monogatari* without the "T:" designation are my own.

15. *GM* 1:135; *Genji*, 73.

16. *GM* 1:218; *Genji*, 120.

17. *GM* 1:229; *Genji*, 127.

18. *GM* 2:31; *Genji*, 244.

19. *GM* 4:174; *Genji*, 761.

20. I use different terms to refer to different aspects of queer critique. I am influenced by Berlant and Warner's preference for "queer commentary" over "queer theory" because "the danger of the label *queer theory* is that it makes queer and nonqueer audiences forget these differences and imagine a context (theory) in which *queer* has a stable referential content and pragmatic force" ("What Does Queer Theory," 344, italics in the original). When I use "queer theory," I don't mean to delimit a unitary category or metatheory. Often, I use "queer approaches" to signal more variance, or "queer studies" for the academic semidiscipline.

21. See, for example, Dinshaw, *Getting Medieval*; and Freccero, *Queer/Early/Modern*.

22. *GM* 1:77; *Genji*, 44.

23. Scholars such as Mitani Kuniaki ("Monogatari no kakukoto," 3) have advocated a phenomenological approach. Regarding how this textualist stance developed in the postwar period, see Yoda, *Gender and National Literature*, 8–12.

24. See Kimura Saeko, "Genji monogatari to feminizumu."

25. See Okada, *Figures*.

26. See Childs, "Chigo Monogatari"; and Atkins, "Chigo in the Medieval Japanese Imagination." For overviews of scholarship on male-male sexuality, see the introductions to Pflugfelder, *Cartographies of Desire*; and Vincent, *Two-Timing Modernity*.

27. See Mann, "Male Bond," 1603–10. She stresses social factors spurring desires for camaraderie among "rootless single males," including kinship and patronage constraints, and a culture of sex-segregated sojourning dependent on male networks.

28. Heldt, "Followers," 1.

29. Schalow, *Poetics*, 3.

30. Schalow, *Poetics*, 83–87, 53, 190.

31. See Schalow, *Poetics*, 116–62; and Sedgwick, *Between Men*, 1–5.

32. Heldt, "Followers," 20.

33. Heldt, "Followers," 25.

34. See Kawazoe, "Sei to bunka," 105.

35. Kawazoe, "Sei to bunka," 106.

36. Kawazoe, "Sei to bunka," 112n10.

37. Vincent, "Queer Reading," 71. He adds, "None of Sedgwick's late work on affect (Sedgwick 2003, 2011) shows any sign of being translated into Japanese," a commentary on queer theory's waning value within the Japanese academy.

38. See Kawazoe, "Sei to bunka"; and Kimura Saeko, *Koisuru monogatari*.

39. See Kimura Saeko, *Chibusa*.

40. Kimura Saeko, "Kuia na yokubō," 37.

41. Freccero, *Queer/Early/Modern*, 5.

42. Freccero, *Queer/Early/Modern*, 6.

43. On the value of indeterminacy within feminist and historical materialist accounts, see Dinshaw, *Getting Medieval*, 12–16.

44. Dinshaw, *Getting Medieval*, 1.

45. Regarding this revolutionary development in the study of Japanese literature, see Bourdaghs, "Overthrowing the Emperor."

46. See Sinfield, *Cultural Politics*, chapter 3; and Nelson, *Pursuing Privacy*, chapter 5. Both of these authors' arguments about containment, secrecy, and contestations over privacy rights draw from Sedgwick's *Epistemology of the Closet*.

47. Berlant and Warner have addressed these issues in their piece "Sex in Public" through a discussion of "intimate public spheres" and the stakes of preserving conditions for the thriving of "queer counterpublics."

48. See Stewart, *Ordinary Affects*, 3.

49. This tack is informed by a historical materialist approach to cultural production that demonstrates the incoherence of discriminatory cultural norms and questions heteronormative mandates.

50. Jagose, "Trouble with Antinormativity," 32.

51. Wiegman and Wilson, "Antinormativity's Queer Conventions," 1–2. The volume in which this essay appears, *Queer Theory without Antinormativity*, gives an extensive treatment of the historical, political, and personal stakes of reassessing this concept. I have found this article and Jagose's "Trouble with Antinormativity" especially helpful in framing the debate.

52. Butler, "Critically Queer," 19.

53. Regarding these mechanisms' hold in the seventeenth and twentieth centuries, Foucault writes, "The first . . . was characterized by the advent of great prohibitions, the exclusive promotion of adult marital sexuality, the imperatives of decency, the obligatory concealment of the body, the reduction to silence and mandatory reticences of language. The second . . . was really less a rupture than an inflexion of the curve: this was the moment when the mechanisms of repression were seen as beginning to loosen their grip" (*History of Sexuality*, 115). Medieval Christianity is the source of these repressive practices. For an illuminating analysis of Foucault's figuration of the Middle Ages, see Dinshaw, *Getting Medieval*, 191–201.

54. Muñoz, *Cruising Utopia*, 1.

55. "Crusading slogan" comes from Sinfield, *Cultural Politics*, x.

56. *New Oxford American Dictionary*, 3rd ed. (2011), s.v. "proximate."

57. Sedgwick, *Touching Feeling*, 8.

58. Sedgwick, *Touching Feeling*, 8.

59. Ahmed, *Cultural Politics*, 149.

60. Berlant, "Intimacy," 286.

61. Berlant, "Intimacy," 286.

62. Berlant, *Cruel Optimism*, 21.

63. Berlant, *Cruel Optimism*, 21.

64. See Wakita and Gay, "Marriage and Property."

65. Freud, "Beyond the Pleasure Principle," 15.

66. Sedgwick, *Between Men*, 1.

67. I thank an anonymous reviewer for this formulation.

68. Heldt, "Followers," 26.

69. LaFleur, *Karma of Words*, 9.

70. I thank an anonymous reviewer for this formulation.

71. Pandey, *Perfumed Sleeves*, 27.

72. Sedgwick, *Touching Feeling*, 125.

73. Cf. Butler's notion of performativity in *The Psychic Life of Power*, especially.

74. Berlant, "Intimacy," 282.

75. Berlant, "Intimacy," 284.

76. See Berlant and Warner "Sex in Public." By contrast, see Bersani and Phillips, *Intimacies*, which posits "impersonal narcissism" as a model of intimate relationality.

77. See Halberstam, *Queer Art of Failure*, introduction and esp. chapter 3. See also Love, *Feeling Backward*; and Muñoz, *Cruising Utopia*.

78. Heldt, "Followers," 19.

79. Ahmed, "Queer Feelings," 156.

80. See the *GLQ* issue *Queer Inhumanisms*, edited by Chen and Luciano.

81. Cerankowski, "Don't You Know That You're Toxic?" See also Ahmed, *Queer Phenomenology*; and Bennett, *Vibrant Matter*.

82. Hayashi Kaoru, "Narrating," 101–2.

83. See Takahashi, *Genji monogatari no taihō*; and Chen, *Animacies*.

84. See R. Jackson, *Textures of Mourning*, esp. introduction and chapter 1.

85. Eng and Kazanjian, *Loss*, 2.

86. See, for example, Love, *Feeling Backward*; and Ahmed, *Cultural Politics*.

87. Freud, "Mourning and Melancholia," 243.

88. Freud, "Mourning and Melancholia," 244–45.

89. Eng and Kazanjian write, "To impute to loss a creative instead of a negative quality may initially seem counterintuitive. As a whole, *Loss* inhabits this counterintuitive perspective. We might say that as soon as the question 'What is lost?' is posed, it invariably slips into the question 'What remains?'" (*Loss*, 2).

90. See Freeman, *Time Binds*, xii–xiii; Eng and Kazanjian, *Loss*, 3.

91. See R. Jackson, "Homosocial Mentorship," 11–15. For the description of the Kiritsubo Consort's death and the Emperor's mourning, see *Genji*, 4–11. On the mourning process that accompanies the Kiritsubo Consort's death, see Amano, *Tonda Genji*, 11–41. Uō Yukihisa notes that the narrative uses death as a plot device to portray diverse perspectives and claims that the Kiritsubo Consort's death influences every subsequent death in the narrative. See Uō, "Genji monogatari to bukkyō."

92. The author writes, "I spent days on end crying terribly. . . . Because all I did was brood like this, mother's heart was troubled, so she sought to lift my spirits by searching for

tales to show me; when she did, I became unconsciously consoled. I read part of the *Genji* plotline involving Murasaki's link to Fujitsubo and longed to read its continuation." *SNKBT* 24:384–85.

93. *GM* 1:208; *Genji*, 115.

CHAPTER 1. TRANSLATION FANTASIES AND FALSE FLAGS

1. *GM* 2:41–43; *Genji*, 250–52.

2. Vincent, "Queer Reading," 75.

3. Sedgwick, "Paranoid Reading," 130.

4. Sedgwick, "Paranoid Reading," 147.

5. Hanson, "The Future's Eve," 105.

6. On the trajectory of queer theory in Japan, see Vincent's *Two-Timing Modernity*, 8–15. For a survey of efforts to analyze queer rhetoric's lexical features in a Western context, see Livia and Hall, *Queerly Phrased*, 3–15.

7. On the terminological distinctions between these and related terms between the transition from Edo to modern discourses on sexuality, see Pflugfelder, *Cartographies of Desire*, 24–44. One premodern term that might be closer to the contemporary American sense of *queer* might be *kabuki*, which preserves some of the valence of "slanted" or "eccentric." See Shively, "Notes on the Word *Kabuki*," 144–49.

8. Sedgwick, "Thinking through Queer Theory," 198–200.

9. Sedgwick, "Thinking through Queer Theory," 198, 200.

10. Sedgwick, *Epistemology of the Closet*, 32.

11. Sedgwick, "Thinking through Queer Theory," 200, italics in the original.

12. Barber and Clark, "Queer Moments," 8.

13. Muñoz, *Cruising Utopia*, 65.

14. Muñoz, *Cruising Utopia*, 65.

15. Ahmed, *Queer Phenomenology*, 161.

16. Merleau-Ponty, *Phenomenology of Perception*, 296, quoted in Ahmed, 4.

17. Bourdaghs, *Sayonara Amerika*, 7.

18. Yoda, *Gender and National Literature*, 34–35.

19. Suyematz Kenchio [Suematsu Kenchō], *Genji monogatari*, xiv; and Uchimura Kanzō, "Kōsei e no saidai ibutsu," 41; as quoted in Suzuki Tomi, "National Literature, Language, and Modernism," 256.

20. I borrow this phrasing from Halperin's *How to Do the History of Homosexuality*, 123. For a literary perspective on modern Japanese ambivalence toward homosexuality, see Vincent, *Two-Timing Modernity*, 1–42.

21. For an overview of this context, see Bourdaghs, "Overthrowing the Emperor."

22. Kamei Hideo outlines trends within this context in "Theories of Language."

23. See Sedgwick's *Between Men*, introduction.

24. Pflugfelder, *Cartographies of Desire*, 5.

25. Schalow, "Generic Innovation."

26. Kimura Saeko, *Sexuality in Premodern Japan*, 41–42. The phrase "legitimate wives" here arguably misconstrues a hierarchy among multiple wives as stable in the mid-Heian context. I thank Edith Sarra for this insight.

27. Gomi, "Inseiki no sei to seiji/buryoku," 34–35.

28. In terms of "sexual preference," Ōishi tallies fifty-nine recorded encounters in *Taiki*: fifty-six with men, one with a woman, and two that are unspecified. See Ōishi, "Inseiki kizokushakai no nanshoku ishiki," 48. Regarding the language used to recount the pleasure experienced, see Gomi, "Inseiki no sei to seiji/buryoku," 35.

29. Ōishi, "Inseiki kizokushakai no nanshoku ishiki," 55–60.

30. Gomi, "Inseiki no sei to seiji/buryoku," 39.

31. Pflugfelder, "Strange Fates," 351.

32. See *Genji*'s "Kiritsubo" chapter for descriptions of Genji's astounding qualities.

33. Kimura Saeko writes, "Textual study . . . reveals that there were two different versions of [*Torikaebaya*], the first written between 1080 and 1100, or possibly 1105, and the revised version written in either 1100, or sometime between 1105 and 1170. Only the revised version is extant" (*Sexuality in Premodern Japan*, 34).

34. Kimura Saeko, "Kuia na yokubō," 37.

35. For more on the rebirth trope's role in maintaining political authority, see Kimura Saeko, "Kenryoku saiseisan shisutemu."

36. Pflugfelder, "Strange Fates," 368.

37. Pflugfelder, "Strange Fates," 368.

38. See, for example, Halperin, *How to Do the History of Homosexuality*, 106.

39. See Foucault, "Nietzsche, Genealogy, History."

40. Halperin, *How to Do the History of Homosexuality*, 109.

41. *GM* 1:38; *Genji*, 24.

42. *GM* 1:77; *Genji*, 44.

43. For an analysis of this relationship, see R. Jackson, "Homosocial Mentorship."

44. Massumi, *Parables for the Virtual*, 35.

45. Yoda, "*Gender and National Literature*," 34–35.

46. Woolf, "The Tale of Genji," 53, 80.

47. Goff, *Noh Drama*, 7.

48. De Gruchy, *Orienting Arthur Waley*, 119.

49. De Gruchy, *Orienting Arthur Waley*, 119. Dennis Washburn notes that "[Waley's] fascination with Heian culture was of a piece with the *Japonisme* that had such a profound effect on European art during his lifetime" (foreword to *The Pillow Book*, 18).

50. Keene, *Chronicles of My Life*, 24.

51. Keene, *Chronicles of My Life*, 24–25.

52. Keene, *Chronicles of My Life*, 24–25.

53. De Gruchy, *Orienting Arthur Waley*, 152.

54. Shikibu, *The Tale of Genji*, trans. Seidensticker, xiv.

55. Waley, *Pillow Book*, 8.

56. Sansom, *Japan: A Short Cultural History*, 238; Sansom, *A History of Japan to 1334*, 178.

57. Morris describes the "Cult of Beauty" in *Shining Prince*, 170–98.

58. Okada, "Displacements of Conquest," 64–65.

59. Field, *Splendor*, 301.

60. Miner, "The Rise of the Radiant Prince," 98.

61. Miyoshi, "Translation as Interpretation," 300–301.

62. Keene, *Landscapes and Portraits*, 34–35.

63. Shikibu, *The Tale of Genji*, trans. Seidensticker, xii.

64. Shikibu, *The Tale of Genji*, trans. Seidensticker, xii.

65. Seidensticker, *Genji Days*, 40, 39.

66. Klein, *Cold War Orientalism*, 36.

67. Klein, *Cold War Orientalism*, 36.

68. Klein, *Cold War Orientalism*, 41.

69. Tyler, "Translating *The Tale of Genji*."

70. Yoda, *Gender and National Literature*, 34–35.

71. Berlant, "Intuitionists," 845–46.

72. *Genji* T: 83, 74.

73. Hinata Kazumasa discusses the physicality of emotional responses in Genji, with particular attention to "worrying" (*monoomohi*) as a "disease" (*yamahi*) that can span from superficial concern to deep mourning. See Hinata, "Genji monogatari to byō."

74. *Genji* T: 328, 240.

75. *Genji* T: 12, 87.

76. *Genji* T: 686–87.

77. *Genji* T: 685.

78. There is an impressive body of literary studies scholarship theorizing the link between queerness, loss, and/or shame. The following lists provide a brief guide. For more on queer loss, see Love, *Feeling Backward*. For the topic of queer shame, see, for example, Moore, *Beyond Shame*; and Halperin and Traub, *Gay Shame*. For more on shame's relation to performativity, see Butler, *Excitable Speech*, esp. 103–26; and Sedgwick, *Touching Feeling*, 35–65.

79. *Genji* T: 3.

80. Halberstam, *In a Queer Time and Place*, 4.

81. Halberstam, *In a Queer Time and Place*, 2.

82. Muñoz, *Cruising Utopia*, 1.

83. See Edelman, *No Future*, introduction.

84. Freccero, *Queer/Early/Modern*, 4.

85. Freccero, *Queer/Early/Modern*, 5.

86. Dinshaw, *How Soon Is Now?*, 5.

87. Freeman, *Time Binds*, xxii.

88. Freeman, *Time Binds*, xxiii. See chapter 2 in that volume for an elaboration of the theory.

89. See Love, *Feeling Backward*, introduction; and Dinshaw, *How Soon Is Now?*, 183.

90. Miyoshi, "Translation as Interpretation," 80–81.

91. See Fujii, *Shigen to genzai*, 233–51.

92. Field, *Splendor*, 27.

93. Shirane, *Bridge of Dreams*, 3–16.

94. Vincent, "Queer Reading," 70.

95. One could fold this literature into a longer trajectory of queer studies, but that might neglect the historical specificity of a postwar concern over analyzing the sexual lives of gay men. This discourse was produced across disciplines of sociology, criminology, psychology, sexology, and professional as well as amateur history. For a recent survey of the influence of such studies on the current state of queer studies, see Love, "Doing Being Deviant." See also Earl Jackson Jr., *Strategies of Deviance*; and Thompson and Gibbs, *Deviance and Deviants*.

96. *GM* 1:20–21; *Genji*, 13–14.

97. On the subject of "anxious masculinity," see Breitenberg, *Anxious Masculinity*, introduction, esp. 2–3.

98. I thank Edith Sarra for pointing this out. Tō no Chūjō has at least fourteen children!

99. Kawazoe, "Genji monogatari no sei to bunka," 106–7.

100. Tateishi, "'Onna nite tatematsuramahoshi' kō," 27–28.

101. On the link between imperial blood and androgynous male beauty, see Yoshikai, "Genji monogatari no danseibi."

102. *GM* 1:4; *Genji*, 3.

103. *Genji*, T: 13.

104. Edelman, *No Future*, 2.

105. Edelman, *No Future*, 3.

106. Edelman, *No Future*, 3.

107. Halberstam, *Queer Time and Place*, 6.

108. Moon, *Small Boy*, 3.

109. Edelman, *No Future*, 3.

110. And yet Edith Sarra astutely notes "that this 'queered tree' is cropped back into (normative) shape by Reizei's non-production of an heir" (personal communication, April 9, 2016).

CHAPTER 2. CHIVALRY IN SHAMBLES

1. Sedgwick, *Between Men*, 1.

2. *GM* 1:110; *Genji*, 60.

3. *GM* 1:111; *Genji*, 60–61.

4. For Koike Miki, this peeping anticipates Yūgao's depiction as beautiful in death. Koike Miki, "Shi ni yuku onna no utsukushisa," 14–15.

5. *GM* 1:112; *Genji*, 61.

6. Heldt, "Followers," 9.

7. *GM* 1:112; *Genji* 61.

8. *GM* 1:112; *Genji*, 61.

9. *GM* 1:37; *Genji*, 24.

10. Field, *Splendor*, 88; *GM* 1:33, 1:38; *Genji*, 22, 24.

11. Shikibu, *The Tale of Genji*, trans. Seidensticker, 38.

12. Pandey, *Perfumed Sleeves*, 60.

13. Schalow, *Poetics*, 117.

14. Tsutamura, "Homosōsharu ni yoru koten bungaku bunseki," 32–36.

15. See Dote, "Yūgao no shi no hitsuzensei," 10.

16. *GM* 1:112–13; *Genji*, 61.

17. Furuta, "Koremitsu no ichizoku," 34.

18. *GM* 1:115; *Genji*, 63.

19. *GM* 1:115–17; *Genji*, 63–64.

20. Murayama, "Genji monogatari no kaiwabun," 99–101.

21. *GM* 1:118–20; *Genji*, 64–65.

22. Field, *Splendor*, 90.

23. Nakanishi, "Inyū to anyū," 107–9.

24. See Ōkubo, "Katari to kanbun sekai," 60–68. For a helpful list aligning the *Genji* phrases with their Chinese referents, see Ōta, "'Yūgao' maki no hikaru genji," 298.

25. Ōta, "Yūgao maki no 'tsuki,'" 133–41.

26. *GM* 1:121–25; *Genji*, 66–68.

27. I thank Edith Sarra for recommending this notion.

28. Hayashi, "Narrating," 87.

29. *Genji*, 67.

30. *GM* 1:125; *Genji*, 68.

31. *GM* 1:126; *Genji*, 68–69.

32. Edith Sarra, personal communication, April 9, 2016.

33. *GM* 1:126; *Genji*, 68–69.

34. See Ueno, "Onna o ushinau hikaru genji," 29–40.

35. *GM* 1:126; *Genji*, 69. This last phrase varies according to different texts, with both "a thousand nights" (千夜) and "a thousand ages/eternity" (千世) appearing as possibilities. I follow Tyler's lead in opting for the slightly ambiguous "a thousand" to maintain both valences. For details, see GM 1:126n8; and Abe, Akiyama, and Imai, *Genji monogatari*, 1:243.

36. Koike Seiji, "'Genji monogatari' ni okeru yotsu no jikan," 4.

37. For more on this trope, see Miller, *Partings at Dawn*, introduction.

38. *GM* 1:126; *Genji*, 69.

39. *GM* 1:126; *Genji*, 69.

40. *GM* 1:127–28; *Genji*, 69.

41. This scene highlights how expressions of grief are prescribed along gendered lines and can prove seductive. Regarding this phenomenon within the context of medieval European masculinity, see Lansing, *Passion and Order*, 187–202.

42. We should note Genji's ability to calibrate his style of crying for different occasions and effects. As one scholar notes, the narrative uses the *nenaki*, or "voiced/audible weeping," phrasing as indicative of an uncommon, calculated willingness to let other people perceive sadness—even from a distance. See Harima, "Genji monogatari no aishū hyōgen," 220.

43. Furuta, "Koremitsu no ichizoku," 34.

44. *GM* 1:127, *Genji*, 69.

45. Miyake, "Yūgao no shi," 73–75.

46. *GM* 1:129, *Genji*, 70.

47. Merleau-Ponty, *Phenomenology of Perception*, 296.

48. *GM* 1:126; *Genji*, 71.

49. *GM* 1:132; *Genji*, 71.

50. *GM* 1:134–35; *Genji*, 72–73.

51. For an overview of more standard Heian mourning practices, see Kobayashi, "Heianki kizokusō."

52. Yi Mi-suk notes that death pollution follows Yūgao's murder, with thirty days, not the standard forty-nine, set aside for mourning her. This period relates more to death pollution than to mourning, irrespective of the deceased's status or fatal circumstances. Interestingly, of the narrative's twelve mentions of pollution, eleven involve death pollution and one refers to menstruation. Yūgao's and Ukifune's deaths are referred to as *kegarai*, or "pollutions"; Murasaki's is not. Yi, "'Genji monogatari' ni okeru shi no 'kegarahi' to 'imi,'" 34–36.

53. Schiesari, *Gendering of Melancholia*, 95.

54. Nakanishi, "Inyū to anyū (4)," 211–12. Comparing the elegies for various female protagonists, Nishida Tadayuki also stresses the use of Chinese allusions for Yūgao's death. See Nishida, "'Genji monogatari' banka kō (ge)," 25–26.

55. *GM* 1:121, *Genji*, 66.

56. *Genji* T: 169, 186.

57. Regarding how this blindness affects Genji's experience of the spatial construction, see Yamamoto, "'Genji monogatari no byōsha hōhō,'" 31–33.

58. *GM* 1:129; *Genji*, 70.

59. *GM* 1:131–32; *Genji*, 71.

60. *GM* 1:132; *Genji*, 71.

61. See Katō, "'Genji monogatari' jūsharon," 3.

62. Ahmed, *Queer Phenomenology*, 161.

63. Phrasing cited from Merleau-Ponty, *Phenomenology of Perception*, 296.

CHAPTER 3. GOING THROUGH THE MOTIONS

1. Bargen, *Mapping Courtship*, 106.

2. *GM* 1:33; *Genji*, 21–22. Tyler inserts the phrase "bosom friend," which, while arguably implied by the text, narrows a sense of the men's potential relationship compared with "companion."

3. Bargen, *Mapping Courtship*, 125.

4. Schalow, *Poetics*, 116.

5. Schalow, *Poetics*, 117.

6. Sedgwick, *Between Men*, 21.

7. Sedgwick, *Between Men*, 22.

8. Gatten, "Weird Ladies," 47.

9. *GM* 1:207; *Genji*, 114.

10. Regarding how Yūgao's death triggers Genji's Suetsumuhana affair, see Ugai, "Tamakazura no 'nadeshiko,'" 30–31.

11. *GM* 1:37; *Genji*, 24.

12. *GM* 1:226; *Genji*, 125.

13. *GM* 1:207; *Genji*, 115. This mention of the house's resemblance to fictional precedents recalls the intertextuality of "Yūgao." On the relation of Suetsumuhana's estate to depictions from "old tales," see Kuriyama, "'Genji monogatari' Suetsumuhana maki ni okeru inyō no shosō," 23–32. Regarding how the dilapidated house motif fits within literary conventions and expectations of female propriety, see Raud, "Heian Literary System," 105–6.

14. The "peering through the hedge gap" (*kaimami*) trope extends from at least the mid-ninth century, pervades the *Tales of Ise* (ca. 930), and intensifies in *Genji*'s depictions. For a bibliographic survey on the practice, see Bargen, *Mapping Courtship*, 261–63n4. For an overview of *kaimami* in *Genji*, with reference to other Heian literature, see Hirota, "'Genji monogatari' 'kaimami' saikō," 143–86. On the trope's revision along less predacious masculine lines, see Sarra, *Fictions of Femininity*, 230–43. See also, Mostow, "Female Readers," esp. 159–65.

15. Bargen, *Mapping Courtship*, 58.

16. Sarra, *Fictions of Femininity*, 26.

17. *GM* 1:208–9; *Genji*, 115–16.

18. *Genji* T: 115.

19. Bargen, *Mapping Courtship*, 128.

20. *GM* 1:209; *Genji*, 116.

21. Hirota, "'Genji monogatari' ni okeru yōshiki to shite no kaimami," 174–78.

22. This nested *kaimami*-esque dynamic raises questions about feminine interiority and agency. Suetsumuhana's case highlights this interiority as a quality potentially overshadowed by the men's homosocial competition. Edith Sarra rightly resists the inclination to unwittingly assume the feminine position to be one of passive objectification or a desire to avoid being seen. Indeed, the events in "Suetsumuhana" are framed by active homosocial gazing of a feminine narrator and gentlewomen who scorn Suetsumuhana. See Sarra, *Fictions of Femininity*, 232–35.

23. Tyler, "Lady Murasaki," 73–74.

24. Tyler, "Lady Murasaki," 73–74.

25. Okada, *Figures*, 11.

26. Regarding the dynamic between central/internal and peripheral/external spaces, see Yasuhara et al., "1–3 'Genji monogatari' ni okeru 'oku' to 'hashi,'" 11–14.

27. *GM* 1:208; *Genji*, 115.

28. *GM* 1:208; *Genji*, 115.

29. *GM* 1:208; *Genji*, 116.

30. *GM* 1:208; *Genji*, 116.

31. *GM* 1:209; *Genji*, 116.

32. *GM* 1:209; *Genji*, 116.

33. See Heldt, "Followers."

34. Heldt, "Followers," 14.

35. *GM* 1:209; *Genji* 116.

36. *GM* 1:209; *Genji*, 116.

37. Both the titles of Secretary Captain and Captain in the Palace Guard fall within the junior fourth-rank, lower grade. But Tō no Chūjō possesses the added title of Secretary, edging Genji out.

38. *GM* 1:209; *Genji*, 116.

39. *GM* 1:208; *Genji*, 116.

40. *GM* 1:209–10; *Genji*, 116. "*On fuedomo fukisusabite*" connotes both playfulness and violence.

41. *GM* 1:209; *Genji* 116.

42. Edith Sarra, personal communication, April 9, 2016.

43. *GM* 1:209; *Genji* 116.

44. No women in *Genji* play flute; it is gendered masculine.

45. *GM* 1:210; *Genji* 116.

46. Kojima Shigekazu, "Genji monogatari kōjō no jikū to sono henyō," 2.

47. *GM* 1:210–11; *Genji* 117.

48. *GM* 1:210; *Genji*, 117.

49. *GM* 1:211; *Genji*, 117.

50. *GM* 1:211; *Genji*, 117.

51. *GM* 1:209; *Genji*, 116.

52. *GM* 1:212; *Genji*, 118.

53. *GM* 1:212; *Genji*, 118.

54. *GM* 1:226–27; *Genji*, 125.

55. *GM* 1:226; *Genji*, 125.

56. *GM* 1:226–27.

57. *GM* 1:213; *Genji*, 118.

58. *GM* 1:216; *Genji*, 119–20.

59. *GM* 1:225; *Genji*, 124.

60. *GM* 1:224; *Genji*, 124.

61. *GM* 1:224; *Genji*, 124.

62. Sasatani Tomoyo reads the nose as an intensely corporeal symbol of externality (*gaibusei*) that Genji abjects to fabricate his Rokujō-in paradise. See Sasatani, "Suetsumu-hana no 'hana,'" 12.

63. *GM* 1:224; *Genji*, 124.

64. *GM* 1:226; *Genji*, 125.

65. *GM* 1:226; *Genji*, 125.

66. See *Genji*, chapters 8–10.

67. *GM* 1:226; *Genji*, 125.

68. *GM* 1:216; *Genji*, 120.

69. *Genji*, 114.

70. For an analysis of these women's life choices, emphasizing the themes of impermanence, stagnation, and death, see Kamiyama, "Genji monogatari kenkyū."

71. *GM* 1:216; *Genji*, 120.

72. Koike Seiji, "'Genji monogatari' ni okeru yotsu no jikan," 5–6.

73. Koike Seiji, "'Genji monogatari' ni okeru yotsu no jikan," 11.

74. *Genji*, 124.

75. *GM* 1:224; *Genji*, 124.

76. *GM* 1:220; *Genji*, 122.

77. *GM* 1:217; *Genji*, 120.

78. *GM* 1:217; *Genji*, 120.

79. *GM* 1:218; *Genji*, 120–21.

80. *Genji*, 120.

81. *GM* 1:229–30; *Genji*, 127.

82. *GM* 1:229; *Genji*, 127.

83. *GM* 1:229; *Genji*, 127. On the "Chinese robe" (*karakoromo*) image in *Genji* and *waka*, see Ueta, "'Genji monogatari' to 'karakoromo.'"

84. *Genji*, 127.

85. Childs, "Coercive Courtship," 127.

86. Childs, "Coercive Courtship," 127–28.

87. *GM* 1: 217–18; *Genji* T: 120.

88. *GM* 1:218–19; *Genji* T: 121.

89. *GM* 1:225; *Genji*, 124.

90. Freud, *Group Psychology*, 81–82.

91. Freud, *Group Psychology*, 63–64.

92. *GM* 1:224; *Genji*, 124. The exceedingly rare "*sarabohu*" links Suetsumuhana to the queer figure Kashiwagi.

93. Butler, *Bodies That Matter*, 95, italics in the original.

94. Butler, *Bodies That Matter*, 94–95.

95. *GM* 1:225; *Genji*, 124.

96. Suetsumuhana resembles women in *Genji* who "hate reproduction" (*seishoku ken'o*) and therefore exclude themselves via Buddhist rites or negligent courtship to avoid subjection to Heian economies. See Nishihara, "'Genji monogatari' no seishoku ken'o."

97. Pandey, *Perfumed Sleeves*, 27.

98. Pandey, *Perfumed Sleeves*, 27.

99. Kahan, *Celibacies*, 4.

100. Following Genji's exile, Suetsumuhana wins restoration of her manor once "Genji appeared from nowhere to see loyally to her needs" (*Genji*, T: 301). I thank Charo D'Etcheverry for this detail.

101. Halberstam, *Queer Time and Place*, 1.

102. Halberstam, *Queer Time and Place*, 1.

CHAPTER 4. QUEER AFFECTIONS IN EXILE

1. See *Genji* T: 217–20.

2. Stockdale, *Imagining*, 2.

3. Charo D'Ectheverry, personal communication, April 9, 2016.

4. Butler and Athanasiou, *Dispossession*, 3.

5. For an overview of exile's significance in Japanese literature and aristocratic consciousness, see Yamaoka, "Bungaku no hassei to kishu ryūritan."

6. Shirane, *Bridge*, 22.

7. Halberstam, *Queer Art of Failure*, 2–3.

8. Kawashima, *Writing Margins*, 12.

9. Stockdale, *Imagining*, 13.

10. See Mann, "Male Bond"; and Heldt, "Between Followers and Friends."

11. Okada, "Displacements of Conquest," 67.

12. Stockdale, *Imagining*, 44, 48.

13. Heldt, "Between Followers and Friends," 5.

14. I thank an anonymous reviewer for this phrasing.

15. *GM* 2:4; *Genji*, 229.

16. *GM* 2:4–5; *Genji*, 229.

17. Tyler notes that "Heian law allowed a man to take his wife into exile, but Genji seems to mean that no one had ever actually done so." *Genji* T: 233n8.

18. *GM* 2:5; *Genji*, 229. Tyler's "many of the ladies he had known even in passing" and Seidensticker's "there were women who" (Shikibu, *The Tale of Genji*, trans. Seidensticker, 220) both specify as female entities whose sex the original leaves unspecified. While mention of Hanachirusato's sadness just before this sentence makes further description of other women's grief plausible, the terms *tokorodokoro* and *hito* can just as well suggest men as belonging to the ranks of "severely heartbroken people" (*hito shirenu kokoro kudaki tamahu hito*) Genji prepares to leave. Despite the editors of this *SNKBT* edition placing the word *woman* in parentheses to gloss the vague phrase (see *GM* 2:5n26), chapters like "Hahakigi" and "Suma," in particular, emphasize yearning for Genji among women and men alike. It therefore seems fitting to preserve the original's ambiguity here.

19. *GM* 2:5–6; *Genji*, 230.

20. *GM* 2:6; *Genji*, 230.

21. *GM* 2:7; *Genji* T: 230. "*Yo wo nogarenamu*" can read more like "flee the world."

22. *Genji* T: 230.

23. *Genji* T: 230.

24. *GM* 2:8; *Genji*, 230.

25. *GM* 2:9; *Genji*, 231.

26. *GM* 2:10; *Genji*, 232.

27. *Genji* T: 232.

28. *Genji* T: 233.

29. *GM* 2:14; *Genji*, 234.

30. *Genji* T: 234–35.

31. *Genji* T: 235.

32. *Genji* T: 236–37.

33. *GM* 2:18; *Genji*, 236–37.

34. Schalow, "Exile from Heian," 70.

35. *GM* 2:18–19; *Genji*, 237.

36. *Genji* T: 237.

37. *Genji* T: 237.

38. *GM* 2:19; *Genji*, 237.

39. *Genji* T: 238.

40. *Genji* T: 238.

41. *GM* 2:22; *Genji*, 239.

42. *GM* 2:22; *Genji*, 239.

43. For a survey of the intertexts of "Suma," see Nakanishi's "Inyū to anyū" series.

44. *GM* 2:22; *Genji*, 239.

45. *GM* 2:23; *Genji*, 239.

46. Regarding how the shifting medieval political landscape affects Suma's literary representation, see Hayakawa, "Heike bunka to 'mumyōzōshi,'" 280–90.

47. *Genji* T: 239–40.

48. *GM* 2:28; *Genji*, 242.

49. *Genji* T: 242.

50. *GM* 2:29; *Genji*, 243.

51. *GM* 2:29; *Genji* T: 243.

52. A similar assertion of authority occurs when Genji fixes Suetsumuhana's manor post exile: "Genji appeared from nowhere to see loyally to her needs." *Genji* T: 301.

53. *GM* 2:31; *Genji* T: 244.

54. *Genji* T: 244.

55. *Genji* T: 244.

56. Regarding painting's significance in relation to the sea, music, and dolls, see Kuzuwata, "E o megutte."

57. For an art historical survey of Suma's depiction in poem-based paintings, see Kimura Suaki, "'Suma' 'Akashi' no keizō."

58. *GM* 2:33; *Genji* T: 244–45.

59. *GM* 2:32; *Genji*, 244.

60. Gotō, "Miyabi otoko no ebisugokoro," 11–20.

61. *GM* 2:33; *Genji* T: 245.

62. Kurata Minoru argues that the asymmetry makes the men regard Genji in an imperial light, even as his grip on the rosary suggests his clinging to Buddhism like he did in "Wakamurasaki." See Kurata, "Genji monogatari 'kaigō no uta,'" 17.

63. *Genji* T: 244.

64. *GM* 2:33; *Genji* T: 245.

65. *GM* 2:37; *Genji*, 248.

66. *Genji* T: 248.

67. *GM* 2:38; *Genji*, 249.

68. *GM* 2:37; *Genji*, 248.

69. *GM* 2:41; *Genji*, 250.

70. *GM* 2:41–42; *Genji*, 250.

71. Koike Seiji, "'Genji monogatari' ni okeru yotsu no jikan," 7.

72. Schalow, "Exile from Heian," 69.

73. *Genji* T: 250.

74. For a comparison of the trope of journeying to Suma and the Western provinces to pursue romance in *Genji* and *Ise*, see Okamura, "Azuma kudari/Suma kudari."

75. *GM* 2:43; *Genji*, 251–52.

76. See Sedgwick, *Between Men*, 2–5. Her discussion focuses on the categorical disparity between the stakes of how the homosocial/homosexual binary plays out among women and men. She stresses that the main difference between sexes rests with the men's schema requiring homophobia, which does not apply for women.

77. The shame felt here could stem from potential contamination from Genji's stripped rank and from Tō no Chūjō's crime of visiting an exile.

78. *GM* 2:42; *Genji* T: 251. Commentators note this phrasing as the narrator's excuse (*katarite no benkai*) for omitting more detailed account of the reunion. See *GM* 2:43n16.

79. *GM* 2:43; *Genji* T: 252.

80. *GM* 2:44; *Genji*, 252.

81. *Genji* T: 252.

82. *GM* 2:44; *Genji*, 252.

83. Tsukahara, *Ise monogatari no shōdan kōsei*, 178. Quoted in Schalow, "Exile from Heian," 66. Regarding male friendship, see Schalow, "Five Portraits." For an English-language treatment of *Ise*, see Newhard, *Knowing the Amorous Man*.

84. *GM* 2:44–45; *Genji* T: 252.

85. *GM* 2:45; *Genji* T: 253.

86. *GM* 2:181; *Genji* T: 328–29.

87. Stockdale, *Imagining*, 61.

88. *GM* 2:43; *Genji* T: 251.

89. *Genji* T: 322.

90. On this phrasing's use in "Eawase," see Okauchi, "Kyōshitsu kara," 14–19.

91. Regarding Chinese writing's reception within "Eawase," see Hashimoto, "'Genji monogatari' eawase maki."

92. *GM* 1:134–35; *Genji*, 73.

93. Hanson, "Future's Eve," 105.

94. I thank Charo D'Etcheverry for this suggestion.

CHAPTER 5. FROM HARSH STARE TO REVERBERANT CARESS

1. Hayashi Kaoru, "Narrating," 103.

2. According to Nagoya Akira, the *Genji Scrolls* represent the earliest, albeit partial, version of *Genji* available; no other complete version exists until the Muromachi period (1336–1573). He calculates that the *Genji Scrolls* represent only 1.8 percent of *The Tale of Genji*'s total lines. Each calligraphic tract averages about 10 percent of each chapter, attesting to the editorial process' selectivity. The calligraphic tracts for "Kashiwagi" are thought to be complete in their extant handscroll form and together represent 16.4 percent of the *Genji* chapter they excerpt. See Nagoya, "Genji monogatari no kohitsu," 258–69.

3. For background on production of the scrolls, see Sano, *Chūsei nihon no monogatari to kaiga*, 87–100.

4. McCormick, *Tosa Mitsunobu*, 39.

5. For a detailed discussion of this painting, see R. Jackson, *Textures of Mourning*, chapter 3. Regarding how grief was expressed in a Heian cultural landscape, see especially 29–32 and 54–62.

6. R. Jackson, *Textures of Mourning*, 57–59.

7. R. Jackson, *Textures of Mourning*, 54.

8. *GM* 4:23; *Genji*, 683.

9. *GM* 4:23; *Genji*, 683.

10. *GM* 4:23; *Genji*, 683.

11. *GM* 4:23.

12. *GM* 4:22–23; *Genji*, 683.

13. *GM* 4:22; *Genji* T: 683.

14. Endō, "Seigenri o chōestusuru dōseikan no kyōkan," 23–29.

15. Suzuki Natsui highlights architectural porosity in Kashiwagi's bedchamber, which lets gentlewomen overhear the men's secrets, gossip, and possibly spy on the men. See Suzuki Natsui, "Tokugawa Gotō bon Genji monogatari emaki."

16. *Genji* T: 691–92.

17. Sedgwick, *Touching Feeling*, 14.

18. *GM* 4:39.

19. Massumi, *Parables for the Virtual*, 35.

20. *GM* 4:48; *Genji*, 697.

21. *GM* 4:53; *Genji*, 699.

22. *GM* 4:54; *Genji*, 700.

23. *GM* 4:54.

24. *GM* 4:54.

25. *GM* 4:54.

26. *GM* 4:55; *Genji* T: 700.

27. *GM* 4:55; *Genji*, 700.

28. On the gendering of musical instruments in Genji and medieval Japanese society, see Iwatsubo, "Genji monogatari ni okeru gengakki no jendaa."

29. *Genji* T: 700.

30. *GM* 4:56–57; *Genji* T: 701.

31. *GM* 4:57.

32. Freud, "Mourning and Melancholia," 246.

33. *GM* 4:58–59; *Genji* T: 702.

34. *GM* 4:31; *Genji*, 687.

35. For a reading of these phenomena, see R. Jackson, *Textures of Mourning*, chapter 3.

36. Freud, "Mourning and Melancholia," 250–51.

37. *GM* 4:60; *Genji*, 703.

38. On Kashiwagi's apparition in relation to concerns about lineage perishing and the flute's symbolism, see Yamahata, "Kashiwagi no bōrei kō."

39. Freud, "Mourning and Melancholia," 250–51.

40. Mann, "Male Bond," 1609.

41. Hayashi Kaoru, "Narrating," 123.

42. *GM* 4:58.

43. *Genji* T: 698.

44. McCormick, *Visual Companion*, 171.

45. See Lippit, "Figure and Facture," 70–72.

46. *GM* 4:59; *Genji* T: 702–3.

47. Mostow, "'Picturing' in *The Tale of Genji*," 6, italics in the original. This essay emphasizes erotic relations. Regarding such phrases more generally, see Hirai, "We ni kakitaru yau naru ni," 46–52.

48. An earlier reference to this trope mentioning breastfeeding appears in the "Usugumo" chapter (*Genji* T: 352). For more on the scenography of "Yokobue," see Lippit, "Figure and Facture," 54–56.

49. Pandey, *Perfumed Sleeves*, 171–72.

50. Narrative and pictorial depictions of scattered rice suggest a spirit's invasion. *GM* 4:51; *Genji*, 698.

51. See R. Jackson, *Textures of Mourning*, chapters 3 and 5.

52. A similar posture appears in "Minori," when Genji refuses Murasaki's tonsure and tries to prevent her death. Regarding this scene and mourning work, see R. Jackson, *Textures of Mourning*, chapter 6.

53. *GM* 4:23; *Genji* T: 683.

54. Edelman, *No Future*, 67.

55. Jacques Derrida formulated an ethics of friendship premised on mourning, in which one friend must die before the other. See Derrida, *Politics of Friendship*, 14.

56. Edelman, *No Future*, 3, italics in the original.

57. Edelman, *No Future*, 3.

58. Edelman, *No Future*, 4.

59. *GM* 4:23; *Genji*, 683.

60. Though committed to creating "an image repertoire of queer modernist melancholia in order to underline both the losses of queer modernity and the deeply ambivalent negotiation of these losses within literature of the period," Love's interest in attachments to the past recalls Edelman's antifuturity project. See Love, *Feeling Backward*, 5.

61. Muñoz, "Race, Sex, and the Incommensurate."

62. Muñoz, "Race, Sex, and the Incommensurate."

63. Berlant, *Cruel Optimism*, 20.

64. Sano Midori discusses the flute's significance and the rhythmic arrangement of male bodies in the "Suzumushi 2" painting. This depiction of musical homosociality complements Yūgiri's mourning. See Sano, "E no bunseki," 104–10.

65. Muñoz, *Cruising Utopia*, 65.
66. Merleau-Ponty, *Phenomenology of Perception*, 296.

CONCLUSION

1. Gilmore, *Golden Gulag*, 247.
2. Miyoshi, "Literary Elaborations," 3.
3. Dinshaw, *How Soon is Now?*, 4.
4. Dinshaw, *How Soon is Now?*, 5.
5. Sedgwick, *Epistemology*, 47.
6. Okada, "Domesticating," 70.
7. See Okada, *Figures of Resistance*, introduction.
8. In her talk "Thinking through Queer Theory," given at Ochanomizu University in Tokyo on October 7, 2000, Sedgwick described the opportunity to lecture in Japan as "exciting" but said that it was "also sobering to speak about important cultural issues while visiting a country with whose history and institutions I am so sadly unfamiliar. Please believe that the insistently American emphasis of these comments does not represent any lack of interest in the very different Japanese experience. Instead, I hope you will hear my lecture as a very heartfelt invitation to join in a comparative conversation that will enable us to share more fully." Eve Sedgwick, *Weather in Proust*, 190. Given her interest in exploring Buddhist nonduality later in her career, one wonders what resources a deeper familiarity with Japanese literature might have lent Sedgwick's critical and pedagogical projects.
9. Sedgwick, "Thinking through Queer Theory," 200.
10. Okada, "Domesticating," 70.
11. See Harney and Moten, *Undercommons*.
12. Okada, "Domesticating," 70.
13. Okada, "Domesticating," 70.

AFTERWORD

1. Okada, "Domesticating," 70.

The place of publication of all Japanese sources is Tokyo unless otherwise noted.

Abe Akio, Akiyama Ken, and Imai Gen'e, eds. *Genji monogatari*. Vols. 12–17 of *Nihon koten bungaku zenshū*. Shōgakukan, 1972–75.

Ahmed, Sara. *The Cultural Politics of Emotion*. New York: Routledge, 2004.

———. *Queer Phenomenology: Orientations, Objects, Others*. Durham, NC: Duke University Press, 2006.

Akiyama Ken. *Ōchō no bungaku kūkan*. Tokyo daigaku shuppan kai, 1984.

Amano Kiyoko. *Tonda Genji monogatari: shi to aitō no hyōgen*. Shintensha, 2009.

Atkins, Paul S. "Chigo in the Medieval Japanese Imagination." *Journal of Asian Studies* 67, no. 3 (August 2008): 947–70.

Barber, Stephen M., and David L. Clark. "Queer Moments: The Performative Temporalities of Eve Kosofsky Sedgwick." In *Regarding Sedgwick: Essays on Queer Culture and Critical Theory*, edited by Stephen M. Barber and David L. Clark, 1–53. New York: Routledge, 2002.

Bargen, Doris. *Mapping Courtship and Kinship in Classical Japan: The Tale of Genji and its Predecessors*. Honolulu: University of Hawai'i Press, 2015.

———. *A Woman's Weapon: Spirit Possession in The Tale of Genji*. Honolulu: University of Hawai'i Press, 1997.

Bennett, Jane. *Vibrant Matter: A Political Ecology of Things*. Durham, NC: Duke University Press, 2009.

Berlant, Lauren. *Cruel Optimism*. Durham, NC: Duke University Press, 2011.

———. "Intimacy." *Critical Inquiry* 24, no. 2 (Winter 1998): 281–88.

———. "Intuitionists: History and the Affective Event." *American Literary History* 20, no. 4 (Winter 2008): 845–60.

Berlant, Lauren, and Michael Warner. "Sex in Public." *Critical Inquiry* 24, no. 2 (Winter 1998): 547–66.

———. "What Does Queer Theory Teach Us about *X*?" *PMLA* 110 (1995): 343–49.

Bersani, Leo, and Adam Phillips. *Intimacies*. Chicago: University of Chicago Press, 2008.

Bourdaghs, Michael K. "Overthrowing the Emperor in Japanese Literary Studies." In *The Linguistic Turn in Contemporary Japanese Literary Studies: Politics, Language, Textuality*, edited by Michael K. Bourdaghs, 1–20. Ann Arbor: Center for Japanese Studies, University of Michigan, 2010.

———. *Sayonara Amerika, Sayonara Nippon: A Geopolitical Prehistory of J-Pop*. New York: Columbia University Press, 2012.

Breitenberg, Mark. *Anxious Masculinity in Early Modern England*. Cambridge: Cambridge University Press, 1996.

Butler, Judith. *Bodies That Matter: On the Discursive Limits of Sex*. New York: Routledge, 1993.

———. "Critically Queer." *GLQ* 1, no. 1 (1993): 17–32.

———. *Excitable Speech: A Politics of the Performative*. New York: Routledge, 1997.

———. *The Psychic Life of Power: Theories in Subjection*. Palo Alto, CA: Stanford University Press, 1997.

Butler, Judith, and Athena Athanasiou. *Dispossession: The Performative in the Political*. Cambridge: Polity Press, 2013.

Cerankowski, Karli June. "'Don't You Know That You're Toxic?': Mel Y. Chen Talks about Race, Toxicity, and Intimacy." Clayman Institute for Gender Research, Stanford University. Last modified Tuesday, April 9, 2013. http://gender.stanford.edu/news/2013/dont-you-know-youre-toxic (link no longer active).

Chen, Mel. *Animacies: Biopolitics, Racial Mattering, and Queer Affect*. Durham, NC: Duke University Press, 2012.

Childs, Margaret. "Chigo Monogatari: Love Stories or Buddhist Sermons?" *Monumenta Nipponica* 35, no. 2 (Summer 1980): 127–51.

———. "Coercive Courtship Strategies and Gendered Goals in Classical Japanese Literature." *Japanese Language and Literature* 44 (October 2010): 119–48.

Crenshaw, Kimberlé. "Demarginalizing the Intersection of Race and Sex: A Black Feminist Critique of Antidiscrimination Doctrine, Feminist Theory and Antiracist Politics." *University of Chicago Legal Forum* 140 (1989): 139–67.

de Gruchy, John Walter. *Orienting Arthur Waley: Japonism, Orientalism, and the Creation of Japanese Literature in English*. Honolulu: University of Hawai'i Press, 2003.

Derrida, Jacques. *The Politics of Friendship*. Translated by George Collins. London: Verso, 2005.

Dinshaw, Carolyn. *Getting Medieval: Sexualities and Communities, Pre- and Postmodern*. Durham, NC: Duke University Press, 1999.

———. *How Soon Is Now? Medieval Texts, Amateur Readers, and the Queerness of Time*. Durham, NC: Duke University Press, 2012.

Dote Shiori. "Yūgao no shi no hitsuzensei: Yūgao no sonzai riyū." *Kokubungakuhō: Onomichi Tanki Daigaku Kokubun Gakkai* 44 (2001): 7–10.

Edelman, Lee. *No Future: Queer Theory and the Death Drive*. Durham, NC: Duke University Press, 2004.

Emmerich, Michael. *The Tale of Genji: Translation, Canonization, and World Literature*. New York: Columbia University Press, 2013.

Endō Kōtarō. "Seigenri o chōestusuru dōseikan no kyōkan: hitomaro banka no seisei o megutte." *Kodai bungaku* 50 (2010): 23–29.

Eng, David L., and David Kazanjian. *Loss: The Politics of Mourning*. Oakland, CA: University of California Press, 2003.

Field, Norma. *The Splendor of Longing in* The Tale of Genji. Princeton, NJ: Princeton University Press, 1987.

———. "'The Way of the World': Japanese Literary Studies in the Postwar United States." In *The Postwar Developments of Japanese Studies in the United States*, edited by Helen Hardacre, 227–93. Leiden: Brill, 1998.

Foucault, Michel. *The History of Sexuality*. Vol. 1, *An Introduction*. New York: Knopf, 1990.

———. "Nietzsche, Genealogy, History." In *Aesthetics, Method and Epistemology: Essential Works of Foucault 1954–1984*, edited by James D. Faubion, 369–92. London: Penguin Books, 2000.

Freccero, Carla. *Queer/Early/Modern*. Durham, NC: Duke University Press, 2005.

Freeman, Elizabeth. *Time Binds: Queer Temporalities, Queer Histories*. Durham, NC: Duke University Press, 2010.

Freud, Sigmund. "Beyond the Pleasure Principle." In *The Standard Edition of the Complete Psychological Works of Sigmund Freud*, vol. 18, translated by James Strachey, 1–23. London: Hogarth Press, 1953–74.

———. *Group Psychology and Analysis of the Ego*. Translated by James Strachey. New York: Norton, 1989.

———. "Mourning and Melancholia." In *The Standard Edition of the Complete Psychological Works of Sigmund Freud*, vol. 14, translated by James Strachey, 243–58. London: Hogarth Press, 1921.

Fujii Sadakazu. *Genji monogatari no shigen to genzai*. San'ichi Shobō, 1972.

Furuta Masayuki. "Koremitsu no ichizoku: 'Genji monogatari' to menoto/menotogo." *Chūkō bungaku* 83 (June 2009): 19–36.

Gatten, Aileen. "Death and Salvation in *Genji Monogatari*." In *New Leaves: Studies and Translations of Japanese Literature in Honor of Edward Seidensticker*, edited by Anthony Hood Chambers and Aileen Gatten, 5–28. Ann Arbor: University of Michigan, 1993.

———. "Weird Ladies: Narrative Strategy in the *Genji monogatari*." *Journal of the Association of Teachers of Japanese* 20, no. 1 (April 1986): 29–48.

Gilmore, Ruth. *Golden Gulag: Prisons, Surplus, Crisis, and Opposition in Globalizing California*. Berkeley: University of California Press, 2007.

Goff, Janet. *Noh Drama and* The Tale of Genji: *The Art of Illusion in Fifteen Classical Plays*. Princeton, NJ: Princeton University Press, 1991.

Gomi Fumihiko. "Inseiki no sei to seiji/buryoku." *Bungaku: Iwanami Shoten* 6, no. 1 (January 1995): 32–39.

Gotō Yasufumi. "Miyabi otoko no ebisugokoro: 'Ise monogatari' dai 15 dan no kaishaku." *Chūko bungaku* 47 (May 1991): 11–20.

Halberstam, Judith. *In a Queer Time and Place: Transgender Bodies, Subcultural Lives*. New York: New York University Press, 2005.

———. *The Queer Art of Failure*. Durham, NC: Duke University Press, 2011.

Halperin, David. *How to Do the History of Homosexuality*. Chicago: University of Chicago Press, 2002.

Halperin, David M., and Valerie Traub, eds. *Gay Shame*. Chicago: University of Chicago Press, 2009.

Hanson, Ellis. "The Future's Eve: Reparative Reading after Sedgwick." *South Atlantic Quarterly* 110, no. 1 (2011): 101–19.

Haraoka Fumiko. "Murasaki no ue no tōjō: shōjo no shintai o ninatte." *Nihon bungaku* 43, no. 6 (June 1994): 40–49.

Harima Yasuhiro. "Genji monogatari no aishū hyōgen: 'nenaku' o chūshin ni." *Tōyō Daigaku Daigakuin kiyō* 39 (2002): 211–24.

Harney, Stefano, and Fred Moten. *The Undercommons: Fugitive Planning and Black Study*. London: Minor Compositions, 2013.

Hashimoto Taka'aki. "'Genji monogatari' eawase maki ni miru chūgoku shoron no jyuyō (ge)." *Wakagi shohō: Kokugakuin Daigaku* 11 (February 2012): 39–47.

———. "'Genji monogatari' eawase maki ni miru chūgoku shoron no jyuyō (jō)." *Wakagi shohō: Kokugakuin Daigaku* 10 (February 2011): 37–45.

Hayakawa Hanayo. "Heike bunka to 'mumyōzōshi': suma no imeeji ga kawaru toki." *Jinken bunka kenkyūka nempyō* 27 (2011): 280–90.

Hayashi, Kaoru. "Narrating Vengeful Spirits and Genealogies in Premodern Japanese Literature." PhD diss., Princeton University, 2018.

Hayashi, Yoshiro. "Mental Illness in *The Tale of Genji*." *Gifudai iki* 51 (2003): 197–200.

Heldt, Gustav. "Between Followers and Friends: Male Homosocial Desire in Heian Court Poetry." *U.S.-Japan Women's Journal* 33 (2007): 3–32.

Hinata Kazumasa, "Genji monogatari to byō: yamai no shujusō to 'monoomohi ni yamahizuku' sekai." *Nihon bungaku* 50, no. 5 (2001): 27–34.

Hirai Yoshiko. "'We ni kakitaru yau naru ni' nado no hyōgen ni tsuite: Genji monogatari no ba'ai." *Jissen kokubungaku* 36 (October 1989): 46–52.

Hirota Osamu. "'Genji monogatari' 'kaimami' saikō." *Jinbungaku/Dōshisha daigaku jinbun gakkai hen* 191 (March 2013): 143–86.

———. "'Genji monogatari' ni okeru yōshiki to shite no kaimami." In *Kodai bungaku no yōshiki to kinō*, edited by Yutaka Tsuchihashi and Tatsumi Hirokawa, 169–86. Ōfūsha, 1988.

Iinuma Kiyoko. "Genji monogatari ni okeru yamai byōsha no imi." *Kokugakuin zasshi* 83, no. 1 (January 1982): 30–45.

Ike Kōzō. "Genji monogatari rokujōin no seikatsu: fūzoku hakubutsukan no shinsō tenji." *Genji kenkyū* 4 (1999): 202–5.

Iwatsubo Takeshi. "Genji monogatari ni okeru gengakki no jendaa: danseisei no gakki to joseisei no gakki." *Shakaikagaku: Dōshisha Daigaku* 43, no. 4 (February 2014): 1–17.

Jackson, Earl, Jr. *Strategies of Deviance: Studies in Gay Male Representation*. Bloomington: Indiana University Press, 1995.

Jackson, Reginald. "Homosocial Mentorship and the Serviceable Female Corpse: Manhood Rituals in *The Tale of Genji*." *Harvard Journal of Asiatic Studies* 76, no. 1 & 2 (2016): 1–41.

———. "Scripting the Moribund: The Genji Scrolls' Aesthetics of Decomposition." In *Reading The Tale of Genji: Its Picture Scrolls, Texts, and Romance*, edited by Richard Stanley-Baker, Murakami Fuminobu, and Jeremy Tambling, 1–36. Leiden: Brill, 2009.

———. *Textures of Mourning: Calligraphy, Mortality, and* The Tale of Genji *Scrolls*. Ann Arbor: University of Michigan Press, 2018.

Jagose, Annamarie. "The Trouble with Antinormativity." *Differences* 26, no. 1 (2015): 26–47.

Kahan, Benjamin. *Celibacies: American Modernism & Sexual Life*. Durham, NC: Duke University Press, 2013.

Kamei, Hideo. "Theories of Language in the Field of Philosophy: Japan in the 1970's." In *The Linguistic Turn in Contemporary Japanese Literary Studies: Politics, Language, Textuality*, edited by Michael K. Bourdaghs, 133–58. Ann Arbor: Center for Japanese Studies, University of Michigan, 2010.

Kamiyama Mio. "Genji monogatari kenkyū: kekkon kyohi no onna kimitachi." *Nihon Bungaku* 108 (March 2012): 55–75.

Katō Matsuji. "'Genji monogatari' jūsharon: Koremitsu no ba'ai, 'Yūgao' maki kara." *Udai kokugo ronkyū: Utsunomiya Daigaku* 16 (April 2005): 1–14.

Kawashima, Terry. *Writing Margins: The Textual Construction of Gender in Heian and Kamakura Japan*. Cambridge, MA: Harvard University Asia Center, 2001.

Kawazoe Fusae. "Genji monogatari no sei to bunka: andorogyunusu to shite no Hikaru Genji." *Bungaku: Iwanami Shoten* 6, no. 4 (October 1995): 104–13.

———. "Hotaru maki no monogatari ron to seisa." *Genji kenkyū* 1 (1996): 91–103.

———. "Media mikkusu jidai no Genji bunka." *Genji kenkyū* 5 (2000): 147–59.

Keene, Donald. *Chronicles of My Life: An American in the Heart of Japan*. New York: Columbia University Press, 2008.

———. *Landscapes and Portraits: Appreciations of Japanese Culture*. London: Secker & Warburg, 1972.

Kimura, Saeko. *A Brief History of Sexuality in Premodern Japan*. Tallinn: TLU Press, 2010.

———. *Chibusa wa dare no mono ka: Nihon chūsei monogatari ni miru sei to kenryoku*. Shinyōsha, 2009.

———. "Genji monogatari to feminizumu." *Kokubungaku kaishaku to kanshō* 73, no. 5 (2008): 72–81.

———. "Kenryoku saiseisan shisutemu to shite no 'sei' no haichi: 'Torikaebaya monogatari' kara 'Yo no nezame' e." *Monogatari kenkyū* 2 (March 2002): 116–35.

———. "Kyūtei monogatari no kuia na yokubō." *Nihon bungaku* 63, no. 5 (May 2014): 32–43.

———. "Love and Sexuality in the Heian Text: 'Productive' and 'Non-productive' Sex." *Proceedings of the Midwest Association for Japanese Literary Studies* 5 (Summer 1999): 47–56.

Kimura Suaki. "'Suma' 'Akashi' no keizō ni tsuite no ikkōsatsu: waka no imeeji o megutte." *Ōtemae Daigaku shigaku kenkyūjo kiyō* 5 (2005): 7–18.

Klein, Christina. *Cold War Orientalism: Asia in the Middlebrow Imagination, 1945–1961*. Berkeley: University of California Press, 2003.

Kobayashi Rie. "Heianki kizokusō ni okeru fukumo shūkan no tenkai." *Nara shien* 59 (2014): 65–80.

Koike Miki. "Shi ni yuku onna no utsukushisa: 'genji monogatari' ga sōzoku suru arata na sekai." *Kindai kokugo kyōiku* 22 (March 2013): 9–20.

Koike Seiji. "Genji monogatari ni okeru shi no imi: monogatari no naibu no shi to gaibu no shi." *Kokubungaku: kaishaku to kyōzai no kenkyū* 53, no. 11 (August 2008): 27–35.

———. "'Genji monogatari' ni okeru yotsu no jikan: susumu jikan, chōfuku jikan, modoru jikan, kūhaku no jikan." *Utsunomiya Daigaku kokusai gakubu kenkyū ronshū* 8 (October 1999): 1–12.

———. "'Genji monogatari' o tenkai saseru gendōryoku to shite no 'shi': 'Genji monogatari' ha kanketsu shiteiru to iu setsu." *Utsunomiya Daigaku kokusai gakubu kenkyū ronshū* 9 (2000): 25–33.

Kojima Naoko. "Hikaru Genji no shintai to sei: ōchō monogatarishi kara." In *Ōchō no sei to shintai: itsudatsu suru monogatari,* edited by Kojima Naoko, 35–70. Shinwasha, 2002.

Kojima Shigekazu. "Genji monogatari kōjō no jikū to sono henyō: yatsushi, madohi, akegure." *Doshisha kokubungaku* 21 (December 1982): 1–14

Kurata Minoru. "Genji monogatari 'kaigō no uta' no igi: iwayuru 'shōwaka' no saikentō." *Ōtsuma Joshi Daigaku kiyō* 44 (March 2012): 13–23.

Kuriyama Motoko. "'Genji monogatari' Suetsumuhana maki ni okeru inyō no shosō." *Waseda Daigaku bungakukai,* 2016.

Kuzuwata, Masakazu. "E o megutte: genji monogatari no shudaironteki bunseki." *Okinawa Kokusai Daigaku nihongo nihonbungaku kenkyū* 4, no. 1 (January 2000): 35–52.

Lafleur, William. *The Karma of Words: Buddhism and the Literary Arts in Medieval Japan.* Berkeley: University of California Press, 1983.

Lansing, Carol. *Passion and Order: Restraint of Grief in the Medieval Italian Communes.* Ithaca, NY: Cornell University Press, 2008.

Lippit, Yukio. "Figure and Facture in the Genji Scrolls." In *Envisioning the Tale of Genji,* edited by Haruo Shirane, 49–80. New York: Columbia University Press, 2010.

Livia, Anna, and Kira Hall, eds. *Queerly Phrased: Language, Gender, and Sexuality.* New York: Oxford University Press, 1997.

Love, Heather. "Doing Being Deviant: Deviance Studies, Description, and the Queer Ordinary." *Differences: A Journal of Feminist Cultural Studies* 26, no. 1 (2015): 74–95.

———. *Feeling Backward: Loss and the Politics of Queer History.* Cambridge, MA: Harvard University Press, 2009.

Mann, Susan. "The Male Bond in Chinese History and Culture." *American Historical Review* 105, no. 5 (December 2000): 1600–1614.

Massumi, Brian. *Parables for the Virtual: Movement, Affect, Sensation.* Durham, NC: Duke University Press, 2002.

Matsui Kenji. *Genji monogatari no seikatsu sekai.* Kanrin Shobo, 2000.

Mbembe, Achille. "Necropolitics." Translated by Libby Meintjes. *Public Culture* 15, no. 1 (2003): 11–40.

McCormick, Melissa. *The Tale of Genji: A Visual Companion.* Princeton, NJ: Princeton University Press, 2018.

———. *Tosa Mitsunobu and the Small Scroll in Medieval Japan.* Seattle: University of Washington Press, 2009.

Merleau-Ponty, Maurice. *Phenomenology of Perception.* Translated by Colin Smith. London: Routledge Classics, 2002.

Miller, Stephen D., ed. *Partings at Dawn: An Anthology of Japanese Gay Literature.* San Francisco: Gay Sunshine Press, 1996.

Miner, Earl. "The Rise of the Radiant Prince." *Times Literary Supplement,* January 28, 1977.

Mitamura Masako. *Genji monogatari: tennō ni narenakatta ōji no monogatari.* Shinchōsha, 2008.

———. *Genji monogatari kankaku no ronri.* Yuseido, 1996.

———. "Yūgiri monogatari no jendaa kisei: 'osanasa,' 'wakawakshisa' to iu hinan kara." *Kokubungaku: Kaishaku to Kanshō* 69, no. 8 (2004): 6–13.

Mitani Kuniaki. "Monogatari to kakukoto: Monogatari bungaku no imisayō arui wa fuzai no bungaku." *Nihonbungaku* 25 (October 1976).

Miyake Saki. "Yūgao no shi: hahakigi sanjō no wakugumi kara." *Nihon bungaku ronkyū* 69 (March 2010): 66–75.

Miyoshi, Masao. "Literary Elaborations." In *Trespasses: Selected Writings of Masao Miyoshi*, edited by Eric Cazdyn, 1–47. Durham, NC: Duke University Press, 2010.

———. "Review Article: Translation as Interpretation." *Journal of Asian Studies* 38, no. 2 (1979): 299–302.

Mizumi Yōichi. "Genji monogatari ni miru josei to bukkyo." *Kokubungaku: Kaishaku to kanshō* 69, no. 8 (August 2004): 136–42.

Moon, Michael. *A Small Boy and Others: Imitation and Initiation in American Culture from Henry James to Andy Warhol*. Durham, NC: Duke University Press, 1998.

Moore, Patrick. *Beyond Shame: Reclaiming the Abandoned History of Radical Gay Sexuality*. Boston: Beacon Press, 2004.

Morris, Ivan. *The World of the Shining Prince: Court Life in Ancient Japan*. New York: Kodansha USA, 1994.

———, trans. *As I Crossed a Bridge of Dreams: Recollections of a Woman in Eleventh-Century Japan*. New York: Penguin Classics, 1975.

Mostow, Joshua. "Female Readers and Early Heian Romances: The *Hakubyō Tales of Ise* Illustrated Scroll Fragments." *Monumenta Nipponica* 62, no. 2 (Summer 2007): 135–77.

———. "'Picturing' in *The Tale of Genji*." *Journal of the Association of Teachers of Japanese* 33, no. 1 (April 1999): 1–25.

Muñoz, José Esteban. *Cruising Utopia: The Then and There of Queer Futurity*. New York: New York University Press, 2009.

———. "Race, Sex, and the Incommensurate: Gary Fisher with Eve Kosofsky Sedgwick." In *Queer Futures: Reconsidering Ethics, Activism, and the Political*, edited by Elane Haschemi Yekani, Eveline Kilian, and Beatrice Michaelis, 103–16. Surrey: Ashgate Publishing, 2013.

Murayama Maki. "Genji monogatari no kaiwabun no bunmatsu hyōgen ni tsuite: Hikaru Genji no josei ni taisuru kaiwa o chūshin ni." *Nihon bungaku* 95 (March 2001): 86–108.

Nagoya Akira. "Genji monogatari no kohitsu." In *Genji monogatari kōza*, vol. 7, *Bi no sekai, miyabi no keishō*, edited by Imai Takuji. (Benseisha, 1992): 258–69.

Nakanishi Susumu. "Inyū to anyū: Genji monogatari ni okeru Hakushimonjū 'Kyōtaku' nado." *Nihon kenkyū* 1 (May 1989): 107–36.

———. "Inyū to anyū (4): Genji monogatari ni okeru Hakushimonjū, 'Chōgonka' (1)." *Nihon kenkyū* 4 (March 1991): 197–224.

Nealon, Christopher. *Foundlings: Lesbian and Gay Historical Emotion before Stonewall*. Durham, NC: Duke University Press, 2001.

Nelson, Deborah. *Pursuing Privacy in Cold War America*. New York: Columbia University Press.

Newhard, Jamie L. *Knowing the Amorous Man: A History of Scholarship on Tales of Ise*. Cambridge, MA: Harvard University Asia Center, 2013.

Nishida Tadayuki. "'Genji monogatari' banka kō (ge)." *Soudai Ajia kenkyū* 22 (March 2001): 28–36.

Nishihara Shiho. "'Genji monogatari' no seishoku ken'o: Onna san no miya no shussan ken'o o chūshin ni." *Kodai bungaku kenkyū: dai niji* 16 (October 2007): 24–38.

Ōishi Mikito. "Inseiki kizokushakai no nanshoku ishiki ni kansuru ikkōsatsu: Fujiwara Yorinaga ni miru nanshoku kankei no seikaku." *Fukushima Kenritsu Hakubutsukan kiyō* 14, (1999): 47–60.

Okada, H. Richard. "Displacements of Conquest, or, Exile." In *Reading The Tale of Genji: Its Picture Scrolls, Texts and Romance*, edited by Richard Stanley-Baker, Murakami Fuminobu, and Jeremy Tambling, 63–79. Leiden: Brill, 2009.

———. "Domesticating *The Tale of Genji*." *Journal of the American Oriental Society* 110, no. 1 (1990): 60–70.

———. *Figures of Resistance: Language, Poetry, and Narrating in the Tale of Genji and Other Mid-Heian Texts*. Durham, NC: Duke University Press, 1992.

Okamura Eiji. "Azuma kudari/Suma kudari: 'Ise monogatari' 'Genji monogatari' shiron." *Tsurumi Daigaku kiyō dai ichi bu nihongo nihonbungaku hen* 50 (March 2013): 25–40.

Okauchi Hiroko. "'Kyōshitsu kara in no onarisama ha, onna nite mitatematsuramahoshiki': 'genji monogatari' eawase," *Kagawa Daigaku kokubun kenkyū* 33 (2008): 14–19.

Ōkubo Yuzuru. "Genji monogatari no katari to kanbun sekai." *Fukui Kōgyō Kōtō Senmon Gakkō kenkyū kiyō jinbun/shakaikagaku* 42 (December 2008): 60–68.

Ōta Yōsuke. "'Yūgao' maki no Hikaru Genji: 'Hakushi monjū' fūyushi o megutte." *Bungaku kenkyū ronshū* 23 (2005): 293–308.

———. "Yūgao maki no 'tsuki': 'Sarashina nikki' to no kankei ni tsuite." *Bunka keishō gakuronshū* 2 (2005): 133–41.

Pandey, Rajyashree. *Perfumed Sleeves and Tangled Hair: Body, Woman, and Desire in Medieval Japanese Narratives*. Honolulu: University of Hawai'i Press, 2017.

Pflugfelder, Gregory M. *Cartographies of Desire: Male-Male Sexuality in Japanese Discourse, 1600–1950*. Berkeley: University of California Press, 2007.

———. "Strange Fates: Sex, Gender, and Sexuality in *Torikaebaya monogatari*." *Monumenta Nipponica* 47, no. 3 (Autumn 1992): 347–68.

Raud, Rein. "Heian Literary System: A Tentative Model." In *Reading East Asian Writing: The Limits of Literary Theory*, edited by Michel Hockx, 114–38. New York: Routledge, 2015.

Reddy, William M. *The Making of Romantic Love: Longing and Sexuality in Europe, South Asia, and Japan, 900–1200 CE*. Chicago: University of Chicago Press, 2012.

Reichert, James. *In the Company of Men: Representations of Male-Male Sexuality in Meiji Literature*. Palo Alto, CA: Stanford University Press, 2006.

Sano Midori. *Chūsei nihon no monogatari to kaiga*. Hōsō daigaku kyōiku shinkōkai, 2004.

———. "E no bunseki wa monogatari no bunseki to dō kakawatte iru no ka: Genji mono-gatari emaki o megutte." *Kokubungaku: kaishaku to kyōzai no kenkyū/Gakutōsha (hen)* 42, no. 2 (1997): 104–10.

Sansom, George. *A History of Japan to 1334*. Palo Alto, CA: Stanford University Press, 1958.

———. *Japan: A Short Cultural History*. Palo Alto, CA: Stanford University Press, 1931.

Sarra, Edith. *Fictions of Femininity: Literary Inventions of Gender in Japanese Court Women's Memoirs*. Palo Alto, CA: Stanford University Press, 1999.

Sasatani Tomoyo. "Suetsumuhana no 'hana': sono karada hyōgen no imi suru mono." *Gunma Kenritsu Joshi Daigaku kokubungaku kenkyū* 26 (March 2006): 1–13.

Schalow, Paul Gordon. "Exile from Heian: Journeying as a Pretext for Male Friendship in *The Tale of Ise* and *The Tale of Genji*." *Proceedings of the Association for Japanese Literary Studies* 8 (Summer 2007): 65–70.

———. "Five Portraits of Male Friendship in the *Ise monogatari*." *Harvard Journal of Asiatic Studies* 60, no. 2 (2000): 445–88.

———. "Generic Innovation and Male Self-Representation in Fujiwara Yorinaga's *Taiki*." Paper presented at the 25th Anniversary Conference of the Nordic Association of Japanese and Korean Studies (NAJKS), Bergen, Norway, August 21–23, 2013.

———. *A Poetics of Courtly Male Friendship in Heian Japan*. Honolulu: University of Hawai'i Press, 2007.

Schiesari, Juliana. *The Gendering of Melancholia: Feminism, Psychoanalysis, and the Symbolics of Loss in Renaissance Literature*. Ithaca, NY: Cornell University Press, 1992.

Sedgwick, Eve Kosofsky. *Between Men: English Literature and Male Homosocial Desire*. New York: Columbia University Press, 1985.

———. *Epistemology of the Closet*. Berkeley: University of California Press, 1990.

———. "Paranoid Reading and Reparative Reading, or, You're So Paranoid, You Probably Think This Essay Is about You." In *Touching Feeling: Affect, Pedagogy, Performativity*, 123–51. Durham, NC: Duke University Press, 2003.

———. "Thinking through Queer Theory." In *The Weather in Proust*, edited by Jonathan Goldberg, 198–200. Durham, NC: Duke University Press, 2012.

Seidensticker, Edward. *Genji Days*. Tokyo: Kodansha International, 1977.

Selden, Lili Iriye. "Discourses of Desire and Female Resistance in *The Tale of Genji*." PhD diss., University of Michigan, 2001.

Shikibu Murasaki. *The Tale of Genji*. Translated by Edward Seidensticker. New York: Knopf, 1976.

———. *The Tale of Genji*. Translated by Royall Tyler. New York: Viking, 2001.

Shimizu Akiko, Tarumi Chie, and Nakagawa Shigemi. "Kuia riidingu to ha nani ka: yomu, arasou, henkaku suru." *Shōwa bungaku kenkyū* 77 (September 2018): 2–30.

Shiomi Yū. "Genji monogatari ni okeru Murasaki no ue no kashi: seishi no kyojitsu." *Monogatari kenkyū* 12 (March 2012): 1–11.

Shirane, Haruo. *The Bridge of Dreams: A Poetics of the Tale of Genji*. Palo Alto, CA: Stanford University Press, 1987.

Shively, Donald. "Notes on the Word *Kabuki*." *Oriens* 10, no. 1 (July 1957): 144–49.

Sinfield, Alan. *Cultural Politics—Queer Reading*. Philadelphia, PA: University of Pennsylvania Press, 1994.

Sono Akemi. "'Genji monogatari' ni okeru 'shi' ni tsuite." *Nihon bungaku shiyō* 47 (1993): 25–37.

Stewart, Kathleen. *Ordinary Affects*. Durham, NC: Duke University Press, 2007.

Stockdale, Jonathan. *Imagining Exile in Heian Japan: Banishment in Law, Literature, and Cult*. Honolulu: University of Hawai'i Press, 2015.

Suzuki Natsui. "Tokugawa Gotō bon Genji monogatari emaki no 'tobari' to 'jinbutsu': Kashiwagi 1 no himitsu o nozoku nyōbōtachi." *Tamamo* 41 (November 2005): 32–43.

Suzuki, Tomi. "*The Tale of Genji*, National Literature, Language, and Modernism." In *Envisioning* The Tale of Genji: *Media, Gender, and Cultural Production*, edited by Haruo Shirane, 243–87. New York: Columbia University Press, 2008.

Takada Nobutaka. "Murasaki no ue sōsō: Minori maki senchū." *Murasaki* 37 (2000): 83–91.

Takahashi Tōru. *Genji monogatari no taihō*. Tokyo daigaku shuppan kai, 1982.

———. "Kashiwagi ha naze mizukara shi o motomeneba naranakatta no ka." *Kokubungaku: kaishaku to kyōzai no kenkyū* 25, no. 6 (1980): 132–35.

———. *Monogatari bungei no hyōgenshi.* Nagoya: Nagoya daigaku shuppan kai, 1987.

Tateishi Kazuhiro. "'Onna nite tatematsuramahoshi' kō: Hikaru Genji no yōshi to ryōseiguyūsei." *Kokugakuin Daigaku* 92, no. 12 (December 1991): 17–30.

Thompson, William E. and Jennifer C. Gibbs. *Deviance and Deviants: A Sociological Approach.* Hoboken, NJ: Wiley-Blackwell, 2016.

Tsukahara Tetsuo. *Ise monogatari no shōdan kōsei.* Shintensha, 1988.

Tsutamura Tomohiko. "Homosōsharu ni yoru koten bungaku bunseki: yūgao maki no 'genji monogatari' ni okeru igi ni tsuite." *Kenkyū kiyō* 8 (December 2009): 27–38.

Tyler, Royall. "Lady Murasaki's Erotic Entertainment: The Early Chapters of *The Tale of Genji.*" *East Asian History* 12 (December 1996): 65–78.

———. "Translating *The Tale of Genji.*" Lecture presented at the Japanese Studies Centre, Monash University, Melbourne, Australia, October, 10, 2003. http://nihongo.monash.edu/tylerlecture.html.

Ueno Tatsuyoshi. "Onna o ushinau Hikaru Genji: seinenki no sōshitsu taiken." *Bungakubu ronshū* 98 (March 2014): 29–40.

Ueta Yasuyo. "'Genji monogatari' to 'karakoromo': From the View Point of the History of the Waka." *Journal of Atomi University Faculty of Literature* 48 (March 2013): 1–14.

Ugai Sachie. "Tamakazura no 'nadeshiko,' 'tai no himegimi,' koshō ni tsuite: 'Yūgao' 'Tokonatsu' to karamenagara." *Tōkyō Joshi Daigaku Kiyō Ronshū* 61 (March 2011): 25–46.

Uō Yukihisa. "Genji monogatari to bukkyō: Kiritsubo kōi no shi o megutte." *Kokubungaku tōsa* 16 (July 1991): 103–14.

Vincent, J. Keith. "Queer Reading and Modern Japanese Literature." In *Routledge Handbook of Modern Japanese Literature*, edited by Rachael Hutchinson and Leith Morton, 69–81. New York: Routledge, 2016.

———. *Two-Timing Modernity: Homosocial Narrative in Modern Japanese Fiction.* Cambridge, MA: Harvard University Asia Center, 2012.

Wakita Haruko, and Suzanne Gay. "Marriage and Property in Premodern Japan from the Perspective of Women's History." *Journal of Japanese Studies* 10, no. 1 (1984): 73–99.

Waley, Arthur, trans. *The Pillow Book of Sei Shonagon: The Diary of a Courtesan in Tenth Century Japan.* North Clarendon, VT: Tuttle, 2011.

Washburn, Dennis. Foreword to *The Pillow Book of Sei Shonagon: The Diary of a Courtesan in Tenth Century Japan*, translated by Arthur Waley, 5–19. North Clarendon, VT: Tuttle, 2011.

Wiegman, Robyn, and Elizabeth A. Wilson. "Introduction: Antinormativity's Queer Conventions." *Differences* 26, no. 1 (2015): 1–25.

Woolf, Virginia. "*The Tale of Genji*: The First Volume of Mr. Arthur Waley's Translation of a Great Japanese Novel by the Lady Murasaki." *Vogue* (UK) 66, no. 2 (July 1925): 53.

Yamahata Sachiko. "'Genji monogatari' Kashiwagi no bōrei kō: 'Yōzei in no onbue' no imi suru mono." *Seishin gobun* 10 (July 2008): 1–11.

Yamamoto Yukari. "'Genji monogatari no byōsha hōhō to kūkan kōchiku: kūkan no meian o jiku to shite." *Nagoya Daigaku kokugo kokubungaku* 99 (December 2006): 29–43.

Yamaoka Yoshikazu. "Bungaku no hassei to kishu ryūritan." *Kokugakuin Daigaku kiyō* 43 (2005): 157–83.

Yanai Shigeshi, Murofushi Shinsuke, Ōasa Yūji, Suzuki Hideo, Fujii Sadakazu, and Imanishi Yūichirō, eds. *Genji monogatari*. Vols. 1–5 of *Shin nihon koten bungaku taikei*. Iwanami shoten, 1997.

Yasuhara Morihiko, Harada Noriko, Iibuchi Kōichi, and Nagai Yasuo. "1–3 'Genji monogatari' ni okeru 'oku' to 'hashi': Heian jidai no kūkan gainen ni kansuru ikkōsatsu." *Nihon kenchiku gakkai tōhoku shibu kenkyū hōkushū* 62 (1999): 11–14.

Yi Mi-suk. "'Genji monogatari' ni okeru shi no 'kegarahi' to 'imi.'" *Kaishaku* 60, no. 3–4 (March 2014): 27–37.

Yoda, Tomiko. *Gender and National Literature: Heian Texts in the Constructions of Japanese Modernity*. Durham, NC: Duke University Press, 2004.

Yoshikai Naoto. "Genji monogatari no danseibi: 'onna nite miru' o megutte." *Fūzoku: Nihon fūzokushi gakkai kaishi* 21, no. 2 (June 1982): 71–82.

INDEX

Page numbers with a *fig.* refer to a figure or a caption; *n* refers to a backnote.

Foucault, Michel, 18
Freccero, Carla, 8, 15, 54–55
Freeman, Elizabeth, 26, 54–55
Freud, Sigmund: on loss of a love-object, 159–60; on mourning, 21, 26, 102; on self-preservation, sex, and herd instinct, 112
Fujii Sadakazu, 56
Fujitsubo (Genji's stepmother): impregnation of, 101; incestuous relationship with, 56, 60, 63, 78–79, 124; and mother's absence, 27
Fujiwara Regents, male-male sex in expanding power, 40
Fujiwara Sukefusa: *Shunki* (journal), 13
Fujiwara Yorinaga (courtier): *Taiki* (diary), 40; on male-male sex, 41–42
Furuta Masayuki, 68, 78

Gatten, Aileen, 89
gay sexuality, deviation/deviance in, 57
geese, as symbol of lifelong partnership, 142
Gender and National Literature: Heian Texts and the Constructions of Japanese Modernity (Yoda), 10
gender binary, androgynous vs., 13
gender identity. *See* sexual identity
gender politics, queer studies in, 14
Gender Trouble (Butler), 14
Genji: affair with stepmother, 56, 60, 63, 78–79, 124; as alpha male, 99, 105; androgynous beauty of, 59–60; apparition preceding Yūgao's death, 71, 74; birth of, 57–58, 60, 61, 62; body language of, 51; charms and allure, 65; children of, 59; clothing of, 31, 66–67, 126–27, 136, 139; and courtship of Suetsumuhana (*see* Suetsumuhana); and courtship of Yūgao (*see* Yūgao); diary of, 122; dominion aspirations nipped in the bud, 174; emasculation of, 29, 64, 73–74, 76, 89, 134; emotional responses of, 77–78, 193nn41–42; in exile (*see* exile); expedient promiscuity of, 59; gender/status axes, 78–79; home space as refuge for, 82–83; Koremitsu role reversal with, 79–85; and loss of lovers, 62 (*see also* Yūgao); love letters of, 89; and mother's passing, 26, 27, 37, 58, 62, 112; and mother's status, 58, 60, 61, 150; noise intolerance, 69; as queer? 43, 44–45; queering of, 5–6; queerness lost in translation, 45–50; and queer temporality of conception, 62; and queer theory, 7; relationship with Kashiwagi (*see* Kashiwagi); relationship with Koremitsu (*see* Koremitsu); relationship with Tō no

Chūjō (*see* Tō no Chūjō); reputation of, 79; residence in disrepair, 134; residence in exile (*see* exile); residence of, 31; sexual prerogatives of, 83; shame of, 142; tendencies to gain advantage, 58; transgression or deviation by, 56; visit to father's tomb, 129
Genji Scrolls, 151*fig*, 153*fig*, 161*fig*, 165*fig*; about, 150–54, 162–63, 165–66, 200n2; pillar in, 162–63, 169
Genji's father (Kiritsubo Emperor). *See* Kiritsubo Emperor
Gilmore, Ruthie, 175
Goff, Janet, 46
Goldberg, Jonathan, 8
Gomi Fumihiko, 42
Gotō Yasufumi, 137
grief. *See* mourning

Halberstam, Judith: on escape from social norms, 121–22; mention, 24; on queer time, 61–62; on reproductive temporality, 54; on Suetsumuhana's willfully eccentric modes of being, 117
Halperin, David, 44
Hanson, Ellis, 33, 147
Harney, Stefano: *Undercommons: Fugitive Planning and Black Study, The*, 180
Hearn, Lafcadio, 46
Heian literature/literary studies: absence of queer treatments in, 11; aristocratic paramours in, 76; "cock's crow" in, 76; courtly male friendship in, 12; "dawn parting" in, 76; and feminist studies, 11; gender studies criticism in, 10; homoeroticism in, 92; and intimacy, 24; psychological complexity of male friendship, 88; queer approaches to, xvii, 175, 176; queer desire across ethnic/species boundaries, 14, 43; queer reading of, 12–15; queer studies connected with, xiii–xv; and queer theory, 7, 9; *Tale of Genji, The*, in, 37; voyeurism in, 90 (*see also* voyeurism)
Heian period: aesthetics of, xvii, 47–48; aristocratic society during, 2; art and poetry of, 37; courtship inequities of, 107; courtship malfunction and tampering during, 118; courtship/wooing, 109, 110, 112; destabilization risk in, 115; diaries from, 40; effeminacy in, 46; female authors' prominence in, 46; and male-female sexuality outlook, 22–23; male-male sexual relations as customary, 40; male-male

Founded in 1893,
UNIVERSITY OF CALIFORNIA PRESS
publishes bold, progressive books and journals
on topics in the arts, humanities, social sciences,
and natural sciences—with a focus on social
justice issues—that inspire thought and action
among readers worldwide.

The UC PRESS FOUNDATION
raises funds to uphold the press's vital role
as an independent, nonprofit publisher, and
receives philanthropic support from a wide
range of individuals and institutions—and from
committed readers like you. To learn more, visit
ucpress.edu/supportus.